IT'S IN THEIR BLOOD

OREGON FOOTBALL COACHES AND THEIR LEGACIES

By Robert F. Gill

EXTRA POINT PUBLISHING

USA

Milwaukie, Oregon

Preface

The careers of Oregon's best football coaches needed to be chronicled. As a sports historian, I expressed my concern. My good friend **Carl Cluff**, the veteran sports writer, agreed and offered me the challenge: "You better get started."

With some reservation, I put my handball and golf games on hold and devoted my time interviewing and researching as much information I could find. The effort became an enjoyable journey. It also became an opportunity to reconnect with a lot of men that I have met over the years and to acquaint myself with others. The experience was energizing. It took three years and became a labor of love. The encouragement grew with each completed biography. The captioned legacies are my editorial input.

"IT'S IN THEIR BLOOD" became an early theme for a title as it was repeated with each sketch. Coaches are special people, and I have a deep respect for them. They love the game of football. Almost all were good players in both high school and college, and as a livelihood, they chose coaching as a career. I feel **Bill Dressell** expressed it best: *"It is impossible to duplicate the pure fun of playing football, but coaching comes close."*

The selection of coaches was personal. I called upon my background as a sports historian and fan of football in Oregon for fifty years. I added biographical sketches until I had a manageable and representative number.

It's my desire to present the collection of biographical sketches not only as a historical reference, but also to honor the coaches' careers and the legacies left to their players.

Acknowledgements

- **The coaches** and family members for their help.
- **Carl Cluff:** For his friendship, encouragement, and editing.
- **John Hilsenteger:** For his valued help by providing those win-loss records.
- **Jerry Long:** For his passionate support propelling me to give my best effort.
- **Allan deLay:** For his timely production of much needed photos.
- **Ken Hess:** For his unselfish help.
- **Sports Information Directors: Dave Williford, Hal Cowan, Larry Sellers, Kelly Bird, Cliff Voliva, Russ Blunck, Chuck Charnquist and Tim Marsh.**
- **Faith Gill:** For the unconditional support of her husband.

Dedicated

to

The memory of Ted, Roy, Fred, Tommy and Pokey.

They could coach the game.

Table of Contents

Preface iii
Acknowledgements......................iii
Dedication iii
Jim Aiken 1
John Allen 4
Dee Andros.......................................6
Bill Austin 10
Pokey Allen 12
Frank Buckiewicz.......................15
Thurman Bell................................18
Hugo Bezdek 20
Rich Brooks 22
Ed Burton.......................................26
Prink Callison 28
Len Casanova 30
Mouse Davis..................................34
Tom DeSylvia.................................38
Bill Dressel 40
Paul Durham..................................42
Darrell Everett...............................45
Jerry Frei 46
Floyd Halvorsen............................48
Marv Heater....................................50
Marv Hiebert 52
Joe Huston......................................56
Mel Ingram 60
Dutch Kawasoe 62
Larry Keck.......................................64
Spec Keene 66

Jerry Lillie......................................68
Jerry Lyons 70
Don Mabee 72
Bill McArthur 75
Don McCarty 78
Gene Morrow..................................80
Jim Nagel......................................82
Ted Ogdahl 84
Jack Patera....................................88
Tommy Prothro 90
George Rallis.................................96
Don Read..98
Don Requa....................................102
Ad Rutschman 104
Doc Savage 108
Tom Smythe 110
Chuck Solberg 114
Fred Spiegelberg.........................116
Gary Stautz 119
Lon Stiner 120
Pete Susick 122
Kip Taylor.....................................126
Roy Thompson.............................129
Dallas Ward 132
Eric Waldorf................................134
Kent Wigle 138
Fred Wilson..................................140
Bibliography v
Photo Credits v

Jim Aiken

- Born : May 28,1899 in Ohio County, W. Va. near Wheeling; moved to Tiltonsville,Ohio
- Died: Oct. 31,1961
- Married: Eleanor
- Son: Jim Aiken Jr. 6/12/19-11/15/89, Jerry Aiken, and daughter Carol Ann
- High School: Martin's Ferry, Ohio
  All-Ohio Valley All-star end

- College: Washington and Jefferson (Washington, Pa.)
  Coach: Earle "Greasy" Neal

COACHING

Jim Aiken was a veteran of 25 years of coaching before the University of Oregon hired him. His college coaching record at Akron and Nevada was very good, but his high school coaching record was phenomenal.

EAST WASHINGTON H.S., PA.

1922	10-0-0	

STEUBENVILLE H.S., OHIO

1923	9-0-0	

FINDLAY H.S., OHIO

1924	8-2-0	
1925	10-0-0	**Ohio State Champions**

SCOTT H.S., TOLEDO, OHIO

1926	6-2-1	
1927	9-1-0	**City and Ohio State Champs**
1928	9-0-0	**City and Ohio State Champs**
1929	9-1-0	**City Champs**
1930	8-1-0	**City Champs**
1931	8-2-0	

McKINLEY H.S., CANTON, OHIO

1932	6-3-0	
1933	9-1-0	
1934	11-0-0	**Ohio State Champs**
1935	6-3-1	

Jim Aiken's friend and coaching rival from Massilon High School in Ohio was **Paul Brown,** who later became the coach of the Cleveland Browns.

Brown gained a lot of respect for Aiken and his coaching. He called Jim Aiken, *"the greatest teacher of football I've ever known."*

Brown's record at Massilon during the 1930s was 81-7-2. Three of those seven losses were to Jim Aiken's McKinley teams in 1932-34.

Jim Aiken: A "great teacher of football," molded 1948 Cotton Bowl team and quarterback Norm Van Brocklin.

UNIVERSITY OF AKRON (19-7-1)

1936	6-2-1	**Ohio Conference Champions**
1937	7-2-0	
1938	6-3-0	

UNIVERSITY OF NEVADA (38-26-4)

1939	5-4-0	**Far West Conf. Champions**
1940	4-4-1	
1941	3-5-1	
1942	4-3-1	
1943	4-1-1	Combined with Reno Air Base
1944	4-4-0	
1945	7-3-0	
1946	7-2-0	

UNIVERSITY OF OREGON

After new athletic director **Leo Harris** signed the *Donald Duck* logo pact with Walt Disney, he went looking for a new football coach. He needed to replace **Gerald "Tex" Oliver** for the 1947 season with someone who could lead the Oregon football fortunes during the post-war era. University of Nevada's Jim Aiken caught his attention. He was hired on a year-to-year basis for $7500.

Even though Jim Aiken's coaching era lasted only four years at Oregon, his immediate impact and his coaching legacy was far reaching. He started fast and molded one of the finest teams in the school's history.

Aiken faced a large rebuilding job. The Ducks had not had a winning season since 1935. His early success was due to his hard work and his coaching genius. He moved a third string tailback, **Norm Van Brocklin**, to quarterback when he installed his T formation.

> " I remember the first time I met Jim Aiken. I was sitting in the stands in MacArthur Court at a basketball game. One of the players came up and said the coach is down on the court and wants to meet me.
>
> "I go down and this gravel voiced man says 'I hear you're one hell of a passer. You'll be my quarterback.' Then he grabs my finger and sticks it up to his nose to smell it and says 'Now stop that damn smoking!' "
>
> **All-American QB Norm Van Brocklin**

Because Van Brocklin had a good passing arm, Aiken put him in the right situation and taught him to be a good quarterback. He put him behind a good blocking line, added good receivers and spent hours teaching him football strategy.

> Jim Aiken's strategic innovation was the **"iron pocket."** It enabled quarterbacks to increase the average yards per completion, the true measure of passing efficiency. It allowed the receivers more time to get deep downfield than any other offensive system. The time spent perfecting the "iron pocket" best exemplifies Aiken's belief and focus on fundamentals.
>
> **Van Brocklin** remembered the time the team was practicing on an area that was surrounded with hedges. He had exited the pocket got knocked into a hedge.
>
> "Aiken came running over and pulled me out of the hedge. He said, 'Van Brocklin, you have a million-dollar arm and a 10 cent head. Keep your ass in the pocket!' "

UNIVERSITY OF OREGON (21-20-0)

1947	7-3-0	PCC 2nd place tie
1948	9-2-0	**PCC Co-Champs (6-0) with Cal (5-0); Cotton Bowl loss to SMU 21-13**
1949	4-6-0	
1950	1-9-0	

In Aiken's era, the head coach did most of the actual coaching. His staff was but four coaches, and he usually was in the middle of the players. When Aiken handled the offense, no one said a word. It was a reflection of the respect the players had for him.

His offense was a combination of single wing features and the T formation. The blocking assignments were generally two-on-one. He wanted the opposition knocked down—not just brushed aside.

> "Aiken's greatest asset was his ability to teach," remembers **Johnny McKay**. "When we went into a game, we were completely prepared offensively, no matter what the other team tried to do."

In 1947, Van Brocklin passed for 939 yards and nine touchdowns leading Oregon to a second place in the conference with a 7-3 record.

> "I was playing intramural football, when Jim Aiken approached with the command: 'You are going to be our right end and catch Van Brocklin's passes next year.' "
>
> "But I drink beer in the spring and am not going to play football," I answered. "Never the less, I played."
>
> **End Dick Wilkins**

THE COTTON BOWL

In 1948, everyone was thinking Rose Bowl. The team welcomed **Johnny McKay**, a transfer from Purdue, **Dick Wilkins,** an end from the basketball team, and **Woodley Lewis** from Los Angeles J.C. to the roster. Aiken, the ardent fundamentalist, stressed perfection and his 1948 team was near perfect.

Van Brocklin had an All-American season when he threw for 1,010 yards. Together with the strong running of **George Bell, Bob Sanders**, **Lewis** and **McKay,** the team won nine games losing only to Michigan 14-0.

Although Oregon and California didn't meet in 1948, they were both undefeated during conference play. It created a co-championship.

The Conference voted California into the Rose Bowl, causing quite a commotion with the fans and students at Oregon. The Conference broke precedence and allowed Oregon to participate in another post season bowl.

The team went to Dallas for the Cotton Bowl where it lost 21-13 before 69,000 to a **Doak Walker** and **Kyle Rote**-led Southern Methodist team.

Oregon ranked ninth in the AP's final poll. The **1949 Cotton Bowl team** was later inducted in the **State of Oregon Sports Hall of Fame** in 1989.

"Most of us were combat veterans in our mid or late 20s. A focused and determined bunch of men," **Dan Garza** said. "We didn't get really psyched up for any game and certainly not the Cotton Bowl...especially when we wanted to go to Pasadena. We just went into each battle, each game, without a lot of fuss or rah-rah, and got the job done.

. "Coach Aiken's strength was that he stressed fundamentals. We practiced blocking and tackling each day. There was also a strong team loyalty that has prevailed throughout the years."

COTTON BOWL LINEUP

E	Dan Garza
E	Dick Wilkins
T	Don Stanton
T	Steve Dotour
G	Ed Chrobot
G	Ted Meland
C	Brad Ecklund
QB	Norm Van Brocklin
HB	George Bell
HB	Woodley Lewis
HB	Johnny McKay
FB	Bob Sanders

"Teamwork was the key to our success," recalled fullback **Bob Sanders**. " We had our stars, but it took the entire unit to get the job done."

NORM VAN BROCKLIN

All the Cotton Bowl starters were offered pro contracts. Van Brocklin forsake his last year of college eligibility to sign with the Los Angeles Rams. He became one of the game's finest quarterbacks, winning two NFL championships, one each with the Rams and the Philadelphia Eagles. The **College** and **NFL Hall of Famer** followed his playing career with head coaching stints with the Minnesota Vikings and the Atlanta Falcons.

JOHNNY McKAY

When Johnny McKay transferred from Purdue to Oregon, his coaching future began to focus. At mid-season of his senior year when he hurt his knee, Jim Aiken invited him to be his backfield coach the next season.

McKay stayed on at Oregon after the Aiken era and worked for new coach **Len Casanova** for an additional eight seasons before he left to become an assistant at Southern Cal.

McKay became the head coach his second season at USC. His 15-year career achieved one of the school's best coaching records. During his tenure, USC had three national titles and seven Rose Bowl teams, three undefeated seasons, and *Heisman* Trophy winners **Mike Garrett** and **O.J. Simpson**. He left USC in 1976 to coach the NFL's new Tampa Bay Buccaneers.

"I learned most of my technical knowledge from Jim Aiken," said **John McKay.** "He had a major influence on my coaching career."

"He taught me that a coach should always do what he believes in, no matter what anyone says. He emphasized that if you listen to your critics you'll start to hunt around, rather than coach. You can only practice so long and only do so many things, so you must stick with what you believe in."

RESIGNATION

Big things for Oregon football were expected in 1949 and 1950, but when Van Brocklin opted to play professional football instead of finishing his senior year, the offense suffered. Jim Aiken, true to his style, worked a little harder. It was his over zealous coaching and recruiting that got him into trouble. It forced his resignation in 1951.

The conference recommended that Aiken be fired for breaking regulations, chiefly for holding extra practices during the summer.

Aiken left Eugene in disgrace. He took a job as a lumber broker in Roseburg.

In 1959, Aiken was hired as the athletic director at Roseburg High School. His genius for athletics was evident as the school responded with winning teams in all sports. Although he dreamed of a "great football team for Roseburg," he wasn't able to see the finale.

Jim Aiken suffered a fatal heart attack October 31, 1961 after addressing a Medford Linebacker luncheon just weeks before Roseburg won the state championship.

John A. Allen

- **John Aloysuis Allen**
- Born: May 18, 1930 in New York, NY
- Parents: John and Mary Allen
- Father was an owner of an international leather goods company.
- Married: Mitzi Lewis 11/17/56
- Family: Tracey Caraluzzi 9/5/57, Kelley Allen 10/23/58, Ardelle Rivera 2/19/60, Sean Allen 9/30/61, Trevor Allen 3/25/65.
- High School: Seattle Prep 1949
  Coach: Dan Melinkovich and John Goodwin
  Position: QB and DB
- Olympic Junior College 1950-51
  Coach: John Zeager
- San Jose State 1952
  Coach: Bob Bronson
- University of Montana 1953
  Coach: Ed Chinske and John Zeager
- Drafted: U.S.Army, Cpl, in 1954-56
- University of Washington
  Degree: B.S. in Psychology and Masters in Social psychology

COACHING START

- "When I was in high school, I always coached my younger brother's teams. Things weren't organized like they are today, so I would surround my brother with players, two to three years older than him, and line up games on the weekend. Then it was Legion baseball in the summers. I can't remember when I wasn't coaching.
- "When I was in Korea, I coached the Army 24th Division. Even though a Major and a Lieutenant were in charge, I did the coaching. The team was a group of mostly officers. 700 turned out for the team. We trimmed it to 50 by tough drills and practices which made me disliked, second only to the Chinese and the North Koreans. We won the Far East Championship and toured the Far East playing against All-Star teams.
- " While I was finishing college at the University of Washington, I gained a great amount of coaching experience at Seattle Prep (1956-58) where I coached the offensive line and the defense."

JESUIT HIGH SCHOOL

Even though Allen was hired as the head coach at Jesuit in 1959, a prior agreement the school made with the previous coach blocked it.

John Allen brought a winning tradition to Jesuit with a military authoritarian style of coaching.

Unhappily he coached the sophomores. But they responded, and Jesuit had a *good football coach.*

"Like the Marines, the kids were proud of playing on a tough team for the toughest coach." As seniors in 1961, the mighty Roseburg players told the Jesuit team after a semi-final game they were… *"the hardest hitting and toughest team we played all year!"* This began what was to become the tradition and source of pride for the next 11 years.

JESUIT HIGH SCHOOL 18yr (120-50-8)

Year	Record	Title
1960	5-2-3	**Wilco Champs**
1961	10-1-0	**Wilco Champs**
1962	8-2-0	**Wilco Champs**
1963	6-3-0	
1964	4-3-2	
1965	8-1-0	**Wilco Champs**
1966	8-2-0	**Wilco Champs**
1967	10-0-2	**Wilco and State Co-Champs** Tied Grants Pass 14-14
1968	12-0-0	**Wilco and State Champs** Beat Marshfield 28-0
1969	10-1-0	**Wilco Champs**
1970	8-1-0	**Metro Champs**
1971	8-1-1	**Metro Champs**
1972	7-2-0	
1973	5-4-0	
1974	3-6-0	
1975	3-6-0	
1976	2-7-0	
1977	1-8-0	

- "It was hard playing football at Jesuit! I ran tough practices. In the 50s, I installed weight training to increase strength, and year-long endurance and speed work to improve performance. It gave us a great edge. And it did work. We had fewer injuries, and we were well known for winning the tough games in the last few minutes against some superior teams because of our endurance. We also had highly motivated teams that wanted to compete.

- "Because money was tight and our equipment poor, one of my first acts in 1960 was to cancel new uniforms to buy six *Riddell* helmets and *Big Hitter* shoulder pads. The six sets we could afford went to the six hardest hitters. It was the beginning of what got called the Jesuit 'Flip Flop Offense.' Opponents knew we moved linemen and backs in varied positions, but didn't know that we were just running to the 'six good helmets.' "

John Allen's original coaching style was modeled on *military authoritarianism* in the 50s and early 60s. It was a successful management style. Later it evolved using the *behaviorist* model with the addition of *personal* and *team accountability* being transferred from the coach to the players.

"For 18 years, John Allen *was* Jesuit High School. It was his football teams, and not always Jesuit's fine academic ranking, that the public heard about most.

"But Allen lived in controversy at Jesuit, both when he was winning everything in sight and when he was losing. If it wasn't accusations from rivals about recruiting, it was the question about his strict discipline."

Norm Maves Jr, *The Oregonian*

Allen left coaching football in 1978 to work for ***The Pacific Institute*** in Seattle.

"It's almost as if John Allen coached football at two different schools for the past 18 years.

"The first 12 years it was 'University of Jesuit.' The past six seasons it has been plain old Jesuit High School.

"Allen took the good with the bad, learned from both. He's moving on now, without bitterness and with plenty of memories."

Dwight Jaynes, *The Journal*

John Allen at 68, still works for The *Pacific Institute*, which is a company that "coaches people in corporations to more easily achieve what they want. Like football coaching, there is an emphasis on winning."

Group success is dependent on each person having an appropriate vision of what they individually need to bring into reality and why. Group success is dependent on the quality contribution of each member. Group and individual success is interdependent. This, like the success of any team, is only a beginning. Next, is helping the players develop themselves.

An important element of this is to help them develop themselves by improving the quality of their automatic thinking which in many instances produces change. When the changes are intended to cause their vision to become reality, our job is to help them do so rapidly, effectively and without stress.

To effectively promote rapid change each person needs to feel that what they need to do is their idea. For example, set their own goals but within the framework of the vision. This is what his coaching experience has enabled him to do.

COACHING HONORS

Oregon Coach of the Year-twice
Metro Coach of the Year
Wilco League Coach of the year-seven times
Oregon Man of the Year- 1968 and 1969

Dee Andros

- **Demosthenes Konstandies Androcopoulos**
- Born: Oct.17, 1924 in Oklahoma City, Okla.
- Parents: Gus and Harriett Andros
- Father was a confectionist who made candy and ran a barbeque stand
- Brothers : Gus and Plato
- Married: Luella Thomas OK'49 Jan 24,1949
- Daughter: Jeanna Andros Baker 7/3/57
- High school: Central High in Oklahoma City Football coach: Dale Arbuckle in 1939 and Olen Williams 1940-42.
- Service: World War II; U.S. Marine Corps; served three years earning the rank of sergeant as a field cook with the 5th Marine Division; Received the Bronze Star for heroism during a field experience when he had volunteered for patrol duty. He helped wipe out three Japanese gun emplacements.
- College: University of Oklahoma 1946-50
- Football: Played guard for coach Jim Tatum in 1946 (Gator Bowl) and Bud Wilkinson 1947-49 (2 Sugar Bowls)
- Honors: 1949 All-American- 2nd team; 1949 Greek All-American; 1946 "Most improved lineman" by OU coaching staff.
- Degree: B.S. and Masters in Education

Dee Andros: "The Great Pumpkin" was one of the game's great motivators. The *"Giant Killers"* personified his best.

ASSISTANT COACH

1950 1951 1952	Oklahoma	Position coach under **Gomer Jones**	**Bud Wilkinson**
1953	Kansas	Off Line Coach	**JV Sikes**
1954 1955	Texas Tech	Off Line Coach	**DeWitt Weaver**
1956	Nebraska	Off Line Coach	**P.Elliott**
1957 1958 1959	California	Off Line Coach Def Line Coach	**P.Elliott**
1960 1961	Illinois	Off Line Coach	**P.Elliott**

When Pete Elliott resigned to take the Illinois job in 1960, Andros became a finalist for the California head coaching position along with **Eddie Erdelatz**. The selection group couldn't break a 5-5 split decision. Andros rejoined Elliott.

UNIVERSITY OF IDAHO

When Andros was hired as the head coach at University of Idaho, he got some advice from his college mentor, **Bud Wilkinson:**

1. "Dee, coach under your own personality. Don't try to mimic me or Pete Elliott (both different from Andros).
2. "Never feel you have all the answers, always be learning and always be a teacher."

"I had the hungriest bunch of kids when I went to Idaho," remembers Andros. "The drawback was recruiting except junior college players. When I sent my assistants out on the road, I would tell them: 'Don't come back until you bring a car load of prospects to Moscow.' "

"After we beat Arizona our first year," recalls Andros. "My kids came over to carry me off the field and they dropped me. That tells you how weak our team was that year. The paper read: *'IDAHO WINS BUT FUMBLES COACH.'* "

UNIVERSITY OF IDAHO (11-16-1)

1962	2-6-1	
1963	5-4-0	
1964	4-6-0	

The 1964 Idaho game performances against the two top Pacific Coast Conference teams contending for the Rose Bowl, OSU and Oregon, and the convincing win over WSU, drew the attention of Oregon State Athletic Director **Slats Gill**.

When OSU coach **Tommy Prothro** resigned to go to UCLA following the 1965 Rose Bowl, Oregon State hired Andros.

OREGON STATE UNIVERSITY

The Staff: Andros brought **John Easterbrook** and **Bud Riley** with him from Idaho; hired **Sam Bogoshian** from UCLA and **Ed Knecht** from Boise High School. Andros recalled, "I wanted a coach with an Oregon State background when I hired **Rich Brooks**. He was a good teacher, so I made him the defensive line coach."

OREGON STATE UNIVERSITY (51-64-1)

1965	5-5-0	
1966	7-3-0	
1967	7-2-1	
1968	7-3-0	
1969	6-4-0	
1970	6-5-0	
1971	5-6-0	
1972	2-9-0	
1973	2-9-0	
1974	3-8-0	
1975	1-10-0	

An Early Lesson: "Learn to beat Oregon! If you are going to live in Oregon, you'd better beat the Ducks."

The Emergence of Pete Pifer: Fullback **Pete Pifer** had only carried the ball one time for ten yards for the '65 Rose Bowl team. "I gave the ball to Pifer 17 straight times against Syracuse for a 13-12 win."

The Andros Image: Applying the wisdom from his mentor, **Bud Wilkinson**, Andros developed his own personality style. He had a special way to motivate his players. While other coaches talked in "coachspeak," Andros spoke from the hip and wasn't afraid to *"guaran-damn-tee"* a Beaver victory.

"I didn't hold back at the beginning of the season and try to play Mickey Mouse with people." Recalls Andros, " If they asked how we were going to do, I'd say 'I *guaran-damn-tee* you we were going to be good.' If I was wrong, well, I've been wrong before."

"The Great Pumpkin:" Andros didn't have that imposing sideline presence of his predecessor Prothro, but he did bring a contagious enthusiasm

for the game that got the most out of his players. It also delighted the media.

> **Harry Missildine** of the *Spokesman-Review* labeled Andros "The Great Pumpkin" after a game at Washington State. The robust coach had led his team onto the field in his orange jacket. It stuck.

The Plan: "Recruit the best athletes." Andros recalls one year when he started 17 players who were either a fullback or a quarterback in high school. Many played elsewhere, sometimes for a year or the remainder of their careers.

Power T Football: Andros believed in power and smashmouth football. "Run the ball up the gut and rely on a rugged defense."

> After carrying the football 45 times for 210 yards against WSU in 1971, **Roger Smith** hugged his coach: "You are the best coach a fullback could have."

THE GIANT KILLERS

1967 was a remarkable year for Oregon State football. It was fortunate to have a schedule that would allow them the opportunity to gain national recognition and the label: "The Giant Killers."

It exemplified the coaching legacy of Dee Andros. It was a masterful job of motivation.

It followed a mid season embarrassing 31-13 loss to Brigham Young, when **Jack Rickard** of the *Gazette Times* wrote: "When you compare the latest AP rankings with the Oregon State schedule, its easy to feel sorry for what lies ahead for the Beaver gridders." USC was No.1, Purdue No.2, and UCLA No.3.

The Purdue Boilermakers still riding high from their win over Notre Dame, were coming off a 41-6 crushing of Ohio State. "No one was giving us a chance," remembers tight-end **Gary Houser**.

"On the night before the game, Andros gathered a few players, most of them seniors, and gave us a pep talk. He spoke softly, and honestly, and looked us in the eye," recalls Houser. "He told us that we could match up with Purdue, and if we played with confidence, and didn't read the press clippings, we could have a great victory. He told us to pass the word that Ol' Coach Andros believes that we will win.

"We did spread the word, and by breakfast everyone was talking about how we were going to win that game. We took the field believing we could win. "I have never forgotten that feeling I had from the trust and confidence that Coach Andros instilled that night." The emotionally charged Beavers won 22-14.

The next week, Oregon State beat winless Washington State at home 35-7, setting the stage for another showdown. UCLA now was ranked No.2.

"There's no way Oregon State can beat 'The Genius' (Prothro) or 'The Great One' (Gary Beban)," a Santa Monica paper wrote.

OSU tackle **Ron Boley** blocked a field goal by **Zeno Andrusyshyn** in the last seconds of the game to preserve a 16-16 tie.

Buoyed with confidence from their achievements, Andros made that famous statement following the game: **"Were tired of fooling around with those #2 teams,"** coach Andros said in his *guaran-damn-tee* you style. **"Bring on No.1!"**

The Fall of Troy: The players picked up on Andros' confidence. They were more focused in practice as any team Andros could remember, yet they maintained an even keel.

"Coach Andros had a great ability to create emotion and focus early in the week that would culminate at game time," recalls linebacker **Skip Vanderbundt**. "His pre-game talk that week was different than most he had given before. His own anticipation was apparent as he spoke in very calm tones emphasizing the importance of what we had to do. He spoke of his pride and the pride the people of Oregon for us as Beaver football players. He reminded us that no one really thought we were for real, especially the USC Trojans, and that the 45 men in that room were really the ones who believed in what we could and would do."

"When the meeting broke up, there was no Knute Rockne cheering, yelling or charging. We left the locker room like men on a mission."

The history of the 3-0 upset and what transpired on that muddy field on Nov.11, 1967, is part of Beaver lore. It is remembered as one of the greatest games in school history. Andros isn't about to object.

"It was the most electrifying game I've ever been around in all my 50 years around athletics." The Great Pumpkin said. "There was just something in the air."

The Beavers finished the 1967 season ranked No.8 after beating Oregon 14-10 in the Civil War. Meanwhile, Indiana pulled a few upsets of its own in the quest for the Rose Bowl. The Hoosier coach, **John Pont**, edged Andros for Coach of the Year honors.

Andros coached at Oregon State until 1976 when he became the athletic director. Some of his best players were:**Paul Brothers, Bob Grim, Pete Pifer, Jack O'Billovich, Rockne Freitas, Jim Wilkin, Skip Diaz, Gary Houser, Dave Marlette, Steve Preece, Bill Enyart, Billy Main, Skip Vanderbundt, John Didion, Jon Sandstrom, Jess Lewis, Harry Gunner, Mel Easley, Jim Sherbert, Jack Turnbull, Jim Lilly, Craig Hanneman, Steve Endicott, Steve Brown, Jeff Hart, Dave Schilling, Greg Krpalek,** and **Bob Horn.**

Dee Andros lives in Corvallis and continues to work with the athletic department helping with fund raising and public relations.

COACHING HONORS

1967	**Regional Coach of the Year**
1968	**Man of the Year Award in Oregon**
1986	**State of Oregon Sports Hall of Fame**
1991	**OSU Athletic Hall of Fame**
1997	**Johnny Vaught Life Achievement Award**

ANDROS LEGACY

Bruce Kannenberg '69 read a letter from **Jim Scheele** who was suffering from Lou Gerhig's Disease: "Coach Andros—the experience was the greatest time of our lives. I want to thank you for being part of the team. To strive for excellence and never give up. Especially for the challenge I now face. Thank you for letting me, be the *"Man in the Glass,"* an Andros favorite.

Craig Hanneman '70 remembers the Oregon game that epitomizes the motivator that Andros was: *"Men, you have 60 minutes of football left...and 40 years to remember,"* was the challenge. "Although we had lost **Steve Endicott** to a broken wrist and we were playing our 4th quarterback, the coach believed in his players on a 4th and long from our own 25 when the defensive players pleaded: 'Coach, let's go for it!' " They made the first down and preserved a 24-9 victory.

Fall of Troy: Dee Andros is congratulated by John McKay while his team carries him off the field following the Beavers upset of the #1 ranked USC 3-0 in 1967.

The 1967 Oregon State University "Giant Killers" staff

William Lee "Bill" Austin

- Born: Oct. 18, 1928 in San Pedro, Calif.
- Parent's names: Larry and Mary Austin
- Father's occupation: 26 yrs US Navy
- Married: Goodrun "Goody" Udbye 6/16/56
- High School: Woodburn H.S. 1945
- Coach: Gerald "Jiggs" Burnett
- Honors: All-League in football, basketball and track
- College: Oregon State College 1945-1948
- Coach: Lon Stiner
- Honors: All-Coast guard in 1948 East-West Shrine Game
- Degree: Physical Education OSC '49
- Professional football draft: Drafted by the NFL NY Giants # 13 in 1949
- Service: US Army 1951-52, corporal with the military police.
- The first year: Played and coached for the Presidio team. On Sundays played for a local pro team, "Horse Trader Ed's San Francisco Broncos" for $50 a game.
- The second year: Played and coached the Camp Drake's football team in Tokyo for the Far East Championship.

An early start

Austin started school two years early. "At age four at Woodburn, I was big for my age, and so active, I must have been quite a problem. So finally my folks sent me to school as a six-year old. I wasn't questioned nor had any trouble keeping up."

PROFESSIONAL FOOTBALL

Bill Austin, at 6'1" and 225, became a New York Giants regular in the National Football League at the young age of 20. Although he was a late round draft pick, he played seven seasons for the Giants. The first year, Austin was a defensive tackle before Coach **Steve Owen** moved him to offensive guard. He later played for Coach **Jim Lee Howell** when he returned from the service, earning All-Pro in 1955.

" Austin excelled at pulling out of the line to lead the wide play. Backs called him smartest of downfield blockers, because he varied his moves to suit the running style of the man carrying the ball behind him," reported his Giant player sketch.   Howell had called him *"the best offensive guard in the NFL."*

Bill Austin: The Oregon State and New York Giant football star was a protégé of Vince Lombardi. He became one of the NFL's finest offensive line coaches.

In 1954, Howell brought a special person to the Giants as their offensive coordinator, a promising coach from West Point, **Vince Lombardi**. Austin played for Lombardi four years while a Giant.

Vince Lombardi, one of the Fordham *"Blocks of Granite,"* was coached by a young line coach, **Frank Leahy**.

Lombardi left a lasting mark on the game. He had been to pro football what Knute Rockne had been to the collegiate sport. He was dedicated to one purpose: winning. To win Lombardi relied upon simple execution of the basics. Intricate defenses and multiple offenses were not for him. "Football," he often said, "is blocking and tackling. If you block and tackle better than the team you're playing, you'll win."

Coached by the hard driving, perfectionist Lombardi, the Green Bay Packers won 5 NFL championships (1961, 1962, 1965, 1966, 1967) and the first two Super Bowls.

When Lombardi became part owner and coach of the listless Washington Redskins, he turned the losing Skins into a winning team posting a 7-5-2 record in 1969. In September of 1970, at the age of 57, Vince Lombardi died of cancer.

COACHING

After surgeries on both knees, Austin decided to retire from playing professional football and pursue his next ambition, to be a college line coach.

In 1958, Austin was hired as a line coach at Wichita State under **Woody Chalmer**. But the college scene only lasted a year before the new Green Bay Packers coach **Vince Lombardi**, hired him on his staff as the offensive line coach. Austin, at age 29, became a professional football coach.

> "It was not surprising that Bill Austin was the first assistant **Vince Lombardi** named at Green Bay and Washington, and the man Lombardi tapped as the Redskins' new coach. Lombardi liked Austin from the first day they met in 1954, when Lombardi joined the New York Giants as line coach and Austin was an all-pro guard.
>
> "'Bill was not very big, but he was smart,' Lombardi later said. He also liked Austin's spunk. Austin was one of the few players who dared speak up to Lombardi.
>
> "I remember telling him every year, 'Vince, when you get that head coaching job, I've got the ideal line coach for you. Me.'
>
> "I was coaching at Wichita State when he called me one day and asked if I was still interested. All I said was, 'When do you want me?' "
>
> **William Gildea, *Washington Post* 1970**

PRO ASSISTANT- LINE COACH

1959 1960 1961 1962 1963 1964	Green Bay Packers Assistant to **Vince Lombardi**	**World Champs in 1961 and 1962**

> Bill Austin admired Lombardi, but, finding his boss's authoritarian rule too stifling, he quit the Packers in 1964 to take an assistant position with the Los Angeles Rams. "I had been around him (for ten years) as a player and a coach. He was a domineering man," said Austin. "After a while, it gets to you… I just thought I had to get away... to see how other people operated."
>
> ***Vince* , a biography by Michael O'Brien**

1965	Los Angeles Rams Assistant to **Harland Svare**	

Bill Austin was offered the St.Louis Cardinal head coaching job before he was coaxed by the **Rooney family** to take the Pittsburg Steeler job. Later Austin claimed, "I should have evaluated the talent better before I made my decision. The Steelers had very average talent."

PITTSBURG STEELERS (11-28-3)

1966	5-8-1	
1967	4-9-1	
1968	2-11-1	

1969	Washington Redskins Assistant to **Vince Lombardi**	

Under the grimmest circumstances, 41 year-old Bill Austin inherited a situation that he never wanted, as Lombardi's successor. His mission was the toughest job, trying to turn the Redskins into winners. "One thing we must recognize that there was only one Vince Lombardi. We do hope to continue things, but I'll be expressing myself as Bill Austin."

WASHINGTON REDSKINS (6-8-0)

1970	6-8-0	

ASSISTANT COACH

1971	Chicago Bears For **Jim Dooley**	Line Coach
1972	St. Louis Cardinals For **Bob Holloway**	Line Coach
1973 to 1977	Washington Redskins For **George Allen**	Line Coach
1979 to 1982	New York Giants For **Ray Perkins**	Line Coach * Playoffs in 1981
1983	New Jersey Generals For **Chuck Fairbanks**	Line Coach
1984	New Jersey Generals For **Walt Micheals**	Line Coach
1985	New York Jets For **Joe Walton**	Line Coach * Playoffs

Austin is retired in Las Vegas, Nevada.

AWARDS AND HONORS

1948	**All-Coast honors at OSC**
1954	**Pro Bowl**
1955	**All-Pro guard New York Giants**
1956	**World Champions NY Giants**
1961 1962	**World Champions GB Packers**
1982	**State Of Oregon Sports Hall Fame**
1990	**Oregon State U. Hall of Fame**

"Pokey" Allen

- **Earnest Duncan Allen Jr**
- Born: Jan. 23,1943 in Superior, Mont.
- Died: Dec. 30,1996
- Parents: Earnest and Esther Allen
- Father was a 23-year Montana Highway Patrolman
- Married: Barbara Rigg July 28,1990
- Daughter: Taylor 10/17/93
- High School: Missoula County H.S. '61
  Football coach: Gene Thompson
  Played QB at 6'1 185 pounds
  Football, basketball, baseball and track
- State champs in basketball in 1959 and 1961
- College: University of Utah
  Coach: Ray Nagel
  Academic All-American Hon. Mention '64

POKEY

Earnest was named "Pokey" after his dad. His father got his nickname, because as a football player at Montana Wesleyan, he was big and slow. It started with "Little Pokey," but as he got older, he lost the "Little" tag of the nickname.

His father was a disciplinarian and was interested in having both his children do well in school and of course having Pokey excel in sports. In Pokey's autobiography, *The Good Fight*, he mentions his dad, "like a lot of fathers who were former athletes and wanted to vicariously relive their athletic success through their sons."

THE PLAYER

1962 1963 1964	Utah	QB and DB for **Ray Nagel** Co-captain and MVP of the Liberty Bowl on '64 team that went 8-2-0
1965 1966 1967	BC Lions	DB and backup QB to Joe Kapp for coach **Dave Skrien** –cut after 4 games in 1967
1967	Edmonton Eskimos	Cut after 2 games
1967	Norfolk Neptunes	Head coach **Gary Glick** Continental League

UTAH

Pokey's senior year, he was co-captain of an 8-2 University of Utah team that was the 1964 WAC co-champion with New Mexico. The Utes received a bid to play in the Liberty Bowl, and their coach **Ray Nagel,** was the *UP* coach of the year.

Pokey Allen could flat out coach. He led Portland State and Boise State to three Division finals. But his legacy may be his courage. He lived it. He never gave up.

Utah beat West Virginia 32-6 with Allen having an all around game. He was 5 for 11 passing for 72 yards, five runs for 28 yards and had an interception on defense. The performance earned him the **MVP award** for the **Liberty Bowl.**

"Pokey was a very smart player. Having him in the defensive secondary was like having another coach on the field."
Utah defensive coach, Ned Alger

CANADIAN FOOTBALL

Allen was not drafted by the NFL, but he did catch the eye of the CFL defending Grey Cup champion, the British Columbia Lions. Allen's three year professional football career ended bumpy. He was cut from the BC Lions after four games, signed with the Edmonton Eskimos for two games, then played out the season with the Norfolk Neptunes of the Continental Football League.

COACHING

Allen wasn't sure what the future held for him. After he moved back to Vancouver, B.C., he earned a securities license through correspondence study. Being a stockbroker seemed like glamorous work, but football was Pokey's passion. When the football season arrived, he gravitated to a coaching job at nearby Simon Fraser University. It would start him on a unique and colorful coaching career.

SIMON FRASER UNIVERSITY

After Allen's five years as an assistant, the vice president in charge of athletics at SFU made an unusual decision. Due to Allen's life style, he opted to have him share the head coaching assignment with **Bob DeJulius** for the next four seasons.

1968	Simon Fraser	DB Assistant for **Lorne**
1969		**Davies**
1970		
1971		
1972		Defensive Coordinator

SIMON FRASER (20-15-0)
Co-head coach with Bob DeJulius

1973	6-2-0	
1974	4-4-0	
1975	5-4-0	
1976	5-5-0	

1977	Montana U.	Defensive Coordinator
1978		for **Gene Carlson**
1979		
1980	Eastern Wash	Defensive Coordinator
1981		for **Dick Zornes**
1982	U of Calif.	Defensive Coordinator for **Joe Kapp**
1983	USFL LA Express	Defensive Coordinator for **Hugh Campbell**
1984	USFL LA Express	Defensive Coordinator for **John Hadl** *fired in mid season
1985	Portland Breakers	Defensive Coordinator for **Dick Coury** *USFL folded

PORTLAND STATE UNIVERSITY

After **Don Read** left for Montana in 1986, Pokey Allen caught the eye of PSU Athletic Director **Roy Love**.

"The thing about Pokey that a lot of people didn't realize is that he and his staff could recruit and flat-out coach," remembers Love. "He would sit back and let his coaches coach. When things went well, he would give them credit. But I tell

you, he knew everything that was going on, on both sides of the ball."

Pokey Allen made Roy Love look good in his selection. He brought a winning style of football to Portland that became the envy of even the state's larger schools.

PORTLAND STATE UNIVERSITY
Western Football Conference (63-26-2) 70%

1986	6-5-0	
1987	11-2-1	***Finals NCAA Div II**
1988	11-3-1	***Finals NCAA Div II**
1989	9-4-0	
1990	6-5-0	
1991	11-3-0	
1992	9-4-0	

Allen coached five playoff teams in seven years. His teams played in the NCAA Div II championship game twice and in the semis twice. He was the **Western Conference Coach of the Year five times**. He coached nine All-Americans and had 15 players in professional football.

His best players were many: **Tracey Eaton, Chris Crawford, Curtis Delgardo, Kevin Wolfolk, Roland Aumueller, Barry Naone, Anthony Spears, Darren Del'Andrae, Bill Duarte, James Fuller, Larry Hall, Ed Yoder, Ted Popson, John Charles, Rais Aho, Henry Newson, Derek Baldwin, Don Finkbonner** and **Matt James.**

Matt James remembered his first trip as a freshman that featured a phone call to his room: "The *Sun Times* wanted an interview in the lobby, wear your jersey, dress up."

The whole freshman group showed up in the lobby. That was Pokey's axiom: *"Don't take football or your place in it too seriously."*

He stressed team....

" I remember we were No.1 in the nation when Pokey called a team meeting. *'Guys, we are in a downward spiral. Your are not bigger than Portland State or the State of Oregon. You need to work harder than when you were 6 and 5. Team success brings individual success.'* "

Chris Crawford QB

GAME PROMOTION

Pokey Allen was more than a football coach. He gained nearly as much attention with his promotional work as he did with his coaching. He became known for his TV and radio commercials on behalf of the PSU program. He rode an elephant, was shot out of a cannon and threatened the viewers that a meteor would land in their back yard if they didn't buy season tickets.

Other coaches had success at Portland State on the football field, but it was Allen that put fans in the stands at Civic Stadium while enhancing the school's football fortunes. Ticket sales grew from 4,000 to 12,000 a game. Fund raising for the PSU went up 500 percent.

BOISE STATE UNVERSITY

Sensing the big time was still out of reach, Pokey Allen viewed the Boise State football program as a sensible target, especially after his Portland State team literally manhandled the Broncos at Boise 51-26 in 1992. Boise State Athletic Director **Glen Bleymaier** took notice of Allen.

After BSU coach **Skip Hall** was fired at the end of the season, Allen was pursued while his own Portland State team continued in the playoffs. Allen charmed the selection committee and became the choice to lead the Boise State football fortunes in 1993.

BOISE STATE UNIVERSITY (24-15-0)

1993	3-8-0	
1994	13-2-0	***Finals NCAA Div I-AA**
1995	7-4-0	
1996	2-10-0	*Moved to Div I-A (Big West Conference)

Duplicating the Portland State experience, the Boise State football team won the Big Sky and advanced to the division finals in the second year, this time at the NCAA Div I-AA level.

Boise State made the second best, one season turn around in Div I-AA history. They lost to top ranked Youngstown 28-14.

> "His thing was, if its not fun, don't do it. To me, he was a breath of fresh air in this profession. He was not locked into that stereotypical image people have of a head coach who is kind of a stuffed shirt with his nose in the air. He was everything that isn't."
> **Assistant coach, Alan Borges**

Pokey Allen wasn't able to realize his big-time coaching goal. Two days after the national title game, he was diagnosed with cancer, **rhabdomyosarcoma**, a form of muscle cancer.

He continued to coach at Boise State for two more seasons and fight the virulent cancer with optimism and a courage that would mark his legacy. Allen died Dec. 30,1996, at age 53.

> *"When Allen retired on Dec. 11, 1996, he met reporters with a quiet courage. Self-pity wasn't part of his game plan. He spoke with supreme confidence of beating cancer, coaching again, retiring. Despite damning evidence to the contrary, he made it seem believable. His was one of the greatest gifts a coach can have:* the ability to inspire faith when none seems justified." **Tim Woodward**, *Idaho Statesman*

COACHING HONORS

	Western Conf. Coach of Year 5 times
1987	**District Coach of the Year**
1988	**Oregon's Coach of the Year Award,** **The Slats Gill Award twice** **NCAA "Small College Coach of Year"**
1994	**Big Sky Coach of the Year Award** **Div I-AA NCAA Region Coach of Year**
1997	**Portland State University Hall of Fame**
1998	**State of Oregon Sports Hall of Fame**

> New Boise State coach, **Houston Nutt**, wanted to start a *Pokey Allen Award*. It would be given to a Bronco player annually. *The Idaho Statesman* wrote: "That's a great idea and a fitting tribute to Allen. The award shouldn't go to the biggest, strongest or fastest player, but to the most determined.
>
> "It should go to the guy whose jersey at the end of the game is torn or bloodied. It should go to the Bronco who hits, gets hit and gets right back up for more.
>
> "It should go to the guy who embodies Allen's spirit of never giving up and never doing anything at half speed."

Frank Buckiewicz Sr.

- Nickname: Buck
- Born April 14, 1930 in Perth Amboy, N.J.
- Parents: Julian and Hedwig Buckiewicz
- Father was a laborer in a metal shop. Parents came over to the U.S. from Poland
- Married : Diane Rimby, in 1953
- Children: Frank Jr., Greg, Gina Jones, Jo Barndse
- High School: Perth Amboy, N.J.
- College: Pacific University 1953
- Degrees: B.S. from Pacific U.in 1953; Masters from Penn State in 1954; Doctorate in Physical Education, U of Oregon in 1974

THE YOUNG ATHLETE

Frank was the youngest of the family of nine children. Since he started school at age four, he was small in high school. In fact, *the man who coached the sport of football for over 26 years did not play high school football.*

The family lived two blocks from a ball park. Frank almost lived there. He was at every event be it basketball, baseball or football.

He was 5'4" and 128 pounds when he graduated from Perth Amboy High School. He played baseball and basketball, but his role during football season was team manager.

SEMI PRO FOOTBALL

Graduating at 16, Buck grew four inches and gained 32 pounds that summer. He played semi-pro football in the fall of 1946 for the Perth Amboy Pros. *The Amboy Evening News* reported that " The Pros opened the season before 5,000 fans…They showed great power on both the offense and defense with little Frank Buckiewicz, the crooning idol of the bobby soxers, making his way into the Hall of Fame scoring two touchdowns." Also, "Frankie 'Rabbit' Buckiewicz pulled down an intercepted pass and raced the length of the field for a 100 yard touchdown to beat Camden…"

Buckiewicz played semi pro football for three years. He was like a coach on the field, taping ankles, coaching and playing. The second year, he played for the upper echelon team.

THE AMBOY DUKES

The Perth Amboy, New Jersey "pipe line" to Pacific University started after WWII. The pioneers of the group, **Joe Morgan** and **Tony Brown** who were at Farragut, Idaho, joined with

After coaching two winning high school programs, **Frank Buckiewicz** returned to Pacific for a challenging 16 seasons.

Gene Lukesozyle, **Bob Logsdon**, **Dick York** and **Walt Staniszewski**, all who were located in California, in a search for a common college to further their education. They selected the hamlet of Forest Grove and Pacific University to play football. Fordham would no longer have the monopoly of Polish athletes. For ten years, six to eight "Amboy Dukes" were on the Pacific football rosters.

When Frank was 19, he followed brother Walt to Pacific to play for **Dr. Paul Stagg**, the son of the legendary Amos Alonzo Stagg. Paul Stagg coached at Pacific from 1947-1961. As an undergraduate student at the University of Chicago, he played for his dad.

FIRST JV GAME

The first week of football, Buck played on the junior varsity team against George Fox and was scheduled to take tickets at the Saturday varsity game. After coach Stagg noticed that Buckiewicz scored five touchdowns, he said "forget the ticket taking, you're going to suit up."

THREE SPORT STAR

Buckiewicz played football, basketball and baseball all four years at **Pacific from 1949-52**. He earned **All-Northwest Conference** honors in all three sports.

Those were the winning years for Pacific. The football team won 30 of its 37 games, earning co-championships three seasons.

Frank Buckiewicz played at 5'8 1/2" and 175 pounds as a tailback in Stagg's single wing T. He was a triple-threat, setting records for rushing, touchdowns and punting. In 1952, he scored 90 points with 13 touchdowns and 12 PATs. He rushed for 1021 yards in 153 attempts. His single game rushing record was 234 yards.

He earned second team **Little All-America** honors in 1952. In 1965, Buck was inducted in the **NAIA Dist II Hall of Fame** as a player.

THE FIRST JOB

After graduation and a marriage, Buckiewicz played summer baseball for the Walla Walla Bears and spent a year at Penn State earning a Masters degree.

With Dr. Stagg's help, Buckiewicz got a call from the Seaside High School principal offering him a job and asking how much he would want to be paid. Buck called back the next day: "$4500 to start and a job for wife at the junior high." He traded in his '49 Plymouth on a new station wagon and headed for the Oregon coast.

SEASIDE HIGH SCHOOL

Buckiewicz produced some fine teams at Seaside. The 1957 team led by **Steve Picard** (who scored 210 points in one season), lost to a **Dutch Kawasoe**-coached Vale 13-6 in the last minute of the AA state championship game. It followed a two-day, 500-mile trip to play on a frozen field at an elevation of 2,245 feet.

The Seaside Seagull team of 1959 returned to Vale again, this time under travel protest with the OSAA, to win 28-21 over a team led by **Dick Fulywyler** and future Oregon and NFL star **Dave Wilcox** for the **AA State Championship.**

SEASIDE HIGH SCHOOL (46-12-1)

1954	6-3-0	
1955	6-3-0	
1956	7-2-1	
1957	9-2-0	**AA finals** lost to Vale 13-6
1958	7-2-0	
1959	11-0-0	**State AA champs** Beat Vale 28-21

GRANT HIGH SCHOOL

Principal **Art Westcott**, with the encouragement of ex-Pacific teammate **Ed Rooney**, recruited Buckiewicz to Grant in 1960.

GRANT HIGH SCHOOL (36-10-1)

1960	6-3-0	
1961	6-2-0	
1962	5-3-0	
1963	10-1-0	**PIL and State CoChamps** Tied North Salem 7-7
1964	9-1-1	**PIL Champs**

Buck's first team in 1960 broke the PIL winning streak of Jefferson in the post **Baker-Renfro** era, 26-14. The 1963 team defeated a **Paul Brothers**-led Roseburg team, 19-14, the weekend of President Kennedy's assassination. Grant tied North Salem 7-7 for the **AAA State Championship.**

PACIFIC UNIVERSITY

When Buckiewicz was hired as the Pacific football coach July 3, 1965, he succeeded **Noah Allen.** After four years of winning football as a player and 11 winning seasons coaching the high school game, Buck found the college level at Pacific a continual challenge.

Not only were budgets small, the coaches were expected to be full-time faculty members.

First, Buck changed the offense from the modified wing T, used by his coach Paul Stagg, to the multiple T offense. Then he re-evaluated his coaching perspective. Buckiewicz stated: "Our number one goal is to get people involved. Naturally, we want to be competitive, to the point where we win our share of games. But it is not the win-or-die approach, though we want to have success; success in participation, success in competition. And then we all strive for excellence, like winning championships."

PACIFIC U. 1965-1980 (38-100-2)

1965	5-3-0	
1966	3-5-1	
1967	3-6-0	
1968	1-7-1	
1969	3-6-0	
1970	0-8-0	
1971	4-5-0	
1972	8-1-0	**NWC 2nd place**
1973	0-9-0	
1974	1-7-0	
1975	1-8-0	
1976	2-7-0	
1977	2-7-0	
1978	4-4-0	
1979	1-8-0	
1980	0-9-0	

NICKERSON TRANSFERS TO PACIFIC

In 1972, star quarterback **Ralph Nickerson** transferred to Pacific after a year at Arizona State. He led the team to a second place finish in the NW Conference. After seven years of frustration, the season energized Buckiewicz.

"Football was fun again," remarked Buckiewicz. "This team makes me a football coach again." Not only was Pacific the top defensive team in the league, they were also second in offense.

Buckiewicz received the **NWC Coach of the Year** and the **NAIA Area I Coach of the Year** awards.

Coaching Philosophy Statement:
"Hard work with a 100 percent commitment. An all-out performance on every play, whether it be practice or during a game. A loyalty to the total program plus a steaming desire to win. Winning with humility and losing with dignity. And most of all, have fun while attaining the above."

A FAMILY AFFAIR

In 1979, Frank Buckiewicz Sr. was coaching the Pacific football team from the sideline seeking advice from son, assistant coach **Frank Jr.**, while other son, quarterback **Greg** led the football team on the field. Wife and mother **Diane,** was high in the stands filming the action with her camera.

THE "BOXER REBELLION"

In 1979, key assistant coach **Jim Weber** left the program. Instead of replacing him, the administration decided to hire one athletic director to replace the women and men's athletic directors who were splitting duties.

The decision added to the frustration of a losing season of a short-handed football program. It caused havoc, which resulted in Buckiewicz being terminated by Pacific University after a tenure of 16 years..

AVOCATION: OFFICIATING

Buck started officiating when he was a high school student in New Jersey. During the school year, he earned money refereeing grade school games for a handful of change.

Buckiewicz' duties as a Pac 8 Conference basketball official have called fouls on some of the best talent in the college game from Lew Alcindor to Bill Walton right down to Ronnie Lee and Lonnie Shelton.

"I look at each game as a special challenge," said Buckiewicz, "The life of a basketball official is one of the loneliest in the world."

ASSISTANT AT LEWIS AND CLARK
In 1982, Lewis and Clark Athletic Director and former coach **Fred Wilson**, had to step in as an interim coach until the new coach, **Tom Smythe**, could take over the position.

Wilson needed some help, so he called upon his friend Frank Buckiewicz, whom he had contested for 16 years, to be his defensive coach.

ASSISTANT COACH

Seven years later in 1989, Buck did return to Pacific to help out as an assistant for three years.

From 1992-1997, Buckiewicz has helped out at the nearby high school at Gaston.

"Serving as an assistant coach at Gaston probably has been the most rewarding of my coaching experiences. The talent is lacking, but the dedication and heart are very visible. It has been fun."

Thurman Russell Bell

- Born: April 10, 1943 in Hanford, Calif.
- Parents: Russell and Veda Bell
- Father: Was a cement contractor
- Married: Tami Sanders 12/23/97
- Sons: Kory Bell 4/12/69, Mark Bell 5/1/70, Jeff Bell 2/15/76
- Step children: Kelli Bell 1/7/70, Stephanie Lowen 4/24/85, MacKenzie Lowen 6/29/89
- High School: Roosevelt, Fresno,Calif. '59
- Coach: Chuck Giardi
- Honors: All-State 3 All-Star games
- College: Oregon State University 1961-1965
- Coach: Tommy Prothro and Dee Andros
- Honors: Most Improved Player in 1965
- Degrees: B.S. in PE OSU; Masters in PE Southern Oregon College; Masters in Counseling OSU

COACHING

Thurman Bell's early dream at age 10, was to be a professional athlete and a coach.

He didn't realize that dream as a pro, but he has as a coach. Bell has become one of the most successful high school coaches in Oregon's history.

Bell had an outstanding three-sport high school career at Roosevelt High School in Fresno, California. When he attracted the interest of **Tommy Prothro**, he went to Oregon State on a football scholarship. There he was able to play both football and baseball for four years.

Bell parlayed his background when he received his coaching start as the head baseball coach at Lebanon and later at Grants Pass. But it was his growth as a football assistant that appealed to Roseburg when they hired him in 1971 as their head football coach.

1966	Lebanon High School
1967	Assistant to **Gleeson Eakin**
1968	
1969	Grants Pass High School
1970	Assistant to **Gary Mires**

Thurman Bell contends that he is the coaching product of five men who have influenced him:

- **"Tommy Prothro** taught me the importance of the technical aspects of the game. He was a tremendous tactician. Even though I felt personally intimidated by him, I learned the importance of discipline and respect."

Thurman Bell has built a football power at Roseburg for 28 years that continues to be a state contender year in and year out...nine final appearances with four championships. He has a passion for winning.

- "From **Dee Andros**, I learned the importance of motivation and how to get the most out of kids."
- "**Gleeson Eakin**, an OCE grad, gave me the first opportunity to coach football when he had me join his varsity staff at Lebanon. He taught me about organization and how to compete."
- "**Barry Adams** guided me when I was starting my career. While at Lebanon, he taught me how to work, and how to spend my time in the gym and on the field."
- "From **Gary Mires** (Grants Pass), I gained a passion for winning. I also learned to work hard and play hard. I'm still learning about the balance."

COACHING PHILOSOPHY

- **"It takes us all to make the one"** is Bell's motto on the team concept. "My own philosophy is that we're all on the same page—first guy to the last. Our team is not a place for individuals." Bell's discipline and organization is reflected in his team's military-like calisthenics over the years that have been his trademark.
- **Encourage participation and discourage specialization.** " I'm from the old school,"

states Bell. "Participate in all sports that you can keep score. Athletes are better if they learn to compete." Bell has coached every sport. He believes high school kids should play as many sports as they have the talent for.

- **Work hard and teach/coach what I know.** "I'm not as smart or knowledgeable as a lot of other coaches, but no one is going to work harder. I'm not in the business of getting athletes scholarships for college. That is just a by-product or a bonus for their hard work. I try to adjust to utilizing the available talent and only teach what I know."

Thurman Bell has coached 28 years at Roseburg High School. He has earned one of the finest coaching records in the strong Southern Oregon Conference and the state of Oregon. His teams have been in the state final nines times winning four times.

Bell claims he will retire from coaching "when I quit becoming emotional about the job. When it becomes work."

ROSEBURG H.S. (221-82-1) 28 years

Year	Record	Notes
1971	1-8-0	
1972	5-4-0	
1973	7-2-0	
1974	8-1-0	
1975	3-6-0	
1976	5-4-0	
1977	8-3-0	
1978	10-3-0	**SOC Champs** **State 4A Finals** Lost to Corvallis 21-14
1979	3-6-0	
1980	6-4-0	
1981	14-0-0	**SOC Champs** **State 4A Champions** Beat Lebanon 22-0
1982	6-4-0	
1983	8-2-0	
1984	8-2-0	
1985	7-3-0	
1986	7-3-0	
1987	11-3-0	**State 4A Finals** Lost to Lakeridge 24-7
1988	11-3-0	**State 4A Finals** Lost to Benson 35-15
1989	11-2-0	**State 4A Finals** Lost to Ashland 24-22
1990	13-0-1	**SOC Champs** **State 4A Co-Champions** Tied Tigard 14-14
1991	6-3-0	
1992	6-4-0	
1993	5-5-0	
1994	6-4-0	
1995	14-0-0	**SOC Champs** **State 4A Champions** Beat Eagle Point 17-12
1996	14-0-0	**SOC Champs** **State 4A Champions** Beat Oregon City 16-7
1997	8-3-0	
1998	10-3-0	**State 4A Finals** Lost to Ashland 29-23
1999		

Some of the best players that have played for Bell have been: **Jeff Loomis, Neil Fuller, Troy Ballard, Rich Ruhl, John Young, Greg Fogle, Heath Howington, Jamie Burke, Matt Morrow, Chris Gibson, Mark Walsh and Jake Cookus.**

Hugo "Bez" Bezdek

- Born: April 1, 1884 in Prague, Czechoslovakia
- Died: Sept. 20,1952
- Came with his family as a child settling in Chicago
- Married: Victoria
- Family: Son, Hugo Jr., daughter, Frances
- College: U. of Chicago, Class of 1905
- Coach: Amos Alonzo Stagg
- Played football first time in college. Stagg enticed him to turn out. Within days, he was in the starting backfield.
  As a 5'7" 175 pound fullback on Captain Walter Eckersall's championship eleven.
  Also played second base on the University's baseball team.
- 1904 Walter Camp's All-Western team
- 1905 Assistant coach at U. of Chicago under Stagg

OREGON

University of Oregon hired Hugo Bezdek at **Amos Alonzo Stagg's** recommendation. "The best player I ever coached," Stagg often said of Bezdek.

OREGON

1906	5-0-1	* 0-0 tie with OAC

Hugo Bezdek's coaching and innovations at Oregon during his first year were impressive. The players learned every position. He inserted the forward pass and perfected a defense that allowed only 9 points. It was just a start for a coach that would have a multi-sport career.

MEDICAL SCHOOL ?

Bezdek left Oregon in 1907 with ambitions to attend medical school in Chicago, but it didn't last long. He accepted a job to coach football and be the athletic director at the University of Arkansas in 1908.
Oregon Ducks Football: 100 Years of Glory

ARKANSAS (29-13-1) 5 years

1908	5-4-0	
1909	7-0-0	
1910	7-1-0	
1911	6-2-1	
1912	4-6-0	

Hugo Bezdek put Oregon on the football map in 1917 with the Rose Bowl win over favored Pennsylvania. When WWI interrupted things, he became an institution at Penn State.

RETURN TO OREGON

Bezdek accepted Oregon's financial offer to return to Oregon in 1913 after the school made a commitment to athletics. He also was the head coach for basketball and baseball until 1915.

Oregon lured Bezdek back to Eugene in 1913. His football philosophy was simple. *"Give me a bunch of boys who can block, and I'll show you an offense,"* he said. *"Give me a bunch of boys who can tackle and I'll show you a defense."* In reality his tactics were often ahead of the opponents. Oregon's teams used the forward pass, and they threw different backfield formations at the competition.
Oregon Ducks Football: 100 Years of Glory

OREGON (30-10-4) 6 years

1913	3-3-1	
1914	4-2-1	
1915	7-2-0	
1916	7-0-1	**Rose Bowl Champs** 14-0 over Penn.
1917	4-3-0	

THE ROSE BOWL OF 1917

Bezdek fielded a veteran team in 1916. **Johnny Parsons, Shy and Hollis Huntington, Orville Montieth,** and **John Beckett** were the stars that were matched against the University of Pennsylvania in the Rose Bowl.

Oregon was a huge underdog to the eastern representative whose lineup included a trio of All-Americans: fullback **Lou Little**; end **Heinie Miller**; and quarterback **Bert Bell**.

Bezdek conferred with his former coach, **Alonzo Stagg**, for a scouting report. Penn didn't have a chance. They never threatened to score. Oregon left Pasadena with a 14-0 victory and the respect of the East.

> The Penn Quakers were stunned by Oregon's win in the 1917 Rose Bowl. They couldn't believe it. "You beat us at our own game," said Coach **Bob Folwell** in congratulating Oregon's Hugo Bezdek. "You have a great team, you deserved to win."
>
> It was a superior defense and a good running attack that got the 1916 Ducks to the Rose Bowl outscoring opponents 244 points to 17.
> ***Oregon Daily Emerald***

ANOTHER ROSE BOWL WIN

After the 1917 season, the **Mare Island Marine** team asked University of Oregon president **P.L.Campbell** to allow Bezdek to coach their team in the Rose Bowl. Bezdek was quite familiar with the service team. Besides beating his Oregon team 27-0 during the season, six of his former Oregon players were on the team. One of them, **Hollis Huntington** became the MVP of the 1918 Rose Bowl.

MARE ISLAND Marines (California)

Jan 1,1918	**Rose Bowl** Coach	Beat Camp Lewis 19-7

PROFESSIONAL BASEBALL MANAGER

Hugo Bezdek had been an outstanding baseball player in his college days at Chicago. The **Pittsburgh Pirates** of the **National League** hired Bezdek to be their manager midway during the baseball season of 1917 to replace legendary **Honus Wagner**. Between the football seasons, Bezdek compiled a 166-187 record in the two-plus seasons with the Pirates from 1917-19.

PENN STATE

Discouraged by the lack of players on the Oregon campus due to the war, Hugo Bezdek secured a release from his University of Oregon contract. He took an army physical conditioning job near State College, Pennsylvania. Subsequently, Penn State needed a football coach. Bezdek was hired. He coached the Nittany Lions for 12 seasons.

PENN STATE (65-30-11) 12 years

1918	1-2-1	
1919	7-1-0	
1920	7-0-2	
1921	8-0-2	
1922	6-4-1	**Rose Bowl** Lost to USC 14-3
1923	6-2-1	
1924	6-3-1	
1925	4-4-1	
1926	5-4-0	
1927	6-2-1	
1928	3-5-1	
1929	6-3-0	

Hugo Bezdek became an institution for Penn State athletics for nearly 20 years.

- His post-war teams were among the best in the country. From 1919-1922, the team went 30 games without a defeat.
- His baseball teams were also among the best in the East. They won 129 while losing 76. At one time they won 29 straight.
- Due to the war, the Nittany Lions found themselves without a **basketball** coach for the 1919 season. Bez volunteered for the job and led the team to a respectful 11-2 record.
- In 1930, Bezdek served as the **Dean of the School of Physical Education** until 1936.

PROFESSIONAL FOOTBALL

In 1937, the Cleveland Rams became the tenth team in the National Football League. The Rams hired Hugo Bezdek as their first head coach.

CLEVELAND RAMS NFL (1-13-0)

1937	1-10-0	
1938	0-3-0	*resigned after 3 games

In 1949, Bez at age 65, returned to football briefly, accepting the dual role of football coach and athletic director at National Agriculture College in Doylestown, PA.(Delaware Valley)

DELAWARE VALLEY COLLEGE (3-5-0)

1949	3-5-0	

HONORS

1954	**NFF College Hall of Fame**
1960	**Helms Foundation Hall of Fame**

Bezdek retired to his chicken farm in Doylestown. He died of a heart attack in 1952 at the age of 68.

Rich Brooks

- **Richard L. Brooks**
- Born: August 20, 1941 in Forest, Calif.
- Parents: Richard and Fern Martin Brooks
- Father was a gold miner
- Family: Wife: Karen Kisky
  Denny 3/20/58, Kasey Holwerda 4/8/64,
  Kerri 5/6/66, Brady 5/3/70
- High school: Nevada Union in Grass Valley,
  Calif., Class of 1959
- Coach :John Valentino
- Sports: Football, basketball, baseball, track
  and boxing. All-league in football and
  basketball, Optimist All-Star Game
- College: Oregon State 1959-1963
  Coach: Tommy Prothro
  Safety and backup-QB for All-American
  Terry Baker. Had five interceptions as a
  senior on the 1962, 9-2 Liberty Bowl team
- Degrees: B. S. in PE at OSU in 1963;
  Masters in Education at OSU in 1964

Rich Brooks: His Oregon legacy will be that final Rose Bowl season...the climax of a determined coaching journey.

Rich Brooks grew up in Alleghany, a remote gold mining town in the California Sierras. At an early age, he was taught to box by a local tavern owner. Brooks competed in the town's "smokers" or boxing matches during his school years. At Oregon State, Brooks earned two all-school boxing titles.

Brooks' meager background and boxing experiences helped mold his strong desire to compete and succeed. They were character traits that sustained him during his future football playing and coaching careers.

ASSISTANT COACHING

1963	OSU freshmen assistant	Tom Prothro
1964	Norte Del Rio H.S. asst.	Bill Tarrow
1965	OSU defensive assist	Dee Andros
1966		
1967		
1968		
1969		
1970	UCLA assistant	Tom Prothro
1971	Los Angeles Rams	Tom Prothro
1972	Special teams and	
	fundamentals coach	
1973	OSU defensive	Dee Andros
	coordinator.	
1974	San Francisco 49ers	Dick Nolan
1975	Defensive backs and	
	special teams	
1976	UCLA linebacker coach	T. Donahue

Rich Brooks became a student of coaching and learned well from his mentors, **Tommy Prothro** and **Dee Andros**.

During the early Andros years 1965-69, Brooks became the "hot" young coach on the Oregon State staff. He built his reputation and respect as a defensive coach. His defensive charges met the challenges against the nation's top teams. Two players, defensive tackles **Jess Lewis** and **Jon Sandstrom** from the 1967 "Giant Killers" team, earned All-American honors.

Brooks knew he could coach, yet he needed to broaden his base to become a head coach.

Pondering an offer to join the UCLA staff, Brooks was reminded by his coaching friend **Jerry Long**: "An Oregon State assistant has never become a head coach." It helped Brooks with his decision to join Prothro at UCLA in 1970. Within a year it became an early opportunity to taste coaching at the professional level.

Coaching Pressure.... Rich Brooks recounted a challenging experience as the Rams' fundamental coach for Prothro in 1971. He was in charge of eight Rams linemen during a *Crowther* sled blocking drill, when **Merlin Olsen** at the head of the line hollered back to **Deacon Jones**: "Hey Deacon, how many years have you been all-pro? Do you need this?"

"I've been all-pro for eight years like you Merlin, but I didn't need this," responded Jones.

SHUNNED AT OREGON STATE

When Dee Andros resigned the Oregon State football job after 11 seasons, Rich Brooks along with **Terry Donahue** and **Craig Fertig** were finalist for the post. The Oregon State Athletic Board chose Fertig leaving Brooks devastated. He almost left the coaching profession.

Meanwhile, Donahue hired him to his UCLA staff. There would be another opportunity for Brooks on the horizon the following year.

UNIVERSITY OF OREGON

University of Oregon Athletic Director **John Caine** had a shopping list for a football coach to succeed **Don Read** in 1976. The list included **Bill Walsh, Jim Mora, Joe Gibbs, Bobby Bowden, Roy Kramer** and Brooks. The only candidate Caine didn't interview was Gibbs, citing he was "too inexperienced and likely not to function well in the Northwest."

When the top candidates pulled out of the search, the 35 year-old Rich Brooks assured the selection committee that he could get the job done. He was hired.

Immediately Brooks was confronted about his Oregon State background. He responded tactfully: *"I'm in a profession where coaching is my job and my business. I was given an opportunity at the University of Oregon that I wasn't given at Oregon State to be a head coach. I appreciate that opportunity and hope to make people glad they had me."*

Rich Brooks learned one lesson well from **Dee Andros**: *"Win the Civil War if you want to live and coach in Oregon."*

"Brooks would attack the Civil War," recalls coach **Joe Schaffeld**. "That's why he stayed so long."

Brooks' Civil War record as a player and coach was 22-3-2. As a player and coach at Oregon State, he was 7-0-1 and as the coach at Oregon he was 14-3-1.

"Rich Brooks is a genuine enigma," commented **Jim Walden,** Iowa State coach who also coached at Washington State. He has done more with less talent than anyone I've seen."

UNIVERSITY OF OREGON
18 years (93-109-4)

1977	2-9-0	
1978	2-9-0	
1979	6-5-0	
1980	6-3-2	
1981	2-9-0	
1982	2-8-1	
1983	4-6-1	
1984	6-5-0	
1985	5-6-0	
1986	5-5-0	
1987	6-5-0	
1988	6-6-0	
1989	8-4-0	**Independence Bowl** Beat Tulsa, 27-24
1990	8-4-0	**Freedom Bowl** Lost to Colorado St, 32-31
1991	3-8-0	
1992	6-6-0	**Independence Bowl** Lost to Wake Forest, 39-35
1993	5-6-0	
1994	9-4-0	**PAC 10 – Rose Bowl** Lost to Penn State, 38-20

In 1981 the team got off to a very poor start. Brooks resorted to tough fundamentals, an approach he learned from **Prothro**. He returned to daily doubles.

"Coach Brooks said we were going to learn to hit, and we hit every day," remembers a player.

Don Pellum made a key tackle the next game against Houston that Brooks credited with saving his job and Oregon football.

"The team could have lost incentive because of how hard I worked them," Brooks said. " I thought *that win* started us on the road to becoming a competitive program."

In 1994, *Oregonian* sports writer **George Pasero** pointed out the strengths of Brooks when he acknowledged in his column:

- "Credit Rich Brooks for making all those in-season trips to Portland--appreciating that there are a lot of UO faithful in the metro area.
- --also for his strong survival stance when recruiting was down and probation hurt badly.
- --for his determination to begin at the bottom and build up on the bowl trail."

IMPROVED FACILITIES

Mike Walter was at Oregon in the early '80s. He remembers fall practice near the track stadium and caring not to step into a crater caused by a hammer-throw practice. The team met in the Autzen Stadium tunnel, and the defensive coach drew plays with chalk on the concrete wall. The locker rooms were littered and cramped; the coaches office in an annex off McArthur Court worse.

In 1983, a new athletic director decided to change things. "We were the worst in the league," athletic director **Bill Byrne** said. "We were convinced Rich Brooks wasn't getting out-coached; he was getting out-recruited. We knew young men bought with their eyes, and if they could come to Oregon and see football was important, we would have a chance."

In 1987, the Ducks upset both USC and Washington. The state went wild over a freshman quarterback, **Bill Musgrave**.

Byrne seized the moment. He raised money to build sky boxes to replace the old press box, and pledged its proceeds to build the Casanova Center, an athletic complex.

The Cas Center and the trip to the Independence Bowl, Oregon's first post-season game in 25 years, brought in a better class of athlete.

Then it was in 1994 that **Kenny Wheaton** ran back an interception of Washington's Damon Huard's pass for 97 yards that propelled the Ducks into the Rose Bowl.

THE 1994 SEASON

1994 was the season of reckoning for Rich Brooks. The pressure was on him. Not only were the fans and alumni soured by the late season collapse of the 1993 team, Brooks was tough on himself. His team came unraveled from within after losing a 30-point lead to California the season's fourth game. No matter how hard he tried, he couldn't remedy it. The Ducks lost six of their last eight games. The 1994 season would be the most critical in his 18 years at Oregon.

Before fall practice, Brooks surrendered the athletic directorship duties he assumed when Bill Byrne left for Nebraska. The team needed his full attention.

He announced for the second year in a row that Oregon was going to be a winner and contend for a post season game and possibly the championship.

Not only had the prognosticators picked the Ducks for the bottom of the PAC 10, Oregon lost games to Hawaii and Utah after beating Portland State. Things didn't look good.

Brooks gathered his coaches together to get their attention. They pulled together. What transpired that season is Duck football lore.

> "Rich Brooks was supposed to be fired. Danny O'Neil was supposed to lose his job as starting quarterback. Oregon was supposed to finish behind everybody else in the Pac-10.
> "But they didn't.
> "What they did was stage one of the most impressive recoveries in conference history. What they did was win, win and win some more, beating all odds as well as the other teams in the Pacific-10 Conference."
> **Don Borst** *Tacoma News Tribune*

The season was magical for Oregon. It personified and climaxed the college coaching career of Rich Brooks.

"I've been at Oregon 18 years and we've had a lot of downs and some up," Brooks said. "To come back the way we did this year is really special. We beat three ranked teams and our young football team started to believe in themselves."

THE ROSE BOWL

"The Rose Bowl is what you coach for," remarked Brooks. " If you are in the PAC 10, you want to win the championship and you want to win the Rose Bowl. It breathes energy and life back into everyone involved in the program, in the community and in the state."

Even the Rose Bowl was an example of Brook's football brilliance. Playing against a heavily favored Penn State, Brooks and his coaches provided the Ducks a competitive game plan for an opportunity to win.

The teams were even 14-14 with 20 minutes to play, before the Nitanny Lions rallied for a 38-20 win. It was a very respectful showing. Oregon's **Danny O'Neil** shattered six individual marks in completing 41 of 61 passes for 456 yards while earning the co-MVP for the game.

> When Rich Brooks accepted the **Bear Bryant Award** for the **National Coach of the Year**, he commented that "the award belonged not to him alone, but to his players and staff and everyone else who contributed."

"Coach Brooks has been a tremendous influence on my career," said **Nick Aliotti**. "He's the head coach, and he always comes in and asks me what we're doing, but for the most part he lets me go with the defensive stuff. He's given me a lot of freedom and a lot of good advice on and off the field in dealing with situations."

"Rich gives me total freedom with the offense and that's a very positive thing," **Mike Bellotti** said. "I appreciate that from him."

While **Joe Schaffeld**, defensive coach of 18 years with Brooks stated, "Rich was great. I always appreciated working for him because you always knew where you stood. You could argue or disagree with him until you were blue in the face. But once it was over, it was over."

PLAYERS

Brooks had many good players at Oregon. Some of the best were **Reggie Ogburn, Vince Goldsmith, Mike Walter, Steve Brown, Gary Zimmerman, Lew Barnes, Dan Ralph, Kevin Hicks, Tony Cherry, Chris Miller, Anthony Newman, Rollin Putzier, Matt Brock, Chris Oldham, Bill Musgrave, Peter Brantley, Derek Loville, Eric Castle, Joe Farwell, Chad Cota, Alex Molden, Herman O'Berry, Danny O'Neil, Ricky Whittle, and Jeremy Asher.**

COACHING HONORS

1979	PAC 10 Coach of the Year AFCA District IX Coach of the Year State of Oregon's Slats Gill Award
1994	Bear Byrant Coach of the Year Award
1994	*Sporting News* Coach of the Year
1994	Football Writers Association of America Coach of the Year
1994	ESPN Coach of the Year
1994	State of Oregon's Slats Gill Award
1994	PAC 10 Coach of the Year

LOS ANGELES / ST. LOUIS RAMS

When Rich Brooks received his accolades for his team's success by receiving the Coach of the Year awards, it became an opportune time to move to the next level. He resigned from Oregon to take the NFL Los Angeles / St. Louis Rams head coaching job.

Brooks found that his new professional team presented major challenges for it to become competitive. But time was not on his side this time.

Lacking a professional coaching reputation, Brooks knew he had to upright the team right away or his position would be vulnerable to the whims of the owners. He was right. Together with the move to St. Louis and into a new stadium, the first two season's progress wasn't enough to satisfy the team owners. Brooks was released with two years remaining on his contract.

ST. LOUIS RAMS   (13-19-0)

1995	7-9-0	
1996	6-10-0	

Atlanta Falcon's Defensive Coordinator

A month after being fired by the St. Louis Rams, the 55 year-old **Rich Brooks** was named the defensive coordinator of the Atlanta Falcons, joining the staff of **Dan Reeves**.

"He knows he's got a challenge," Reeves said. "And he's willing to accept it. It is exciting to me that he knows what he's got to do. But he's excited about it. He really thinks he can turn this thing around."

Brooks did get things turned around on the defensive side of the ball. Within two years, the Atlanta improved their NFL defensive ranking from 29th to 8th. They were 2nd against the rush, first in take-ways and fumble recoveries. It contributed to the success of the team. The Atlanta Falcons played in the 1999 Super Bowl.

Brooks feels confident he can be successful as a head coach in the NFL. But to his disappointment, the eight NFL coaching positions that turned over in 1998 were filled before he was available to be interviewed.

Ed Burton

- Born: June 16, 1941 in Longview, Wash.
- Parents: George and Donna Burton
- Father's occupation: Construction worker
- High School: Modesto, Calif., Class of 1960
- Coach: Jay Pattee
- Honors: Played football (QB and FB), basketball and baseball on championship teams. Student body president
- College: Modesto Junior College
- Coach: Stan Pavko
- Honors: All league guard in 1960
- College: Chico State
- Coach: George Maderos
- Honors:1961-62 All-Far West Conf end, 2nd team Little All-American, set game, season and career records for most receptions.
  Chico State's All-Centennial Football team and Hall of Fame
- Family: Married Penny Young 6/20/64
  Sons: Derek 1/31/68, Doug 12/29/69
- Degrees:1964 Chico State B.S. Education; 1972 Masters Chico State
- Service: Viet Nam 1966-68

COACHING CAREER

When Burton was eight while living in Modesto, his brother, his only sibling, drowned in an irrigation ditch. His junior year in high school, his parents divorced, leaving him alone to support himself.

"I was a tremendously angry kid in high school," remembered Burton. "I should have been a juvenile delinquent. But thanks to some help from some special people, I found I could release those feelings on the athletic field and get a pat on the back for it."

"As I grew up, competition became a way of life," Burton said " I felt I was judged if I won or lost."

ASSISTANT COACHING

1966	San Ramon HS assistant
1968-1972	Biggs HS Asst football coach Head wrestling and baseball coach
1972-1977	Roseburg HS Asst football coach for **Thurman Bell** – Head wrestling coach 1975-1977
1977-1983	Oregon City HS Asst football coach for **Don McCarty**- Head wrestling coach 1978-1984
1984-1985	Assistant football to Mike Mitchell

When **Ed Burton** blended coaching philosophies to balance his competitive intensity, he had 11 successful football seasons at Oregon City.

OREGON CITY

Ed Burton started as a wrestling coach at Biggs, Roseburg and Oregon City. He assisted in football.

When Burton applied his strengths as a wrestling coach to the game of football, his coaching stock grew. Oregon City Athletic Director **Paul Poetsch** hired him as Oregon City's football coach in 1986.

His competitive desire became so consuming, that it eventually affected his relationship with his family and players. The search for a deeper meaning of winning became a concern.

About that time, Burton met **Frosty Westering**, a coach that had mastered that same struggle. The resulting *After Glow* rituals and other Westering concepts became an answer to Burton's frustration. It gave him the opportunity to reach the next level of career and personal satisfaction.

For Burton, it was no longer a selfish ego coaching journey. He coached the game with a new zeal, a lot of encouragement, and a lot of hugs. Relationships with the players became his number one priority

The kids responded. There became no limit to their talent development.

"The After Glow"

The after-game event, that the Ed Burton-coached Oregon City players and fans experienced, was an expression of love and care that earmarked the Burton coaching legacy.

As a coach, Burton had been influenced by his mentors, **Thurman Bell** and **Don McCarty**.

"Bell has a tremendous competitive spirit," Burton said. "His philosophy and style of doing things are a part of my life. McCarty taught me about the quality of life."

Frosty Westering, the football coach at Pacific Lutheran University, whom he became acquainted when son Doug was being recruited, helped him create a bridge between the two influences.

"He taught me you can have it all," Burton said. "Its OK to want to win, but don't be consumed by the scoreboard."

Burton realized that the victories aren't necessarily on the scoreboard. The winners are the kids on the field by overcoming obstacles with discipline, hard work, and dedication.

The **After Glow** postgame ritual borrowed from Westering is designed for parents, fans and players to share the game's positive experiences. Win or lose. Home or away. The captains acknowledge and applaud their teammate's victories. *The game of football and the game of life being kept in a proper prospective.*

The 1996 state championship game against Roseburg, became the highlight of Ed Burton's coaching career. It was a match-up with his former mentor **Thurman Bell**.

Oregon City had played well in the playoffs, until they met the strong Roseburg team. The Pioneers lost in a hard fought battle, 16-7.

Burton intensity hasn't mellowed, but his wisdom and success has eased the bitterness and anger that dominated his early life.

Ed Burton retired from high school coaching at the end of the school year. He was replaced by his assistant **Mark Bell**, Thurman's son.

In Burton's 11 years as the Pioneers' head coach, his team's had an 80-37 record, reaching the playoffs 10 seasons. He recorded the most wins in the history of the school.

The most recognized players during the Burton era were: **Gary Hoxit, Ian Shields, Ben Schroeder, Adam White, Lance Oliver, Tony Rants, Bryan Piaski, Anthony Spencer, Joe Daiker, Jeremy Boyd, Travis Miller, Todd Hunter, Jason Taroli, Tyler Kemhus, Scott Ackerman, David Rothwell, Brandon Hubbard, and Nate Wante.**

Burton's love for coaching couldn't keep him off the sidelines. He joined **Tim Walsh's** staff at Portland State to coach linebackers for the Viking's 1998 season.

COACHING HONORS

1996	**Class 4A Coach of the Year** *Oregonian* **and TRL**
1997	Shrine Bowl head coach- North team

OREGON CITY HIGH SCHOOL
11 years (80-37-0)

1986	6-5-0	
1987	8-3-0	
1988	9-2-0	**Three Rivers League champs**
1989	6-4-0	
1990	7-5-0	
1991	8-2-0	**Three Rivers League champs**
1992	5-5-0	
1993	6-3-0	
1994	5-5-0	
1995	8-3-0	**Three Rivers League champs**
1996	12-1-0	**TRL Champs** **State 4A Finals** **Lost to Roseburg 16-7**

"Prink" Callison

- **Prince Gary Callison**
- Born: Aug. 15, 1899 in Pleasant Hill, Ore.
- Died: 1987
- High School: Eugene High School
- Lettered three years in football and basketball
- College: University of Oregon 1923
- Four year letterman 1919-1922
- Coach: Shy Huntington
- Position: Center
- Honors: All-Coast center in his junior and senior year-earned the title "60 Minute Man" for his skill and stamina
- Medford: Coached all four major sports for the Tigers. Out of 19 seasons for all major sports in the Southern Oregon Conference, teams were victorious 18 times.
- Considered by many, the top high school coach on the Pacific Coast.

MEDFORD HIGH SCHOOL (45-2-2)

1923	5-2-0	SO champs
1924	5-0-2	SO champs
1925	9-0-0	SO and Western Oregon Championships *
1926	9-0-0	SO and State Champs beat Grant 24-6 in finals *
1927	8-0-0	SO and State Champs beat McHi (MF) 44-0 in finals *
1928	9-0-0	SO and State Champs beat Benson Tech 39-0 in final *

*unoffical state championships during this era

The **legacy of Callison's** as a high school coach can be documented by the careers of his players. Of the 21 players on the championship team of 1928, 11 went on to play college football. Three members of that team turned to coaching careers and three players made their mark in the pros.

Probably the best known players on that team was **Bill Bowerman**, who returned to coach at Medford High School and then became the head track coach for the University of Oregon. Then there was **Bill Morgan** who played tackle at Oregon and later became all-pro for the New York Giants. **Bernie Hughes** also played at Oregon before he played eight straight years of pro ball for the Chicago Cardinals.

1929-1931	University of Oregon Freshmen Coach whose teams lost only two games in three years

Prink Callison: A tough innovative disciplinarian type coach whose football was executed with precision. A winner.

After three years as a successful freshman coach, Prink Callison at the age of 34, was selected to replace the controversial Oregon coach, **Clarence "Doc" Spears**.

UNIVERSITY OF OREGON (33-23-2)

1932	6-3-1	
1933	9-1-0	**Co-champions**
1934	6-4-0	
1935	6-3-0	
1936	2-6-1	
1937	4-6-0	

The first season, 1933, found All-American fullback **Mike "Iron Mike" Mikulak** teamed up with his former Medford players and stars, **Bernie Hughes, Bill Morgan** and **Bill Bowerman**. The team finished 5-3-1 and was invited to play Southeastern Conference champion LSU in Baton Rouge in December in what would be a forerunner to the Sugar Bowl game. On a bitter cold day when both the team water bottles and the band instruments froze, Oregon beat LSU 12-0.

Callison's squad won a share of the Pacific Coast Conference championship in 1933. Despite a 9-1 record, Oregon lost the bid to play in the Rose Bowl when it lost to USC 26-6.

Oregon was 18-19-1 in the next four seasons, and Callison resigned at the end of the 1937 schedule.

Other star players during Callison's reign at Oregon were **Alex Eagle, Ray "Butch" Morse, Del Bjork, Bob Smith and Jay Graybeal**

Ross Carter, a guard on the 1934-35 teams, remembers Callison as "a stern disciplinarian who was very technique oriented. He expected his offense, the 'Notre Dame Box,' to be executed with precision. He was one of the toughest coaches of the time, but he was tough with everyone."

"I've got nothing but nice things to say about Callison," commented Carter. "He taught me enough to allow me to succeed in both football and life. It has allowed me to play four years of professional football with the Chicago Cardinals."

Ray "Butch" Morse, a star end, considered Callison quite an innovator. "He developed an end around play that I liked. I scored three times on that play in one season."

Mike "Iron Mike" Mikulak, remembers *"the cruncher play,"* that fit his style of running. "It was designed for me to make my own interference if it wasn't there. I would position myself so my thighs were like pistons, yet I needed to run with good balance." About Callison, the 1935 all-pro player remembers, "Prink was really a fine man. He was a great tactician."

Prink Callison retired from the game of football at the age of 41. He ran Lucky's Cigar and Pool Hall in Eugene, did a lot of fishing in Alaska until he moved to Laguna Hills, California. He died in June 1986.

Leonard J. "Cas" Casanova

- Born: June 12, 1905 in Ferndale, Calif.
- Parents: John and Marie Casanova
- Father's occupation: teamster
- Married: Dixie Simmers 1931,
  Margaret 8/17/63
  Daughters: Margo Wells 1934,
  Andrea Casanova 1944
- High School: Ferndale in Humboldt County
  , Calif. in a class of 14 in 1923
- College: Santa Clara 1923-1927
- Coach: Eddie Keinholz 1923-24,
  Adam Walsh 1925-26
- Position:HB-known as a ferocious
  competitor and is still remembered for a 98
  yard punt against St. Marys in 1923
- Service: Commander USN WWII – Was in
  charge of West Coast physical training
  program
- Played one season with the San Francsico
  Oympic Club football team in 1927.

THE MAN

"Many years ago when visiting in Ferndale, California, I happened upon a jewelry store. In the window was a display of coaching pictures and paraphernalia of Len Casanova.

I stepped inside and introduced myself to a small crippled jeweler, **Walt Guilari**, who told the following story: 'Cas was my friend in high school during the 20s here at Ferndale. The school had high front steps and everyday before school started, Cas would carry me in my wheelchair up those stairs to class. That's the kind of guy he was. He's been my hero ever since.' "

Fitz Brewer

Len Casanova was a caring man. That quality characterized his life and his coaching career. The respect received from his players and his coaching honors are testimony to his success.

HIGH SCHOOL COACHING

1928	Belmont Military Academy	

SEQUOIA H.S. Redwood City, CA (36-10-4)

1931	8-3-0	
1932	6-1-3	
1933	8-2-0	
1934	6-3-1	
1935	8-1-0	

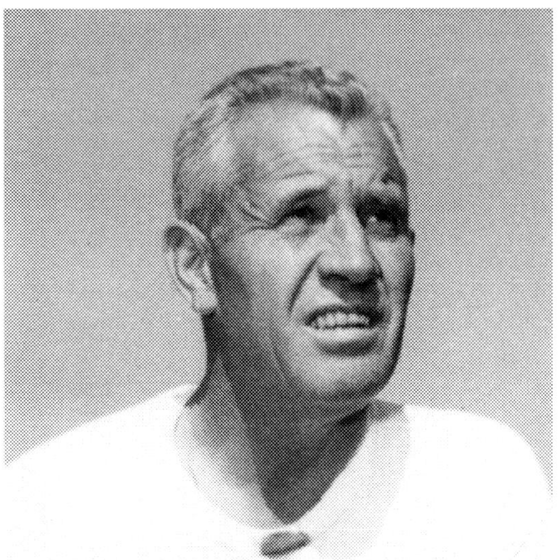

Cas: "A gentleman with dignity" had coaching tenures at Santa Clara and the University of Oregon that earned him the game's highest honor, the induction into **The National College Hall of Fame.**

COLLEGE COACHING

Casanova returned to his alma mater, Santa Clara, in 1936 to be a college assistant coach for **Lawrence "Buck" Shaw**. And what an opportunity it became. Santa Clara won the Sugar Bowl in 1937 and 1938, both over Louisiana State. The undefeated and stingy 1937 squad gave up but nine points on defense.

1936	8-1-0	Santa Clara (Asst to Shaw)
1937	9-0-0	
1938	6-2-0	
1939	5-1-3	
1940	6-1-1	
1941	6-3-0	
1942	7-2-0	

Buck Shaw, a Notre Dame graduate, coached Santa Clara seven seasons 1935-41, (47-10-4), before he moved on to the NFL San Francisco 49ers from 1944 to 1954. He became the Air Force Academy's first coach in 1956, and then returned to the NFL in 1958 as the head coach of the Philadelphia Eagles. In 1960 with quarterback **Norm Van Brocklin** at the helm, they captured the World Championship, and for his efforts, Shaw was named the NFL's Coach of the Year.

After World War II, Len Casanova was hired to lead the Bronco's grid fortunes following the program's three-year layoff.

SANTA CLARA (21-13-3)

1946	2-5-1	
1947	4-4-1	
1948	7-2-1	
1949	8-2-1	**Orange Bowl**

NATIONAL RECOGNITION

Len Casanova's coaching record in 1948 and 1949 at Santa Clara against many of the nation's top teams highlighted his career nationally.

SANTA CLARA 1948- Won 7 Lost 2 Tied 1

19 California 41	* Rose Bowl team
20 Oklahoma 17	* Sugar Bowl team
45 Fresno State 7	
27 Stanford 14	
47 Loyola (Calif) 0	
0 SMU 33	* Cotton Bowl team
25 San Francisco 13	
14 Nevada 0	
10 St. Mary's 7	
21 Michigan St 21	

1949- Won 8 Lost 2 Tied 1

7 California 21	* Rose Bowl team
14 San Jose St 13	
53 Fresno State 0	
26 Portland 13	
14 UCLA 0	
27 Loyola (Cal) 19	
7 Stanford 7	
13 San Francisco 7	
21 Oklahoma 28	* Sugar Bowl team
21 Kentucky 13	**Coached
Orange Bowl	by **Paul "Bear" Byrant**

UNIVERSITY OF PITTSBURG

Casanova was ready for a new coaching challenge when he accepted the University of Pittsburg job. The program was rebuilding after de-emphasizing football a few years earlier. "Pitt was a city school," remembered Casanova. " No campus to speak of and I had a hard time conscientiously trying to sell the school."

PITTSBURG (1-8-0)

1950	1-8-0	

After a disappointing 1-8 season in 1950, Casanova was frustrated with the outlook at Pittsburg. Promises to improve facilities didn't occur.

When the Oregon football post was vacated by **Jim Aiken**, Pittsburg Athletic Director **Tom Hamilton** allowed Cas out of his contract so he could accept the opening.

OREGON

The Oregon football program in 1951 was a huge challenge for Casanova when he and his inherited assistant **Johnny McKay** evaluated the available talent.

"It was a little tough when I first came to Oregon. It was during the Korean War and because of the lack of players, freshmen were eligible," remembered Casanova. " I inherited only 15 letterman and had to play 23 freshmen that season."

But one of those incoming freshmen was **George Shaw**, a heralded quarterback off two state championships at Grant High School. He made a major contribution his first year by intercepting 13 passes for a NCAA record. The versatile Shaw left his mark on the program by becoming a six-way player. His senior year, he led the nation in total offense before he became the "bonus pick," the number one choice in the NFL draft by the Baltimore Colts. Other members of that freshmen class were linemen **Jack Patera, Hal Reeve and Ron Phiester.**

UNIVERSITY OF OREGON (82-73-8)

1951	2-8-0	
1952	2-7-1	
1953	4-5-1	
1954	6-4-0	
1955	6-4-0	
1956	4-4-2	
1957	7-4-0	**Tie for PCC Championship** **Rose Bowl lost to Ohio St**
1958	4-6-0	
1959	8-2-0	
1960	7-3-1	**Liberty Bowl** Lost to Penn State 41-12
1961	4-6-0	
1962	6-3-1	
1963	8-3-0	**Sun Bowl** beat SMU 21-14
1964	7-2-1	
1965	4-5-1	
1966	3-7-0	

ROSE BOWL

It wasn't until the 1957 season that a Casanova-coached team had success in the competitive Pacific Coast Conference. The close-knit team had good leadership and speed. It squeaked out some close wins to tie Oregon

State for the title. Due to the "no-repeat" rule, the Ducks made their first trip to the Rose Bowl in 37 years.

The Rose Bowl game with Ohio State was billed by the LA scribes as the "biggest mismatch in Rose Bowl history." But the game was anything but a mismatch. Ohio State won the game 10-7, but they were out-gained in yardage 351-304 and in first downs 21-19 by the scrappy Oregon team. The Duck quarterback **Jack Crabtree** was named the Rose Bowl MVP.

During Cas' tenure, the Pacific Coast Conference, long in turmoil because of blatant recruiting violations by some of its members, fell apart. The game of football also changed with the arrival of two-platoon football.

Casanova operated for years under the recruiting handicap of poor facilities, and having to play the big games in Portland. But despite the disadvantages, only a few key plays kept his teams out of at least three post season bowls.

Casanova's teams had many outstanding players such as **Monte Brethauer, Emery Barnes, George Shaw, Ron Phiester, Jack Patera, Dick James, Phil McHugh, Jim Shanley, Steve Barnett, Bob Grottkau, Bob Peterson, Dave Tobey, Willie West, Dave Wilcox, Mel Renfro**, and **Bob Berry.**

At Oregon, Casanova always operated with a small budget, a small staff, and a small squad. But a mark of his coaching genius was the preparation of the backup players. They were coached well enough to step up when and where they were needed.

> **Advice from Cas:**
> *"Go into coaching for the kids, not for what the kids can do for you,"* remembered **Joe Schaffeld** before embarking on a 38 year career.

LEGACY OF COACHES

Johnny McKay	College and pro coach
Jack Patera	Pro coach
Jerry Frei	College and pro coach
Jack Roche	College coach
Bruce Synder	College and pro coach
John Robinson	College and pro coach
Phil McHugh	College coach
Joe Schaffeld	H.S. and college coach
Spike Hillstrom	H.S. and college coach
Ron Phiester	H.S. and college coach
Tom Keele	H.S. and college coach
Bill Tarrow	H.S. and college coach
Dick Arbuckle	H.S. and college coach

Of his career, Casanova said in 1970, "All those years working with young people made it worthwhile."

"When I look back at the tremendous number of kids who have made it, who have succeeded, I'm proud to think I may have been an influence; that my participation might have helped."

"It really irritates me when people still talk about dumb football players. Some of the kids I've had at Oregon and Santa Clara have become doctors, attorneys, dentists, big businessmen, coaches, high school principals, judges…"

Like Casanova's players, they have learned loyalty and practiced it. Of all the cornerstones Cas has preached over the years, it is the most enduring.

> In 1977, when Casanova was inducted into the **NFF College Hall of Fame**, his successor, **Jerry Frei**, spoke for the many who had come to know him as "Cas" over the years. "Cas will always be a symbol," Frei said. " He goes down in everyone's book as a gentleman, *a gentleman with dignity."*

Year	COACHING HONORS
1977	**NFF College Hall of Fame**
1980	**State of Oregon Sports Hall of Fame**
1992	**U of Oregon Athletic Hall of Fame**
1957	**Oregon Coach of the Year** **Slats Gill Award- Hayward Banquet**
1990	**Amos Alonzo Stagg Award by AFCA** **for his contibution to football**
1991	**Named new athletic center at Autzen** **Stadium in honor of Len Casanova**
	Coached in three East-West games **Two Hula Bowls** **One College All-American game**
1959	*United Press* **"Coach of the Week"** **following 20-3 upset of Air Force**
	Santa Clara Hall of Fame
	President of the American Football **Coaches Association**

Athletic Director at Oregon 1967-70
Private business 1970-72
Athletic Director Emeritus 1972-present

1958 Rose Bowl Staff: Bill Hammer, Jerry Frei, Cas, Johnny McKay, and Jack Roche

ROCHE: A CASANOVA PROTÉGÉ

In 1936, Jack Roche, a senior football player at Sequoia High School, was invited to live with his football coach, **Len Casanova**, while his dad, a greyhound owner, was racing dogs in Florida. It began a long relationship and a career opportunity.

> Jack Roche was a well developed athlete and wore the same size clothing as Cas. This was a real asset to Roche since he borrowed Cas' clothes, shoes and car while dating Renne, who he eventually married.

Roche matriculated to Santa Clara to rejoin Casanova, who had been hired by **Buck Shaw** as an assistant. Roche was a tailback on some of Santa Clara's finest teams.

Following student teaching, Roche became a bomber pilot teacher during World War II.

When Casanova became the Santa Clara coach in 1946, he invited Roche to join his staff.

Roche learned his job well. He became a defensive specialist. He followed Cas first to Pittsburg and then to the University of Oregon in 1951.

"Roche was brilliant," remembers **Jerry Frei**. "His strength was that he was creative each week. He would research and the scout the opponent, then come up with a defense that always looked different."

In 1960 when Roche led the Ducks for the Cal game (subbing for Cas), he was drained from the stress. He didn't like the pressure and was happy to be an assistant until he retired from the University of Oregon.

Darrel "Mouse" Davis

- Born: Sept. 6, 1932 in Palouse,Wash.
- Parents: Lu and Nate Davis
  Father was a farmer and truck driver
- Brothers:Don and Gale
- Married: Beverly Warren 9/10/55
- Children: Brad 10/23/57, Debbie 7/6/60,
  Brent 4/25/62, D'Ann 5/9/65
- High School: Independence , Oreg.
  Coach: John Mathis
  QB- All-League 1949
- College: Oregon College of Education
  Graduated in 1955 B.S., Education   and
  University of Oregon with a Masters in 1960
- Played football, basketball and baseball
  Coach: Bill McArthur
- Played at 5'6" 165 as QB, RB, and DB,
  making All-Oregon Collegiate Conference
  recognition in both 1953 and 1954.
  Williamson System All-American in 1954
- Service: Drafted in the U.S. Navy in 1955

THE NICKNAME: "MOUSE"

> "When I was younger, my father used to call me 'Burrow Mouse.'" Davis said. "I'm not sure why. I also remember playing second base on the varsity in my freshman year in high school when my brother Don , the catcher, threw the ball to me and I dropped it. He said, 'Nice hands, *Mouse.*' That's where it all started."

COACHING

1957	Assistant at OCE for **Bill McArthur**
1958	

JEFFERSON OREGON, H.S.

1959	9-1-0	**League Champs**

GRANT HIGH SCHOOL

1960	Freshman Coach for
1961	**Frank Buckiewicz**

COACH BILL MCARTHUR

" Bill had a great influence on my coaching. His coaching principals were: Keep it simple, but allow for great flexibility; Team is the most important; Believe in the player by allowing him an opportunity to contribute to the system.

"Personally, Bill always had time for me. He treated me like an equal and still commanded the respect necessary to be the coach. He loved football and loved to coach."

Mouse Davis: Turned football programs around with an innovative passing offense. The consummate teacher, possibly one the best at developing passing quarterbacks the game has seen.

THE " RUN-AND-SHOOT" OFFENSE

Mouse Davis' name is synonymous with the football term "**run-and-shoot**," which refers to a passing offense. After 34 years at different 14 coaching stops, the Davis offense might be better described as the "pass and score" offense.

"I think we've got an excellent offense," he said. "And I would like to give credit to everyone. **Tiger Ellison** (a former high school coach in Middletowne, Ohio) wrote a book called *The Run-and-Shoot Offense* in the early 1960s. What we do isn't what Tiger did, but I stole from him. I'm sold on what we do. Its important that what we do, we do it well," comments Davis.

Davis introduced the run-and-shoot offense in 1963, his first coaching job at Milwaukie.

MILWAUKIE HIGH SCHOOL (18-9-0)

1962	7-2-0	
1963	5-4-0	
1964	6-3-0	

SUNSET HIGH SCHOOL (36-13-6)

1965	4-3-2	
1966	5-4-0	
1967	6-2-1	
1968	5-2-2	
1969	7-1-1	
1970	9-1-0	**Metro Champs**

HILLSBORO HIGH SCHOOL (25-7-0)

1971	5-4-0	
1972	9-2-0	
1973	11-1-0	**AAA State Champions** Beat Medford 35-21

COLLEGE ASSISTANT

In 1974, Davis joined the college ranks by becoming the offensive assistant for a struggling Portland State program. Davis succeeded head coach **Ron Stratton** at the season's end.

PORTLAND STATE COLLEGE

1975 was a "make or break" year for the Portland State football program. It was facing extinction, when **President Joe Blumel** and Davis worked out a bare budget plan for one more season.

Davis enlisted the services of transfer quarterback **June Jones** to lead the Vikings grid fortunes. And what a player he found. Jones lit up the scoreboard and flourished with the run-and-shoot offense. In just two seasons, Jones had 5590 career yards of offense. *It saved PSU football* and Davis's start in college football.

PORTLAND STATE UNIVERSITY (42-24-0)

1975	8-3-0	
1976	8-3-0	
1977	7-4-0	
1978	5-6-0	
1979	6-5-0	
1980	8-3-0	

During Davis' tenure, the Viking offense averaged 486 yards and 37.8 points per game, led the NCAA in passing and total offense each year, and in scoring four of the six years. He coached five first-team Division I-AA All-Americans. Davis was named **State of Oregon Coach of the Year** in 1976.

The All-Americans were **June Jones, Dave Steif, Stuart Gaussion, Kurt Ivanoff, and Neil Lomax.** Other good players were **Fred Norgren, Jeff and John Urness, Jeff Rudolph, Joel Sigel, Scott Saxton, Ron Seawell, Art Dickson, Rob Pflugrad, Clint Didier and Mel DeLaura.**

NEIL LOMAX

The development of Neil Lomax as the most prolific passing quarterback in college football was the peak accomplishment of Mouse Davis' coaching career.

He finished his college career with 13,220 yards and 106 touchdowns in 42 games. He completed 938 of 1,607 passes. One game against Delaware State in 1980, Lomax threw for eight touchdowns in a 105-0 win. Two weeks earlier, Portland State scored 93 points against Cal Poly-Pomona.

Lomax was inducted into the first class of the College Division Hall of Fame in 1996.

CALIFORNIA ASSISTANT

Davis left Portland State after All-American quarterback **Neil Lomax** finished his career in hopes to take his own coaching career to the next level. Being overlooked by both major Oregon schools, he settled on being a Cal assistant in 1981. He left at mid-season when the Cal coach, **Roger Theder**, reneged on his commitment to the run-and-shoot offense.

Mouse Davis' coaching career shifted to the professional game.

COACHING PHILOSOPHY

"Total belief in our plan, which included a commitment to our offense and defensive approach. With work and dedication to that commitment, we always got better and better as the season progressed. Execution is the key, not how smart you attempt to be.

"The good players all want to believe and will if you do. It brings out the greatness in the individual player and shows up as a great team attitude. All my quarterbacks I had were an extension of my beliefs."

Quarterback

" The quarterback has been the backbone of our programs. We put him on display as no other offense can and they have responded with great production. We ask them to do every thing which one expects the leader of an operation to do, i.e. leadership, technique, study the game and become an extension of the coach and the system. He must believe, to have the team believe. Our belief has been that if one gives them a chance to become the *guy*, they will raise their production in every way. If they do not produce, we must find another QB, even if that QB is not physically gifted. This has happened twice in all my years coaching, once in high school and once at Portland State. In each case, the next quarterback that took over became more productive. They both set state and national records for production.

"The journey of quarterback development somewhat parallels the evolution of the offense. Improved techniques and the coaching of the quarterback as we continued to evolve the offense into an unstoppable producer. There is every confidence we could start the offense tomorrow at any level and have great success which parallel or exceed the production when we stopped the evolution at the last coaching stop in New York."

Under Davis' direction, the system works:

In Davis' six seasons as coach at Portland State, the Vikings led all schools within their division in total offense and passing each year.

In the Canadian Football League, directing the run-and-shoot as an assistant with the Toronto Argonauts in 1982, Davis helped turn around a team that had finished 2-14 in 1981 behind the CFL's worst- ranking passing game. The Argos went 9-6-1 in 1982 with the league's No.2 aerial attack, averaging 315 passing yards per game.

PROFESSIONAL FOOTBALL

1982	Toronto CFL	Assistant
1984	*Houston Gamblers USFL*	*Assistant*

Davis moved to the United States Football League in 1984, serving as offensive coordinator for the Houston Gamblers. With quarterback **Jim Kelly** at the controls, the run-and-shoot amassed 5,793 passing yards in 18 games, and averaged 34.3 points. The following season, Davis was named the coach of the Denver Gold. With likes of **Vince Evans** and **Bob Gagliano** at quarterback, the Gold finished 11-7 with the USFL's No.2 rated offense.

DENVER GOLD USFL (11-7)

1985	11-7-0	Head Coach

Backers of the run-and-shoot concede that personnel will determine how well, not if, the offense will work. "The number one way to stop it," Davis said, "is to have far superior people, but we'll still win a lot of the battles. If the personnel is even, we'll win 75 percent. If we're better than those who we are playing, we will never lose."

ARENA FOOTBALL

Davis helped get the Arena Football League on its feet in 1986, serving as the league's Director of Operations.

1986	Director of Operations	
1987	St.Louis Lightning	Team folded

The Arena St.Louis Lightning approached Davis to coach the second year. "But some of the owners didn't come up with the money and we never started," remembers Davis.

DETROIT LIONS NFL

1988	Offensive Assistant	**Wayne Fontes**
1989		
1990		

Davis had earned a reputation during his journey through three collegiate levels and four pro leagues and hoped to bring his "show" to the big time, the NFL. The first opportunity came when Detroit coach **Wayne Fontes** decided to open up his offense when he hired both Davis and **June Jones** to install their offense in 1988. It was tabbed the "silver stretch." The offense had moderate success, but drew criticism from some NFL purists who thought that a tight end was essential in its offense.

NYNJ KNIGHTS WFL (21-17-0)

1991	11-8-0	Head Coach
1992	10-9-0	Head Coach

"The Knights was a great football job. The kids were stars in college but not in the 'super' class. The World League owned the teams and had good administration, but the most difficult part was making the trips to Europe and controlling everything."

TORONTO

1993	Toronto CFL	Assistant

" As an offensive coordinator, I had a big influence on the Canadian game. When I first went up there in 1982, we introduced trips and quads and a lot of motion. Eleven years later when I came back, everyone was doing it."

ATLANTA FALCONS

When **Rankin Smith**, the Falcon owner, decided to replace **Jerry Granville** at the end of the 1993 season, he cast his lot with Granville's offensive coordinator, **June Jones**.

1994	Atlanta Falcons	Assistant to **June Jones**
1995	Atlanta Falcons	Assistant
1996	Atlanta Falcons	Assistant

In selecting his staff, Jones turned to Davis, who was an assistant with Toronto, to help him with the offense. Davis, realizing that often-criticized offense might be facing extinction in the NFL, cast his lot for three years to help his former pupil and friend, June Jones. Davis and Jones had worked together at Toronto, Houston (Gamblers), Denver and Detroit. "We've waited 16 to 18 years," Jones said, "16 to 18 years of frustration for this opportunity and it may not come again."

Davis had the opportunity to work with the much traveled quarterback **Jeff George**, whom he considered had the best "rocket" passing arm in the game. It was ideal for the offense. It was rumored that drills could last 20-30 minutes without a dropped pass.

Even with Davis helping Jones on the practice field and from the press box, George's salary squabbles and his on-the-field behavior led to team problems. June Jones' head coaching stint with the Atlanta Falcons ended in 1996 after only two years. It may have ended the "run-and-shoot" era in the NFL.

Davis retired after 50 years in the game. He presently resides in Las Vegas.

COACHING HONORS

1975	**The PSU Charles Withers Award**
1976	**The Slats Gill Coach of the Year Award**
1997	**Portland State Hall of Fame**
1997	**NFF Walk of Champions Award 1973 AAA Champs-Hillsboro H.S.**

"Hey 'Big Kid', its show time." Those were the words that I heard my freshman year at Portland State when it was my time. My time to take center stage for the most explosive offense in the game today that was orchestrated by the master coach **Darrel "Mouse" Davis**. Portland State was the proving ground for my ten year career in the NFL. But it was more than football that I learned from Mouse. Don't be mistaken, we spent countless hours on game films and defensive strategies that could slow down our potent run-and-shoot offense. This knowledge that I learned from Mouse made it easy for me to adapt to the pro game and all of its complicated defenses.

Neil Lomax , PSU QB

THE MOUSE DAVIS LEGACY: DEVELOPING QUARTERBACKS

Jerry Costanzo	Milwaukie H.S.
Grant Spencer	Milwaukie H.S.
Chris Maletis	Sunset H. S.
Brent Curtis	Sunset H. S.
Matt James	Sunset H. S.
Curt Nohavec	Sunset H. S.
Bob Nicholl	Hillsboro H. S.
Dick Judah	Hillsboro H.S.
Mark Neffendorf	Hillsboro H.S.
Mike Gardner	Portland State
June Jones	Portland State
Lloyd LaFrance	Portland State
Mike Atwood	Portland State
Neil Lomax	Portland State
Gale Gilbert	U of California
Conridge Holloway	Toronto Argos
Joe Barnes	Toronto Argos
Vince Evans	Denver Gold
Jim Kelly	Houston Gamblers
Rodney Pete	Detroit Lions
Eric Kramer	Detroit Lions
Bob Gagliano	Detroit Lions Denver Gold
Reggie Slack	NY NJ Knights Toronto Argos
Jeff George	Atlanta Falcons
Bobby Hebert	Atlanta Falcons

Tom Elias DeSylvia

- Born: Sept. 29, 1924 in Butte, Mont.
- Parents: Elias and Mary Burns DeSylvia
  Father was an immigrant from the Azores, Portugal. He worked his way to Montana as a "cattle puncher." There he worked in the copper mines.
- Married: Vernell Anderson 8/7/51
- Sons: Terry 4/5/43, Mike 5/7/52 and Dan 4/21/57 Daughter: Jeri Ann 6/4/55
- High School: Butte Public '43
  Coach: Harry "Swede" Dahlberg
  Tackle sophomore and junior year
  All state fullback senior year
- Navy 1943-46
  Farragut, Idaho USN dental corpsman
  Played on winning football team
- College: Oregon State College 1946-50
  Coach: Lon Stiner 1946-48
  Coach: Kip Taylor 1949
- Honors: East-West Shrine Game,
  2nd team *AP* All-Coast
- Degree: B.S. in PE in 1950

HIGH SCHOOL

Tom DeSylvia's high school football career is legendary in Montana. At 5'11" 190 pounds, he was All-State three years and performed on two state championship teams. His playing and coaching career was impacted by his coach, **Swede Dahlberg**, who coached at Butte High for 44 years, winning 21 league titles.

COLLEGE

When DeSylvia was discharged from the Navy in 1946, he found his way to Eugene, planning for a football future at the University of Oregon. But football coach **Tex Oliver** disappointed him: "You don't have a ride here."

Subsequently some Montana friends encouraged DeSylvia to consider Oregon State College. He was welcomed with open arms by coaches **Lon Stiner** and **Jim Dixon.**

And what a football player the Beavers landed. The husky and strong DeSylvia had an outstanding college career as a guard and tackle. He played on both sides of the ball. He is recognized as *the only player to have played in every game for four years at Oregon State.*

His senior year, DeSylvia was selected team captain for new coach **Kip Taylor**. He led them to a 7-3 winning season. The upset of Michigan State in Portland was the highlight.

Tom DeSylvia was inducted in the **Oregon Sports Hall of Fame** in 1997. He coached some of the finest football players, Terry Baker and Mel Renfro, and teams that have played in the State of Oregon.

PRO FOOTBALL

DeSylvia was drafted by the NFL champion Philadelphia Eagles in 1950, but an unfortunate incident ended his tryout prematurely.

In practice the week after the College All-Star game, DeSylvia inadvertently injured one of the Eagle's stars, **Bucko Kilroy,** in a collision. The coach reacted by releasing DeSylvia.

Former OSC teammate **Bill Austin**, who played and coached many years in the NFL, claims DeSylvia was a player and could have played in the pros.

ASSISTANT COACHING

DeSylvia returned to Portland to start his career as a football coach. He was assigned to assist **Ted Ogdahl** at Grant High School.

JEFFERSON HIGH SCHOOL

The following season, DeSylvia was transferred to Jefferson to assist the legendary **Eric Waldorf**, who had been coaching there since 1927.

The young enthusiastic coach was eager to make an impact on the program, but it wasn't Waldorf's style to utilize DeSylvia talents until the second year.

DeSylvia's coaching strength, which earmarked his coaching career, was developing strong blocking and tackling linemen. Waldorf began to utilize those talents.

After the senior-laden 1952 Jeff team won the city championship, Waldorf called it quits. He left the coaching opportunity for DeSylvia with the parting remark: "You'll be fortunate to win three games next year."

DeSylvia was up to the challenge. His first team, with only a handful of returning lettermen, won eight games, losing only their second game in the state semifinals.

DeSylvia's coaching success at Jefferson included seven league titles and two state championships in just nine years. *The best, the 1958 team, led the nation in offense with 4,989 yards; scoring 512 points in 12 games while giving up only 51. Four players became college All-Americans; Heisman winner **Terry Baker**, NFL Hall of Famer **Mel Renfro**, and small college All-Americans **Mick Hergert** and **Bill Hartman**.*

Other recognized players from that winning era were **Ray Renfro, Harvey Jackson, Doug White, Mike Henselman, Dennis Prozinski, Ken Kearney, Herb Washburn, John Theis, Mike Barnes and Rance Spruill.**

DeSylvia molded tough teams that played with a lot of enthusiasm. When he praised his players, they always performed at their best.

JEFFERSON HIGH SCHOOL (74-15-0)

1953	8-2-0	PIL 2nd	Semis
1954	7-2-0	PIL 1st	Quarters
1955	8-1-0	PIL 1st	Semis
1956	3-5-0		
1957	11-0-0	PIL 1st	**State Champs**
1958	12-0-0	PIL 1st	**State Champs**
1959	11-1-0	PIL 1st	**Finals**
1960	8-2-0	PIL 1st	Quarters
1961	6-2-0	PIL 1st	Quarters

PORTLAND STATE COLLEGE

In the summer of 1962, DeSylvia jumped at the opportunity to coach at the college level when the Portland State job became available.

Tom DeSylvia was naive when he thought coaching football at the young urban college might be as easy as it was at Jefferson.

So with his usual enthusiasm, DeSylvia took up the challenge and made a big impact on Portland State. He was the first "name coach" hired to lead their fortunes. With a small staff, he was able to achieve respect and attract quality players. The best were **Billy White, Jerry Humphries, Andy Berkis, Mike Shrunk, Ray Renfro, Mike Henselman, Jay Lillie, Ron Simonson and Jim Hollingsworth.**

PORTLAND STATE COLLEGE

1962	4-4-0

DeSylvia experienced shock and mixed emotion his first college game. On the opening kickoff, Lewis and Clark's **Mick Hergert**, the Jeff star of 1958, ran it back 93 yards for a touchdown. 11 of his former Jeff players were on the opposing Lewis and Clark roster.

But Portland State College wasn't prepared to upgrade their football program fast enough to satisfy DeSylvia. Frustrated and impatient, he abruptly resigned after one season. At age 37 and at the height of his coaching career, DeSylvia was without a job.

SAN MATEO HIGH SCHOOL

Former Oregon State teammates, **Arvid Niemi** and **Yale Rohlff** lured DeSylvia to San Mateo High School in California as an assistant football coach in 1963. The following year, DeSylvia became the head coach.

SAN MATEO HIGH SCHOOL

1964	4-5-0	

DAVID DOUGLAS

At the urging of another former college teammate, David Douglas Athletic Director **Dick Miller**, DeSylvia returned to Portland. **Marv Hiebert** added him to his staff in 1965. He became the defensive coach.

DeSylvia remained at Douglas for 21 years mainly as an assistant coach with the exception of a two game head coaching stint in 1969. A head injury in a fall at home forced him to the sidelines. DeSylvia retired in 1985.

DAVID DOUGLAS HIGH SCHOOL

1969	1-1-0	

HONORS

1959	**Hayward Banquet Man of the Year**
1982	**Martin Luther King Award**
1988	**NFF Walk of Champions Award**
1991	**Butte, Montana Athletic Hall of Fame**
1994	**Oregon State U. Hall of Fame**
1997	**State of Oregon Sports Hall of Fame**

Bill Dressel

- **Leonard William Dressel**
- Born: Dec. 28, 1939 in Newberg, Oreg.
- Parents: Leonard and Maryan Dressel
- Father was a logger
- Married: Gaynelle Gaibler September 5,1958
- Children: Kimra Corada 4/18/58, Kevin Dressel 2/5/62
- High School: Newberg , 1954-1958
- Football coach: Tom Poulton and Glenn Benedict Jr.
- Position: Running back/safety- 6'165 lbs
- Honors: All TYV League 1957-58
- College: Linfield College 1958-1962
- Coach: Paul Durham
- Running back – Honorable mention All NWC and Honorable mention All-American
- Degrees: B.S. in PE and Health in 1962; Masters in Education in 1965 from Linfield

YOUNG BILL DRESSEL

The person that turned Bill Dressel on to sports was his junior high coach, **Glenn Benedict**. Dressel played football, basketball, baseball and track for him in the 6th, 7th, and 8th grades.

Dressel fell in love with football. He loved everything about the game. There was more action than baseball and basketball. He felt his temperament also fit better with football. He loved running with the ball. He remembers that "nothing compared to either out-running, running over, making an opponent miss a tackle or breaking loose on a long run."

"It was such a rush, I think that is why I enjoyed coaching so much. I know what the players are feeling when they make a good run, score a touchdown, make a good tackle or a goal line stand. *It is impossible to duplicate the pure fun of playing football, but coaching comes close.*"

Varsity coach **Keith Moore** got Dressel involved as a running back in the Newberg offense both his sophomore and junior year. He also challenged him to learn the assignments of every team position.

The Newberg's team record during Dressel's high school career wasn't remarkable, but his individual 20 touchdowns were. It earned him all-league recognition and a scholarship to Linfield College.

Bill Dressel had 27 winning football seasons during the 34 years he coached the sport. *"The football field was the classroom...the games the weekly tests... the final exam is life."*

LINFIELD COLLEGE

Dressel had a great experience at Linfield. **Paul Durham's** teams were starting a long string of winning seasons. He earned letters all four years on some very good teams as a prime receiver and a running back. His senior year, Dressel played a big part when the Wildcats rolled to 10 straight victories before losing in the NAIA final (the Camellia Bowl) to Pittsburg State of Kansas 12-7.

COACHING

Bill Dressel had some interest in becoming a coach when he was in high school, but it became solidified with the Linfield experience. **Paul Durham, Roy Helser and Ted Wilson** showed him how to coach by their good example and teaching.

When Dressel starting his coaching career at Academy Junior High in Dallas, he coached football and basketball. His basketball team would compete against his own junior high mentor's (**Glen Benedict**) team from Newberg. Dressel remembers: "It wouldn't make *Sports Illustrated* but it was big stuff for me."

Dressel followed his eighth grade charges to Dallas High School to help and assist **Wes Ediger**. The following season at the age of 24, Bill Dressel was the head coach at a 3A school.

CAREER COACHING RECORD (224-112-2)

1962	Frosh football coach	Academy Jr High Dallas, Oregon
1963	Varsity Assistant	Dallas H. S.

DALLAS HIGH SCHOOL (28-27-1)

1964	2-6-1	
1965	7-2-0	
1966	1-8-0	
1967	5-4-0	
1968	4-5-0	
1969	9-2-0	**TYV Champs**

It took Dressel six seasons before his team won the TYV championship in 1969. He was chosen **Oregon High School Coach of the Year**. He was successful and was in demand.

Central Catholic hired Dressel to coach football in the strong Metro League. There he coached for seven seasons against the likes of **Don Mathews, Mouse Davis, John Allen and Greg McMackin.**

CENTRAL CATHOLIC H.S. (36-26-1)

1970	7-2-0	
1971	7-2-0	
1972	5-3-1	
1973	3-6-0	
1974	5-4-0	
1975	3-6-0	
1976	8-3-0	

In 1976, when Benson Principal **Harold Anderson** went looking for a coach to replace **Mike Lopez,** who had just received the Aloha football job, he asked Vice Principal **Dick Hennessy** for input.

"Well Harold, what are you looking for, a high-key coach or a low-key coach?" asked Hennessy.

Anderson replied, "Both you and Mike were high-key coaches. Maybe we should try a low-key one for a change."

"I know just the guy," said Hennessy. "He's over at Central Catholic." Dressel was hired.

Since then, Benson and the PIL were rewarded with 21 years of solid football. By his retirement after the 1997 season, Dressel's Benson gridders won or shared seven PIL championships. They reached the playoffs 18 times.

His best team in **1988** won the **State Championship**. It earned him another **Coach of the Year** awards by his contemporaries.

BENSON TECH (160-59-0)

1977	5-3-0	**3 way PIL 1st place tie**
1978	7-3-0	
1979	7-4-0	
1980	8-2-0	**PIL Champs**
1981	7-3-0	
1982	7-3-0	
1983	5-4-0	
1984	9-1-0	**PIL Champs**
1985	8-2-0	
1986	11-2-0	
1987	11-1-0	**PIL Champs**
1988	14-0-0	**PIL and State 4A Champs** Beat Roseburg 35-15 **Won *Prefontaine* team Award**
1989	11-1-0	**PIL Champs**
1990	9-2-0	**PIL 1st place tie**
1991	6-4-0	
1992	4-6-0	
1993	7-3-0	
1994	6-4-0	
1995	4-5-0	
1996	7-3-0	
1997	7-3-0	

COACHING HONORS

1969-70	**Oregon High School Coach of Year**
1988-89	**Oregon High School Coach of Year PIL Coach of the Year**
1989	Head Shrine Coach

COACHING PHILOSOPHY

The football field is a classroom. The coaches are teachers. The players are students. The curriculum: individual sacrifice, cooperation, team work, respect, character, dedication, work ethic, self discipline, motivation, integrity, confidence and courage. The games are weekly tests. The final exam is life.

Bill Dressel

Paul Durham

- Born: Oct. 18, 1913 in Portland,Oreg.
- Parents: Darr and Greta Durham
- Father's occupation: Printer-owned *Durham and Downey Printing Co* in Portland
- Married: Amelia Litzenberger
- Family: Jeff 4/21/40, Terry 5/3/45, Cathy Devine 7/21/47
- High School: Franklin, 1927-32
  Coach: Football-Harvey "Pop" George, Basketball-Larry Devlin
  Track- Rein Jackson
- College: Linfield 1932-36
  Coach: Football-Henry Lever
- Played fullback at 6'2" 225 pounds
- Played basketball and track
- Degree: B.S. Linfield (history) '36; Masters of Education Uof Ore '41

HIGH SCHOOL

Paul Durham started Franklin High School in 1928, but dropped out after a year and a half to work. "Jobs were hard to get, but schools were still open during the Great Depression." So Durham entered Linfield in 1932.

LINFIELD

"Coach **Henry Lever** was a great man and had a wonderful influence on his students and athletes. He was an excellent and solid coach. He was also an outstanding example of the kind of life a man should live. I admired and loved him greatly.

Paul Durham earned 10 varsity letters at Linfield in football, basketball and track.

In 1935, Linfield won the school's first Northwest Conference championship

HIGH SCHOOL COACHING

YAMHILL H.S.

1936	Coached basketball and baseball. School did not have a football program
1937	
1938	
1939	

"It was my first coaching job, and it was wonderful. Life of a coach in a small town is really unparalleled. My four years at Yamhill were as much fun and brought me as much happiness any four working years of my life."

FRANKLIN H.S.

1940	JV Football coach
1941	

Paul Durham developed and formed the winning philosophy that continues today at Linfield.

"I was the Franklin JV football coach and had terrific young men who went undefeated under **George Emigh, Arne Faust and Johnny Londahl**."

COMMERCE H.S.

1942	Football Assistant, head basketball and baseball coach
1943	
1944	
1945	

"Paul Durham was my first varsity coach at Commerce, and he became a strong influence in my life. One major event happened during my junior year during a PE class when Durham became irritated with my 'horseplay' and marched me into his office.

"Don't you realize you have a chance to receive an athletic scholarship if you get serious once in a while?

"Coming from a low-income family, I had not given consideration to attending college. This was the first time anyone suggested the subject.

"I had so much respect for Paul Durham because of the time he gave his athletes and his positive attitude, I decided I wanted to be a teacher and coach."

Mel Krause

"I assisted Ed Warren (a wonderful man and great coach) in football. **Mel Krause, Jim Peccia, Chuck Bafaro and Whitey Palmquist** were great athletes."

FRANKLIN H.S. (6-9-1)

1946	4-4-0	Head football, basketball and baseball coach
1947	2-5-1	Head football and baseball

COLLEGE FOOTBALL

In 1948, Paul Durham started his college coaching career at his alma mater. He was ahead of his time in developing a strong program. He was an exceptionally smart and sound football coach. He formed a winning philosophy that continues today at Linfield.

LINFIELD COLLEGE   20 years   (122-51-10)

1948	3-6-0	
1949	4-4-0	Added athletic directorship
1950	6-3-0	
1951	3-3-3	
1952	5-3-1	
1953	5-4-0	
1954	3-6-0	
1955	3-6-0	
1956	6-1-2	**NWC 1st**
1957	8-1-0	**NWC 1st**
1958	7-1-1	
1959	5-3-1	
1960	7-2-0	
1961	10-1-0	**NWC 1st Camellia Bowl Lost to Pitt State 12-7**
1962	8-0-1	**NWC 1st**
1963	8-1-0	
1964	8-1-1	**NWC 1st**
1965	8-2-0	**NWC 1st Lost to St.Johns Minn 33-0**
1966	7-2-0	
1967	8-1-0	**NWC 1st**

In the 20 years that Paul Durham was the football coach at Linfield, his record was 122-51-10 for a 69.4 winning percentage.

The last twelve years, from 1956-1967, Durham's Linfield teams had winning seasons, dominating the Northwest Conference with seven championships and four runner-ups. It was the foundation of the national record for consecutive winning seasons the school earned in 1998.

DURHAM'S WINNING PHILOSOPHY

The phenomenal success of the Linfield football coach and athletic director baffled his conference rivals. How did he do it?

- **Superior coaching staff :** "**Roy Helser**, one of the best college baseball coaches and **Ted Wilson** the basketball coach were fine assistants in football."

- **An exacting brand of football:** The running offense depended on perfect timing, bristling with trap plays, counters and quick openers. His passing attack was full of fakes to the fullback or halfback. His skill and deception extends to the defense where his writing on the subject became worthy of national publications.

- **Psychological preparation:** "My belief about football is that a great percentage of the game is mental and emotional. All the close games are won by the team best prepared in these phases. The coach can do something about it, but basically it has to be done by the older players. This is where the pride, respect for the institution and such should enter in the picture. It's when these older players begin to absorb what the coaches have been trying to teach them and lead the others along, that success follows. These old-timers have to lead through the way they play, not say. If you have this, you're in business."

- **Dedication:** Durham's winning formula required a fanatical dedication to the game, being more dedicated than the opponent. So he fused the feeling into his players, that no one could out-condition them. He summed up the stamina and dedication need with this: "When a boy is dropping physically and then turns over to head and heart and takes the next step no matter what the pain, he's arrived."

- **Recruiting:** Durham had strong bonds with his players after graduation. At least 250 graduates were actively coaching in the Pacific Northwest, and another 55 are in administration. "They were our greatest sources in recruiting," he says. "They interested people in our institution and it pretty much perpetuated itself." Durham maintained miraculous contact with his graduates through personal contact and a periodic newsletter. On the other side of the ledger is the respect that the men who have played under him hold for him and the school.

> "We firmly believed and worked on the premise that if we told a potential recruit about his future help at Linfield, he would get it even if he didn't turn out to be a championship performer. We tried to treat our team members as though they were members of our families."
>
> **Paul Durham**

Coaching wish: Durham's primary wish was to produce good coaches. "When a principal called me and says he has a Linfield man on his staff, not asking more, it makes me feel we're doing our job," Durham commented. " We concentrated on making the good coaches. We didn't want them to push kids around and swear at them. That placed a strong requirement on our coaching staff, but they lived by what they said. They are terrific examples."

Head coaches that have played for Paul Durham

Mel Fox	North Salem
Mel Krause	University of Oregon
Ad Rutschman	Hillsboro and Linfield
Marv Heater	South Salem
Randy Harrison	Albany
Ray Olson	Dallas
Harry Schibel	Central Catholic
Pat Smith	Clackamas
Connie Sproul	Newberg and Tigard
Ray Simonson	Sheridan
Cliff Saxton	North Salem
Bob Scofield	
Charlie Driggers	Canby
Vern Marshall	Grant
Joe Brock	Stayton
Cliff Allen	Park Rose
Bob Haack	Forest Grove
Ron August	Dallas
Jeff Durham	Forest Grove
Jim Bernhardt	Scappose
Gene Forman	Riddle
Dick Flood	Gresham
Larry Binkard	Hillsboro
Gary Yates	Pendleton
Coy Zimmerman	Barlow
Larry Miller	
Howard Morris	Oregon Tech
Norm Musser	Grants Pass and Medford
Ron Parrish	North Marion
Bill Parrish	Astoria
Gary Walls	Madison
Fred vonAppen	U of Hawaii
Dave Kocer	Jackson, Wilson

ATHLETIC DIRECTOR

Durham's ability to select the right people for the right jobs had a tremendous impact on the success of other sports programs at Linfield.

1. Chose **Roy Helser** , his college teammate, to coach baseball.
2. Chose **Ted Wilson** to coach basketball for 20 years.
3. Recruited **Ad Rutschman**, a three sport athlete from Hillsboro H.S., and later a protege who would succeed him as the football coach.

Durham was also the sports editor of the *Daily McMinnville News Register*. His columns became essential reading by sports enthusiasts across Oregon.

> "Dad would get up early in the summer, go down to the paper, write his column *"Dodging with Durham,"* return to teach classes at the college and then go down to take charge and run the McMinnville Park and Recreation program."
>
> **Son Jeff Durham**

During the last two seasons, that Paul Durham coached football at Linfield, he suffered from the pressure of coaching. He resigned in favor of **Ad Rutschman.**

Durham would have stayed on as athletic director, but **President Harry Dillon** wanted to cut his salary. It was timely for Durham's career when he was offered the athletic directorship at the University of Hawaii in 1968.

HONORS

	NAIA Football Coaches Hall of Fame
	Helms Athletic Hall of Fame in L.A.
1989	**Oregon Sports Hall of Fame**
1961	**Oregon's Man of the Year Award**
1962	**NAIA National Coach of the Year**
1997	**U. of Hawaii Sports Circle of Honor**

ATHLETIC DIRECTOR AT U. OF HAWAII 1968-1975

Durham resigned in 1975 and remained on the faculty in Health and Physical Education and with the College of Education from 1975 through 1981.

Durham resides in Hawaii.

Darrell Everett

- Born: July 23, 1931 in Portland,Oreg.
- Died: Feb. 27, 1985
- Parents: Charlie and Goldie Varner; was adopted by step father, Ray Everett
- Occupation: Ray worked at the post office
- Family: Daughters Teri Everett 2/12/58, Cindy Murphy 4/2/58
- Married: Patsy Annula
- High School: Roosevelt 1945-1949
- Football coach: Mike DeLotto
- Honors: All-City on co-champion team
- College: Gray's Harbor Junior College '50
- Coach: Dan Melinkovich
- Honors: Junior College All-American
- College: Lewis and Clark College 1952-55 Coach: Joe Huston
- Honors: Captain, All-Northwest Conference and Little All-American on championship team in 1954 as a tackle
- Lewis and Clark Hall of Fame in 1980

MARSHALL HIGH SCHOOL

In 1960, when Marshall High School first opened its doors in southeast Portland, Athletic Director **Ralph Harper** knew the type of person that was necessary to coach its football team. He wanted a man who would build character as well as teach a good brand of football.

Harper didn't have to look far. He recruited a promising student teacher he had five years earlier at Benson Tech and at that time an assistant football coach at Lincoln, Darrell Everett.

Harper and Marshall High School got what they bargained for. What transpired in the school's first 21 years will be remembered as the "Darrell Everett Era."

Besides Everett's excellent coaching record (100-82-4), his impact on the lives of hundreds of Minutemen will be remembered.

Harper remarked about Everett's rapport with kids, his ability to understand them, to inspire them and to maximize their potential making them all "winners," building a feeling of self-worth.

Darrell Everett coached the Marshall varsity football team for 21 years before health forced him from the game in 1982. Everett's style of coaching included a deep sense of loyalty, pride and team unity. He taught his teams songs that would create those qualities such as *"We are the Mighty Minutemen, When the Minutemen hit the tartan,* and *We've been there baby, we've been*

The **Darrell Everett** era at Marshall embodied a deep sense of loyalty, pride and team unity. His team's were tough.

there!" His teams were proudly known as the "Red Hats."

The 1970 team won the PIL championship losing to Medford in the semi-finals. Everett was named **Oregon State High School Coach of the Year** and was the head coach of the winning North Shrine team in 1971.

MARSHALL HIGH SCHOOL (100-82-4)

1961	1-7-0	
1962	2-5-1	
1963	5-4-0	
1964	5-3-0	
1965	2-7-0	
1966	5-4-0	
1967	4-2-2	
1968	2-6-0	
1969	5-3-1	
1970	10-1-0	**PIL champs**
1971	8-1-1	**PIL champs**
1972	6-3-0	
1973	9-1-1	**PIL champs**
1974	6-3-0	
1975	7-2-0	
1976	6-3-0	
1977	7-2-0	
1978	5-4-0	
1979	1-7-0	
1980	2-7-0	
1981	2-7-0	

Heart problems forced Everett from coaching in 1982. He died Feb. 27, 1985, at the age of 54.

Jerry Frei

- Born: June 3, 1924 in Brooklyn, Wis.
  Parents: George and Gertrude Frei
- Father's occupation: livestock dealer
- Married: Marian Benson 12/25/45
- Sons: David 4/4/49, Terry 1/1/55
- Daughters: Judith Kaplan 2/2/52, Susan
  Earley 6/4/59, Nancy McCormick 1/24/62
- High School: Stoughton, Wis., 1941
- Coach: Ray Myrick
- Honors: All-league tackle
- College: University of Wisconsin 1948
- Coach: Harry Stuhldreher
- Position: Played guard on a team that had
  Pat Harder, Dave Schreiner and Elroy
  Hirsch in 1942, 1946-7
- Degree: B.S. '48; Masters Wisc. '50
- Service: WW II, Army Air Force, 1st Lt.
  P-38 pilot; flew 67 photo reconnaissance
  flights in the South Pacific

THE MOVE TO OREGON

After experiencing an exceptionally cold winter his last year at Wisconsin, Jerry Frei remembered the favorable reference about the city of Portland by an Air Force friend, **Don Gabarino.**

" So on a whim, I wanted to go to Oregon to see what's it like," remembered Frei. He took his wife Marian in their Nash automobile and paid his service chum a visit in August of 1948

Frei must have liked Portland, for he made application for employment with the school district. He was interviewed by Grant principal **Colton Meek** to help coach football but was disappointed that a teaching position wasn't available. Within a couple of days, Meek found that teaching opening, and hired Jerry Frei to his first coaching job as an assistant to another eager first year coach, **Ted Ogdahl.** And what a coaching combination they made. Within two years, the Grant Generals were the undefeated Oregon high school champions.

Jerry Frei changed jobs to become the Lincoln High School head coach for the 1950 and 1951 seasons before he moved on again to Willamette University to rejoin **Ted Ogdahl,** who was now a promising college coach.

Oregon's football coach **Len Casanova** had heard about the good line coach from Wisconsin and offered him a position on his staff twice. The second offer was considered seriously and accepted by Frei. He wanted to advance his coaching career.

Jerry Frei was a player's coach. During his five-year tenure, Oregon had some of the school's best athletes and played some of their most exciting football.

Frei first joined Casanova's staff in 1955 as the freshman coach and later became the varsity line coach.

COACHING CAREER

1948	Grant H.S.	Assistant to **Ted**
1949	Portland	**Ogdahl**
1950	1-6-1	Head Coach
1951	4-4-0	Lincoln H.S.
1952	Willamette U.	Assist to **Ted Ogdahl**
1953		
1954		
1955	University of	Assist to **Len**
1956	Oregon	**Casanova**
1957		Freshmen Coach
1958		
1959		Line Coach
1960		
1961		
1962		
1963		
1964		
1965		
1966		

When athletic director **Leo Harris** retired in January 1967, after 20 years service, Casanova took over the reins and hand-picked his own successor, his loyal 12 year veteran line coach, Jerry Frei.

UNIVERSITY OF OREGON (22-29-2)

1967	2-8-0	
1968	4-6-0	
1969	5-5-1	
1970	6-4-1	
1971	5-6-0	

Like Cas, Frei was also a player's coach. During his five-year tenure, Oregon had some of the school's best athletes and played some of the school's most exciting football.

True belief in the players...

George Dames remembers well the 1967 Civil War game against the "Giant Killers."

"Coach Frei had jumped up on a bench to give a pep talk to the team when he sensed his message was not inspirational. He abruptly stopped. He started to cry. 'Go out and beat them. I know you can.' "

The Ducks played well. They led until the final minutes of the game before OSU won 14-10.

"It spoke volumes," said Dames. "Frei showed at a special moment how much he believed in his players."

Recognized players were **Jim Smith, Omri Hildreth, George Dames, Claxton Welch, Tom Blanchard, Bobby Moore/Ahmad Rashad, Tom Drougas, Tim Stokes, Andy Mauer, Tom Graham, Bob Newland, Steve Rennie, Leland Glass and Dan Fouts.**

Frei's five-year record at Oregon was only 22-29-2, due to its competitive conference and heavy non-conference schedule; the likes of Ohio State, Nebraska, Oklahoma, and Notre Dame. Then add the five Civil War losses with a series of inopportune injuries, it didn't keep the pressure off the coaching staff.

Sadly, in January of 1972, Jerry Frei fell victim to poor administrative leadership. Disgruntled alumni exerted pressure on the first year-athletic director, **Norv Ritchey**, to have the football coach make some staff changes. Frustrated, but true to his coaching principles, Jerry Frei felt undermined and resigned.

PROFESSIONAL FOOTBALL

1972-1975	Denver Broncos	Offensive line coach For **John Ralston**
1976-1977	Tampa Bay Bucs	Offensive line coach For **Johnny McKay**
1978-1980	Chicago Bears	Offensive line coach For **Neil Armstrong**
1981-1982	Denver Broncos	Line coach For **Dan Reeves**
1983-1994	Denver Broncos	Pro scout
1995-1999	Denver Broncos	Consultant

Jerry Frei was a good football coach. He turned to the professional level where he could focus entirely on the game. The next 26 years, he has coached for the Broncos, Bucs and the Bears. His highlights have been the five Super Bowl experiences with the Broncos.

Frei lives in Denver.

Floyd Emil Halvorsen

- Born: March 18, 1939 in Williston, N.D.
- Parents: William and Vivian Halvorsen
- Father was a copper miner in Butte,Mont.
  Family: Married Patricia Price 11/25/61
  Marie Wyatt 9/29/62 , Floyd 11/28/63,
  Timothy 12/21/65, and Robyn 5/10/73
- High School: Butte Central , 1957
- Football coach: Jim Sweeney '53-54 and Ed Simonich "55-56
- Honors: All-State tailback
  Most returns for touchdowns, career and one game, Montana state records still stands.
- Baseball, track and wrestling
- College:Carroll College (Helena) '61
- Coach: Jim Hunthousen
- Honors: 4 year starter All-Frontier League for 3 years (NAIA)
  Carroll College Hall of Fame in 1993
  Butte Sports Hall of Fame in 1995
- Degrees: B.A. Carroll 1961; and Masters from U of Oregon 1985

CARROLL COLLEGE

Floyd Halvorsen was described by his teammates as epitomizing the Carroll athlete, playing both football and baseball carrying a demanding academic schedule.

"His speed, agility, determination and athletic ability made him one of the greatest breakaway runners ever in Montana. His positive attitude towards the game contributed greatly to the team's tremendous successes. His unselfish play continually amazed and inspired his team. He was an All-Conference senior who, despite a separated shoulder and cracked ribs, would continue to run, block, and tackle with intensity. Floyd Halvorsen was Carroll College Football at its very finest."
Carroll College Hall of Fame induction 1993

COACHING CAREER

1961	Cental Catholic H.S. Portland	Assistant coach to **Al Yanzik**
1962 1963	Central Catholic	Assistant coach to **Joe Schaffeld**

Floyd Halvorsen brought winning football to Churchill High School, two state finals and 10 league championships in 25 years.

COACHING RECORD 29 years (186-103-5)
JOHN F. KENNEDY, MT. ANGEL (10-22-4)
First year for private coed school of 300 students (2A). Head foootball and track coach

1964	0-9-0	
1965	3-4-2	
1966	4-4-1	
1967	3-5-1	

ASSISTANT COACHING

1968	Grants Pass H.S.	Assist. to **Mel Ingram**
1969 1970 1971	Grants Pass H.S.	Assistant to **Gary Mires ***

* Other assistants at Grants Pass that coached with Halvorsen were **Thurman Bell** and **Darrell Thornton.**

CHURCHILL H.S. 25 years (176-81-1)
10 Mid Western League championships
14 consecutive playoffs 1976-89 (18-14-1)

Year	Record	
1972	4-5-0	
1973	5-4-0	
1974	4-5-0	
1975	8-1-0	**Tie for League championship**
1976	8-2-0	**League champs**
1977	11-1-1	**League champs Co-State Champs – tied Medford 7-7**
1978	10-1-0	**League champs**
1979	11-3-0	**State finals- lost to Corvallis 15-14**
1980	7-4-0	
1981	8-3-0	
1982	9-1-0	**League champs**
1983	10-1-0	**League champs**
1984	10-2-0	**League champs**
1985	13-1-0	**League champs State finals lost to Medford 14-13**
1986	8-2-0	**League champs**
1987	10-1-0	**League champs**
1988	6-4-0	
1989	6-4-0	
1990	3-6-0	
1991	2-7-0	
1992	4-6-0	
1993	4-5-0	
1994	5-4-0	
1995	6-3-0	
1996	4-5-0	

"At the beginning of each season Coach Halvorsen would require every player who turned out to get his haircut above the ears. His reasoning to the players was that it was a safety issue since short hair was required to insure the proper fit of the old suspension helmet. Long hair was the 'in' thing during the mid-seventies and many players chose to pass on football rather than cut their hair. This included two of my best friends who were also good players.

"It wasn't until I began my own coaching that I realized cutting our hair wasn't about safety but rather commitment and sacrifices. Floyd only wanted those players out who were willing to make those sacrifices. The year we lost my two buddies was also the first championship year of Churchill football. When you played a Halvorsen-coached team you had to defeat a team, not a collection of individuals. His philosophy toward the team and working together as one has stuck with me throughout my career."   **Steve Greatwood, USC line coach**

Frank Spear, who assisted Halvorsen for 20 years in football, thought one of Halvorsen's strengths as a coach was his ability to delegate responsibility. "If he hired you to coach, he let you coach," Spear said.

More than a coach…

One of Halvorsen's former players, **Kevin Leonard,** often saw his coach as loyal to his players as he was to his assistant coaches.

"He was more than just my coach," said Leonard, an all-league player in football and basketball in the late 1970s. "When I was a sophomore, I had problems. I wanted to be a big man on campus, but I had a hard time understanding what that meant. He gave me a different outlook on football and on life.

"My grandmother did a good job of raising me, but I didn't have a male influence. If I wouldn't have had him, I don't think I would have made it through high school. He made me fill out weekly grade reports and monitored me through every class. He helped me get through high school.."

And after Leonard graduated, Halvorsen didn't give up on him. He hired him as an assistant coach five years ago.

Dave Kayfes *The Register-Guard* **1997**

LEGACY OF PLAYERS

1974	**Roy Nelson**	Colorado State
1976	**Steve Greatwood**	U of Oregon
1978	**Marty Louthan**	Air Force Acad.
1979	**Rick Geyer**	Stanford
1984	**Kelly Skipper**	Fresno State

COACHING HONORS

1993	**National High School Coach of the Year Region 7**
1977	**Oregon Coaches Association Football Coach of the Year**
1977	**Northwest Coach of the Year**
9 years	**Mid Western League Coach of the Year**
7 years	**State Shrine Bowl Coach**

As a secondary teacher, Halvorsen has taught all levels of mathematics from Basic Math Skills up to Calculus.

He has been the **athletic director** at Churchill High School from 1995-1999.

Marvin Earl Heater

- Born: Aug. 31, 1929 in Newberg, Ore.
- Parents: Clarence and Lenora Heater
- Father was an auto mechanic, volunteer fireman and fire chief at Newberg
- Married: Jeanne Effenberger Nov. 19, 1951
- Family: Janeen Allen 2/8/54, Pamela Heater-Brown 1/30/55, Ann Martin 12/22/59, Brian Heater 5/4/64.
- High School: Newberg 1947
  Coach: Loren Douglas '43-44
  Earl Gillis '45-46
- Honors: All-League guard in the TVL
- College: Oregon State 1947-48
  Freshman coach: Al Cox
- Linfield College 1949-51
  Coach: Paul Durham
  Honors: All-NWC
- Service: Captain in the National Guard
- Degree: Business Administration
  P.E. Linfield College

Marv Heater won state championships at Central and South Salem due to his ability to discipline, to communicate and adjust to the talent of his players.

CAREER

Banking or coaching? Marv Heater was majoring in business administration at Linfield and was ready to enter a banking program.

"I had this sad feeling that my experience with athletics was about to end," remembers Heater. "I guess **Paul Durham** could read me because he offered me a job assisting him. The idea was that I could take a fifth year of college and get a degree in physical education. If he hadn't made the offer, I'm sure I would have entered the banking program and never would have gotten into coaching."

- 1952 Central H.S. Assistant coach for **Sam Bell** (Football, basketball and baseball)

DRAIN (16-9-3)

1953	9-1-0	Quarters
1954	3-5-1	
1955	4-3-2	

- 1956 When Sam Bell left Central, he recommended Heater for the position.

CENTRAL (43-5-2) Capitol League

1956	9-1-1	League Champ
1957	7-2-0	
1958	8-0-1	
1959	7-2-0	Co-League Champ
1960	12-0-0	League and State 3A Champs Beat Myrtle Point. 20-13

SOUTH SALEM (67-34-6) 11 years

1961	3-6-0	
1962	6-2-1	
1963	4-4-1	
1964	4-5-0	
1965	5-2-2	Co-league champs
1966	11-1-0	State finals Lost to Hillsboro 17-2
1967	9-1-1	State semis
1968	3-5-1	
1969	5-4-0	
1970	7-2-0	Co-league champs
1971	10-2-0	State AAA Champions Beat Grants Pass 20-6

THE COACH

"He's big enough to be a drill sergeant but his disposition is that of a chaplain's. He knows there are all kinds of people but he doesn't try to change them unless they ask for it. Most of the changing he's done has been boys into men.

"His method has been no fear, all respect. He's had that from more than hundreds of kids than maybe anyone in town. He's living proof that nice guys don't finish last because he finished right at the top."

"The kids who played for him learned to use their heads for more than something to hit opponents with. He encouraged students to become scholars and also made them smart football players."

Marc Faulconer, *the Statesman-Journal*

COACHING PHILOSOPHY

Discipline: "Football still is and always will be a sport that demands great discipline. I have become more liberal in my attitude about such things as dress and long hair and I've probably mellowed some, but I'm still convinced that discipline is key to a good program."

Communication: "Probably the biggest challenge in coaching is to find out what the players are capable of doing and then bring out the best in each individual," Heater said. It is difficult to do this without knowing the player on a personal basis. Time is a coach's worst enemy in this regard."

Always learning: "The learning process goes on and on for a coach," Heater said. "I laugh every time I think back when I took my first job at Drain. Every young guy who comes out of college and goes into coaching has the same experience. You think that you know so much, then you step onto the field and find that you don't know a thing."

Adjusting: Heater always showed a knack for adjusting to the times and to personnel.

"We've almost always been pass-oriented at South, but we've tried many different things," he said. "We used the flanker-T offense when we had **Gary Edmonds** at quarterback, we tried the I formation one year when we had only one good running back and we went with the Kansas City-I for its play-action features for awhile."

When **Phil Brus**, the Saxon's all-state quarterback, came along, the situation called for an offense featuring plays for the drop-back passer. So, the South Salem staff moved in that direction, obviously with success.

Bob Robinson *The Oregonian*

- **Athletic Director at Sprague High School**
- **Assistant Principal at South Salem**
- **Principal at McKay High School**
- **Executive Director Oregon High School Coaches Association**

"Coach Marv Heater and his staff at South Salem were excellent teachers of the game. Heater was a great motivator. A lot of what I learned and experienced from him later helped me through my college and professional career.

"I am certainly grateful to have had the influence of Coach Marv Heater in my life."

Jeff Hart

LEGACY

Twelve players of Heater's South Salem teams received Divison I scholarships: Four made the professional football grade; **Craig Hanneman, Jeff Hart, Bob Horn, and Greg Specht.**

Marv Hiebert

- Born: May 15, 1925 at Mt. Lake, Minn.
- Parents: Nick and Marie Hiebert
  After the family moved to Dallas, Ore. in 1940, father joined the Navy
- High School: Dallas, 1941-44
  Sports: played football, basketball, baseball, wrestling and golf
  Football coach: Andy Anderson
  1944-All-league halfback with 14 TDs
  Played end, quarterback and halfback
- Service: WWII 1944-1946 Navy- Gunner's Mate; saw action at Okinawa, Saipan and Iwo Jima
- Married: Marianne "Sam" July 20, 1978
- Family: Joan Hiebert 4/8/49, Susan McFarland 7/28/52, Marilynn Wollmuth 6/1/55, Diana Hiebert-Betteridge 7/21/59, Scott Galbreath 9/27/70
- College: Oregon College of Education
  FB coach: Bill McArthur
  End, running back and defensive back, NAIA Dist II Hall of Fame
- Degrees: B.S. in Ed OCE 1950;
  Masters in Ed from U of Oregon 1960

Hiebert was a student of the game, but it was his incredible ability to focus and teach those proven details that led to his success.

COLLEGE

Upon being discharged from the Navy, Marv Hiebert enrolled at the University of Oregon in the fall of 1946 hoping to play tailback for Coach **Tex Oliver's** single wing offense.

But Hiebert sustained a serious toe injury while working in a cannery before the start of the football season causing him to withdraw and re-enroll at Oregon College of Education in Monmouth.

The toe injury limited his playing time during that first football season at OCE, that Hiebert claimed, "we had the worst college team in America."

McARTHUR'S FIRST RECRUIT

The next summer in 1947, when Hiebert was ready to transfer back to the University of Oregon to play for their new coach, **Jim Aiken,** an encounter changed his mind.

Hiebert remembers: "I was at the Monmouth bus depot located in a drug store to purchase a ticket to Eugene when a newcomer to the community walked in to introduce himself to the drugstore owner as the newly-hired OCE football coach. His name was **Bill McArthur.** I was impressed with his personal mannerism so I introduced myself to him and told him of my plan to transfer to the University of Oregon to play football. Needless to say, he persuaded me to stay and continue my football and college career at OCE."

A McARTHUR LEGACY

Marv Hiebert played a lot of football at OCE. He was given the opportunity to play many positions; even in the same game. "I experienced and learned great organization and game plan preparation. Besides learning the basic football fundamentals as a total picture as how the game should be played," related Hiebert. "It had a big impact on my decision to become a teacher and a coach."

MOLLALA

The first teaching job in 1950 was at Mollala Jr. High. But the summer semi-pro baseball experience for the town lumber mill got Hiebert thinking about other job opportunities. He was offered a job as a sawyer with serious thought of becoming a lumber broker.

But with a turn of events, things changed. His employer encouraged Hiebert to apply for an unexpected coaching opportunity at the high school. The football and wrestling coach had been drafted into the Korean War.

"Three hours before the interview for the position," remembers Hiebert, "I came by the school and asked the janitor if he would allow me access to the facilities and the equipment room. I found it a mess. The equipment was torn, wet and moldy "

"When it came my turn to interview, they asked me why I wanted the job," recounts Hiebert. "I told them I wasn't so sure after what I had just seen. I would not allow my son to play with that football gear. I asked them if they were willing to upgrade and replace the worn out equipment and do what was necessary to help the program succeed, then I would be interested in the position."

Nobody had a question. The interview ended.

Hiebert did get the coaching job and most of his demands. The 26 year-old stayed in education and became an outstanding football coach.

MOLLALA HIGH SCHOOL (19-21-2)

1951	3-5-0	
1952	3-4-1	
1953	8-2-0	
1954	3-5-0	
1955	2-5-1	

During his four year-coaching stint at Mollala, Hiebert's football teams had a 19-21-2 record. His wrestling teams were Willamette League champs in 1953 and 1954 finishing 2nd and 3rd respectively at the state meets.

DAVID DOUGLAS

When David Douglas High School opened in 1955, the head football coach **Dick Miller** hired Marv Hiebert at the encouragement of principal, **Howard Horner.**

Horner had been Hiebert's football coach his freshman year at Dallas High School in 1941. He had been following his career through high school, college and at Mollala High School.

Within four years, Dick Miller retired from football at the end of the 1958 season, Hiebert became Howard Horner's selection to be David Douglas' second head football coach.

WINNING FOOTBALL

Hiebert had become a student of coaching. He dedicated himself to learning every facet of the game. Football books and clinics helped him, but it was *his incredible ability to focus and to immerse himself into teaching those proven details of the game that would lead to his success.*

DAVID DOUGLAS (76-18-6)

1959	9-2-0	**Metro Champs**
1960	11-1-0	**Metro and State Champs**
1961	6-2-1	
1962	6-2-1	
1963	3-6-0	
1964	7-1-1	
1965	12-0-0	**Metro and State Champs**
1966	7-0-2	
1967	5-3-1	
1968	10-1-0	**Semis**

Hiebert's first year was sensational for a rookie coach whose team was picked to place last in the very tough Metro League.

He immediately established a new offense. He replaced Miller's single-wing with a more productive T-formation.

From a bumpy start in 1959, the Scots rallied to win the school's first Metro League football championship by prevailing in many close games.

Hiebert and his staff made believers of his young players. *Believers that they could become winners.* And winners they became. The 1959 team finished with an impressive 9-2 record, losing to a **Mel Renfro**-led Jefferson team in the playoffs.

THE STATE CHAMPIONSHIP

The experienced 1960 team not only repeated winning the Metro title, they won the state championship.

It might be recorded as one of the finest coaching efforts in the history of Oregon high school football. It reflected the coaching genius of Marv Hiebert.

The David Douglas team defeated the PIL champion Jefferson 13-6 in a re-match of the previous year's playoffs. But it was the upset of the defending state champion Medford that was huge. It was testimony to Hiebert's game preparation and his ability to motivate to beat a team of Medford's stature.

The 1960 Medford team might have been the strongest, fastest, and most dominating of the 31 teams that the legendary **Fred Spiegelberg** coached. The record indicated that they ran roughshod over their opponents by an average of 41 points. The team deserved to be a three-touchdown favorite, but their "Achille's heel" was that they were never challenged.

Hiebert's defensive game plan was masterful. The defensive linemen played off the line of scrimmage to throw off Medford's offensive timing, and the Scots would stand up the ball carriers while others made an effort to strip the ball. On offense, ball control kept the game close until quarterback **Terry DeSylvia** scooted around the end to put his team ahead, 20-14.

The touted Medford offense, unaccustomed to being behind, fumbled twice and threw an interception to end the game.

"It was my biggest game ever," remarked Hiebert. "We were a much smaller team than Medford. On paper, we were not their equal, but that is the beauty of football, you still have to do it on the field."

David Douglas defeated North Salem 34-20 the following week before 12,963 fans in Multnomah Stadium for the school's first state football championship, 34-20.

ANOTHER STATE CHAMPIONSHIP

Hiebert continued to work his coaching magic as good athletes and teams developed in the suburban school of 2,800-3,300 students.

The 1965 team was a powerhouse that would go undefeated by visiting another Southern Oregon Conference defending state champion, the Grants Pass Cavemen. In a driving rainstorm, they played a mistake-free game to win 19-7. The final game victory in Civic Stadium's mud was a businesslike 20-13 score over a tough **Dutch Kawasoe**-coached Reynolds team.

> "Marv is basically a good organizer. He has good assistants and he'll take his game plan and stay with it until he beats you. He's that bullheaded," remembers **Mouse Davis** of a Sunset-David Douglas game. "He won't figure out how he's beat you until after the game, but while its going on he just keeps knocking you down."
>
> Davis remembers "we had Hiebert down 14-0 with something like eight minutes to go in the fourth quarter and he won 20-14. It was my worst loss."

THE COMMUNITY COLLEGE

When Mt. Hood Community College, located in Gresham, Oregon, opened its doors in 1969, **President Dr. Earl Klapstein** and **Athletic Director Dutch Triebwasser** selected Marv Hiebert to become its first football coach. As it turned out, Hiebert had the unique opportunity to lead the Saints' program for the nine years of its existence.

Mt. Hood competed in the Northwest Community College Athletic Association League, which in 1970 included Yakima, Olympia, Walla Walla, Spokane, Grays Harbor, Everett, Treasure Valley, Columbia Basin and Wenatchee.

Hiebert's teams won 56 and lost 26, but the most satisfaction he gained was having 145 of his players receive athletic scholarships to assist them to play football and pursue their academic interest at various colleges and universities.

JC COACHING PHILOSOPHY

Hiebert found that at the junior college level, it was important to have a realistic game plan that is implemented during the week of practice and to be executed during the game. This allowed the players to establish realistic goals that were obtainable. Through this coaching philosophy, the player did gain confidence in his ability to perform at a higher level of success.

MOUNT HOOD C.C. (56-28-0)

1970	2-7-0	
1971	6-3-0	
1972	2-7-0	
1973	7-2-0	
1974	5-4-0	
1975	10-0-0	**NWAACC Champs**
1976	9-1-0	**Western Div Champs**
1977	8-1-0	**NWAACC Champs**
1978	7-3-0	**Western Div Champs**

> Recruiting overlooked kids for the Mt.Hood program became Hiebert strength. "We try to sell them on junior college football, and we think there are advantages," Hiebert stressed. "A kid can play right now if he comes here, play 18 to 20 football games before he leaves."

The last four seasons, Mt.Hood dominated the junior college play. They were undefeated in 1975 and were heart broken again in 1976 when they didn't receive the bid to play in the touted Junior College Little Rose Bowl. In 1977, the Saints were ranked No.1 in the nation most of the year.

Hiebert produced four Junior College All-Americans: **Willie Brock, Randy Gill, Dennis Adams and Stafford Mays.**

But the cost of success and growth of the program presented problems balancing the school's athletic budget. By February of 1979, the community college board got involved with serious cutbacks.

It was either cutting out six other sports or "biting the bullet" as **Dutch Triebwasser** called it by dropping the football program. Mt. Hood by that time was the only Oregon community college west of the Cascades fielding a football team. The decision had one alternative. Football was dropped.

Hiebert continued teaching at Mt. Hood until his retirement in 1988.

WRESTLING

Hiebert has been involved with the sport of wrestling for 48 years, as a wrestler, a coach and as an official. He has served as a commissioner and many other leadership positions.

COACHING HONORS

- **NWAACC Football Coach of the year (1975,1976,1977)**
- **NFF Walk of Champions award Honored for the David Douglas AAA State Championship teams**
- **Mt. Hood CC Athletic Hall of Fame**
- **NWAACC Hall of Fame**
- **1997 National Wrestling Hall of Fame**

Joseph Kline Huston

- Born: March 10, 1915 in Colfax, Wash.
- Died: March 21, 1975 in Portland, Ore.
- Parents: J. Karl and Rosa Huston; mother died of pneumonia shortly after birth.
- Married: Bernadine Lenhart 7/13/41
- Daughter: Jodine "Jody" Huston 11/12/46
- High School: Herbert Hoover in Glendale, Calif. 1934
- Glendale J.C. '34, 35
- College: University of Oregon, '36, '37
  Coach: Prink Callison
  Position: Guard and place kicker—"Little Joe with the educated toe." He and Tony Amato were the "Small Blocks of Granite"
  Honors: All-Coast
  Degree: B.S. in Education U of Oregon
- Service: WWII; 1st Lieutenant in U.S. Navy

COACHING PROFESSION

In 1939, Joe Huston started his coaching career when he was an assistant freshman coach at the University of Oregon under Coach **Tex Oliver.**

Joe Huston took his coaching seriously. His first head-coaching job was at Bend High School. He had immediate success. He resurrected their football program in 1940 and guided the Lava Bears to Oregon's first prep football championship by beating Medford on its field, 20-7.

BEND HIGH SCHOOL (8-1-1)

1940	8-1-1	Oregon State Prep Champs

ROOSEVELT HIGH SCHOOL (5-2-1)

1941	5-2-1	

GRANT HIGH SCHOOL (10-0-0)

1946	10-0-0	Oregon State Prep Champs

When Joe Huston returned from the service, he was hired by **Colton Meek** to replace **Jim Torson** at Portland's Grant High School. Torson was moving to the University of Portland basketball coaching position. With the help of assistant **John Lewis**, he guided another team to the 1946 Oregon High School championship. The Generals beat a tough Hood River team, 7-6, when **Tom Shaw** fired a long pass to an outstanding athlete **Pat Duff** for the winning score.

Joe Huston: An excellent teacher...a perfectionist when it came to fundamentals. His record and teams reflected that legacy.

Quarterback **Tom Shaw**, who became a star at Stanford, reflected back: "Joe Huston was a fine high school coach," he said. " He was a man you could play for and learn from. Although he was tough and decisive, he made us pay attention so we could improve. But he was a realistic guy, he would put us in situations where we could perform well."

LEWIS AND CLARK COLLEGE

In 1947, Lewis and Clark football coach **Robert "Matty" Mathews,** a prestigous coach from Portland University and Idaho, was looking forward to his 38th coaching year with a special zeal. L&C had rejoined the Northwest Conference, and most of his players were returning from the previous season. Mathews figured to field a championship contender right away.

But Matty Mathews died suddenly September 1st after the team had gathered for fall practice.

Lewis and Clark President **Morgan S. Odell** began a search for his replacement. He attracted one of the state's outstanding young coaches in Joe Huston. For a couple weeks, Huston had to coach both teams; the defending state champions, the Grant Generals, and his new college team, the Lewis and Clark Pioneers.

LEWIS AND CLARK (100-52-7) 18 years

1947	2-3-3	
1948	6-2-0	NWC 2nd
1949	6-3-0	**NWC tie for 1st with Cof I**
1950	9-0-0	**NWC 1st Pear Bowl Champs**
1951	6-2-0	**NWC tie for 1st**
1952	1-6-0	
1953	4-5-1	
1954	8-2-0	**NWC tie for 1st**
1955	6-2-0	**NWC tie for 1st**
1956	7-3-0	
1957	4-6-0	
1958	4-4-1	
1959	4-5-0	
1960	6-4-0	
1961	6-3-0	
1962	7-1-1	
1963	8-0-0	**NWC 1st**
1964	6-1-1	

"Joe Huston seemed to be one step ahead of everyone else during his coaching career," remembers **Dick Hennessy '52**. Its no wonder high school and college coaches could be seen on the Lewis and Clark campus during the off season."

Huston was an excellent teacher of the game, and he was a perfectionist when it came to fundamentals. Hennessy remembered a course he took from Huston called *Fundamentals of Football*. " Huston said a common mistake made by many coaches was they got involved in devising a game plan and spent too much time teaching assignments. When that happens, you ignore fundamentals and that is when you stop improving."

"As a player for Joe, I remember him as very strict and business like," **Fred Wilson** recalled. "I played for him during his younger years when he was a very intense young man, so intense it got to the point where he would personally get down and demonstrate his techniques. He had nothing but respect for his players. He was not an emotional man as far as pep talks or firing people up," Wilson remembers. "He had a pet statement: *You fellows know what has to be done and if you have any pride in yourself you will go out and get it done.*"

THE 1950 LEWIS AND CLARK TEAM

Huston had two undefeated teams in his tenure, but it was the 1950 team that is talked about with awe

The team was considered one of the best small college teams ever to play in this area. It won the eight regular season games without being pressed. They outscored their opponents 256-24 while holding their opponents to a meager 50 yards per game.

Then it demolished previously undefeated San Francisco State, 61-7, before 12,000 fans in the post-season Pear Bowl in Medford.

Of the 37 players, 11 earned first team all-conference honors and 12 others gained honorable mention. Five players were named to all-American teams. They were fullback **Ruben Baisch**, linebacker **Bud Cox**, halfback **Stan Blair**, tackle **Bill O'Hara** and defensive back **Fred Wilson**.

George Pasero of the *Oregon Journal* wrote: "One of the finest clubs in fundamentals with vicious tackling and exceptional blocking."

L.H. Gregory of the *Oregonian* sports editor, who covered Oregon and Oregon State in 1950, called the Pioneers "the top football team in Oregon."

Bill Hulen of *The Oregonian* wrote: "Lewis and Clark's football team was the very best I've seen in its class of competition."

In 1951, Huston wanted to bring the first ever college football game to **Bend, Oregon**. He had coached Bend High School to Oregon's first prep state championship in 1940. His team did not let him down as Lewis and Clark defeated Southern Oregon 50-7.

THE 1963 UNDEFEATED TEAM

Joe Huston's 1963 team was "undefeated, untied, and uninvited" after winning eight straight in impressive fashion before being passed over when the NAIA picked their playoff teams (OCE, complaining of injuries, begged out of the needed ninth game for consideration.) That team included All-American **Mick Hergert** who led the nation in rushing offense, lineman **Gary Boggs** and defensive tackle **Mike Kostraba**.

"Hergert is the greatest back I ever coached," commented Huston in an *Oregonian* article by **Don Fair**.

"I was fortunate enough to have played for two great football coaches, **Tom DeSylvia** at Jefferson and **Joe Huston** at Lewis and Clark. Whereas Tom was the great physical motivator, Joe was the emotional/mental motivator. Joe was the gentleman coach, a father figure of sorts to me, who demanded perfection and the best from his players. I cannot recall ever hearing a harsh word of criticism or ever an 'in your face' attitude toward any player. In practices, his style was to spit in his hands, rub them together and say ' run the same play again.' You knew he was pleased with the results then. In my own coaching career, I tried to emulate Joe in the way he handled players. Except for spitting in my hands of course."

1963 All-American, Mick Hergert

COACHING HONORS

1963	**Oregon's Man of the Year Hayward Banquet Coach of the Year**
1963	**Runnerup National NAIA Coach of the year award**
1963	**NAIA Dist II Coach of the Year**
1967	**NAIA District and National Hall of Fames**
1991	**State of Oregon Sports Hall of Fame**

Joe Huston retired from football at the end of the 1964 season at the age of 48, when he became the athletic director. In addition to coaching and teaching, Huston served as the Dean of Men at the college from 1951 to 1960. He retired in 1972 after 25 years of service to Lewis and Clark College.

Joe Huston died March 21, 1975 at the age of 60.

Joe Huston was an excellent teacher of the game, and he was a perfectionist when it came to fundamentals

Melvin "Mel" Ingram

- Born: July 4, 1903 in Acton, N.C.
- Died: October 28, 1979 in Medford, Ore.
- Parents: B.F. Ingram, One of five children; Mel came west with folks when he was six years old.
- Married: Marion in 1927, Sybil Pearson in 1977
- Son: Michael S. Ingram , Daughter: Marion "Mimi" Hislop
- High School: Weatherwax High School in Aberdeen, Wash.
- College: Gonzaga University 1928
- Football, basketball, track and baseball
- Pittsburg Pirates baseball in 1929

INGRAM THE ATHLETE

> At Weatherwax High in Aberdeen, Wash., Ingram "could and did almost everything with a football; was possessor of an amazing shiftiness and tackle-evading pace. Added to this was speed equalled by few, plus possession of a keen football sense."
>
> ***"Punts and Passes" by Fred Hampson 1928***

Ingram matriculated at Gonzaga University in Spokane where he was hailed as the greatest athlete that ever attended the University at barely 160 pounds. He lettered in four sports in all four years.

> "After looking over Ingram in his four years of athletics at Gonzaga, we have speculated as to which game he performed best. In the fall we thought he was the greatest as a halfback; in the winter, it seemed he could not be as good a halfback as he was a forward in basketball; then in the spring there was the difficult choice: he excelled as a sprinter, broad jumper or baseball player? Now that we have seen him in several games this year, there seems no longer any question. Baseball is his best game and he can play it."
>
> **Bob Phillips, columnist in Spokane**

Ingram's greatest achievement as an athlete came on the field of baseball. He was signed by the Pittsburg Pirates in 1929 but refused to enter into a contract until he was promised an early release by the end of the summer. It was important to return to the West where he could begin his coaching career at Wallace, Idaho on September 1st. Ingram received his share of the 1929 World Series second-place money since he

Mel Ingram brought an intense competitiveness to Grants Pass football. Five state finals in 22 years and the many outstanding teams speak to his success as a coach.

played so well that season.

It wasn't just coaching for Ingram, however, during the 1930s. He achieved fame as a baseball player. He was a member of the touring House of David team, whiskers and all, for several seasons. He played on the same team with the legendary **Satchel Paige**. In other years he played on clubs in the Idaho-Washington League.

WALLACE, IDAHO H.S. (63-19-2)
15 years 1929 to 1943 *yearly record unavailable

> At Wallace, Ingram's team won 63 football games, lost 19, and tied two. In the 15 years, he had nine all-Panhandle football teams including three North Idaho Championship teams. One of the teams was rated first in the entire state of Idaho. Ingram's teams were never below fourth in competition, nor were ever beaten twice in any one year by one team.
>
> **Rollie Brunning** *North Idaho Press*

ROSEBURG, OR., H.S. 3 years (16-9-0)

1944	4-4-0	
1945	4-4-0	
1946	8-1-0	**State playoffs**

GRANTS PASS, OR., H.S. 22 yrs (142-49-19)

1947	5-3-0	
1948	10-1-1	**State Champions** Beat Jefferson 6-0
1949	7-1-0	
1950	9-0-0	Undefeated * League tie but Prineville voted to state
1951	11-0-1	**State Champions** Tie-beat Grant on yardage
1952	5-3-1	
1953	7-3-2	**State Finals** Lost to Central Catholic 14-13
1954	6-2-1	
1955	3-3-2	
1956	6-3-0	
1957	6-2-1	
1958	4-1-3	
1959	4-5-0	
1960	5-3-1	
1961	4-5-0	
1962	5-2-1	
1963	7-1-1	
1964	10-1-1	**State Champions** Beat Corvallis 7-0
1965	10-1-0	**State Semis**
1966	5-4-0	
1967	9-0-3	**State Co-Champions** Tied Jesuit 14-14
1968	4-5-0	

Mel Ingram who succeeded **Mel Johnson** put Grants Pass on the map in Oregon prep football. "He was an institution," said athletic director **Jesse Loffer**. "He was responsible for building up the football program at Grants Pass to where it is now. Grants Pass hadn't done much in football until he came."

Grants Pass had its first state championship in Ingram's second year in 1948. While undoubtedly one of the highlights of Ingram's long career, it will also be remembered for the tragedy that occurred following the championship game when the team bus crashed on Mount Sexton killing two players, **Al Newman,** and **Sterling Heater.**

Mel Ingram built a dynasty at Grants Pass during his early years. They were undefeated in 1950 and the 1951 team scored 452 points in 12 games.

Ingram called 1964, "a building year" to deflect the pressure. But the team had one of the more improbable finishes of any team considering the few expectations.

"Risky, gutsy call, but golden"
Ingram's competitiveness-- was evident on the last moments of the playoff deciding final game against Medford in 1964.

Grants Pass had more yards in a 21-21 tie game and would make it to the playoffs, but Ingram wasn't satisfied when a penalty flag offered one last play. He called for a pass. **Tom Blanchard** hit **Terry Crenshaw** with a 22 yard TD.

Ingram preferred teaching and coaching at the high school level. He turned down offers to become a college coach because he preferred to work with younger boys. He was always striving to "make men out of boys" and points with pride to literally thousands of men scattered over the United Sates who are important citizens in their communities due in a large part to the intense interest Ingram took in them in their early years.
Jerry Acklen Sports Editor *G P Courier*

Some of the top players during the Imgram years were **Dick James, Tom Blanchard, Jerry Sherk, Mark Brandt, Bruce Fry** and **Steve Endicott.**

COACHING CAREER, 40 years (220-74-21)

HONORS

1968	**National H.S. Coach of the Year**
1976	**National H.S. Coaches Hall of Fame**
1980	**Grants Pass H.S. field named Ingram Field**
	Head Shrine coach five times
1979	**Gonzaga U. Hall of Fame**
1972	**Inland Empire Sports Hall of Fame**

" *We all had the same first name...*"
At the 50-year reunion of the 1948 state championship team when 21 of the 25 members returned to Grants Pass, the story surfaced about Ingram addressing the players by the same first name. "It was always *Dammit* Craft, *Dammit* Donovan, *Dammit* Bayless,etc."

Melvin "Dutch" Kawasoe

- Born: Nov. 8, 1925 in North Powder, Ore.
- Parents: George and Mausko Kawasoe
- Father's occupation: Cook and farmer
- Married: Mary Ann 2/65
- Family: Marcia Housten 1/27/55, Mari Anne Leipzig 8/23/57, and John Kawasoe 4/15/66
- High School: Weiser, Idaho '45
- Coach: Ace Lloyd
- Honors: All-league guard
- College: University of Idaho F-'45
- Coach: Babe Brown
- College: College Of Idaho '46-'49
- Coach: Clem Parbarry
- Honors: All- Northwest Conference 1948
- Degrees: B.A. in Education in 1949

"Dutch"

"I got the nickname in 1930 when I was six years old. The chief of police, who was the father of my best friend, caught us riding our bikes down the wrong side of the street. "You're always in 'Dutch,' " he told me. "From that time forward my friend called me 'Dutch.' " The name stuck.

At 5'7", 230 pounds, Kawosoe started at guard for the University of Idaho his freshman year in college. He played against the University of Washington and University of Montana before he "blew-out" his knee against Washington State.

Worried that he couldn't play again, Kawasoe decided to go home and farm. But College of Idaho's **Clem Parbarry** contacted him. "You can play in the Northwest Conference on one leg," he said. "I think I can tape it." Kawasoe made All-NWC in 1948. College of Idaho defeated Southern Oregon in the Pear Bowl that season.

COACHING

1949	Parma, Idaho H.S. assist to **Wes Johnson**
1950	Vale H.S. assist to **Jerry Camman**
1951	
1952	
1953	

Jerry Camman commented to Kawasoe when he resigned in 1954: " I hate to give up this job to you, because you won't win five games with this bunch."

Dutch Kawasoe had a brilliant football mind. He applied it successfully to coaching and scouting.

It was enough motivation for Dutch Kawasoe to prove he was a football coach. His first year as a head coach, he went undefeated and won the state championship.

Kawasoe's Vale teams were dominating; three state championships in four seasons. Key players were **Tony Arana, John** and **Dave Wilcox**.

VALE HIGH SCHOOL (40-2-1)

1954	11-0-0	**State AA Champions** Beat St. Helens 14-7
1955	11-0-0	**State AA Champions** Beat Dallas 45-0
1956	8-2-0	
1957	10-0-1	**State AA Champions** Beat Seaside 13-6

Kawasoe's best coaching memory...

was the state championship game against Seaside in 1957.

After Oregon State assistant **Bob Zelinka** informed Kawasoe that Seaside might be four to five touchdowns better than his young Vale squad, which started eight sophomores, he took up the challenge again.

Kawasoe reviewed Seaside game film for 25 hours before he was certain of a game plan. Vale upset Seaside 13-6 for the state championship.

Oregon State coach **Tommy Prothro** who viewed the game from the stands, called it "the greatest job of defense I've seen in high school football."

Kawasoe developed a mutual admiration with Prothro. They shared their coaching philosophies together.

Kawasoe regretted the next challenge he took when he moved to Portland to upright the Franklin football program, which hadn't won a game in two years. Kawasoe, content at Vale with a veteran team returning, felt "conned" by a persistent group of Franklin administrators and coaches.

He remembers, it was a response to Franklin's coach **Gene Tanselli's** prodding: "Take the Franklin job Dutch. That's the only way you'll know if you can coach football."

FRANKLIN HIGH SCHOOL (11-21-3)

1958	2-7-0	
1959	4-4-1	
1960	2-6-1	
1961	3-4-1	

Dutch Kawasoe knew that he could coach football. He was an advocate of the balanced line single wing. He believed in strong fundamentals and execution. But the Franklin experience wasn't one that Kawasoe wanted to remember in regards to his coaching record. He remembers tossing 10 players off the team his first year, but salvaged a promising lineman in **Lynn Hewitt**.

REYNOLDS HIGH SCHOOL (22-6-2)

1963	5-4-0	
1964	6-1-2	
1965	11-1-0	**Wilco Champs State Finals** Lost to David Douglas 20-13

Reynolds was more responsive to Kawasoe's coaching. The players developed. The team won, and within three years, Reynolds won the league

championship. The Lancers proceeded to the state finals before falling to David Douglas. **Mike DeBois, Danny Walter, Butch Woodward and Mike Blackwell** were the stars.

- 1966-68 Kawasoe left education to work for a construction company.

SCOUTING

In 1968, when Kawasoe became the career education coordinator at Grant High School, he also became the scouting coordinator at Mt. Hood Community College for **Marv Hiebert**. He became a key asset for the Saint's success the next ten years.

"Dutch had a great football background. I respected his judgement and knowledge of the game. He was invaluable as my scouting coordinator.

" He was the type of guy that didn't need a lot of written material. He kept his scouting notes on a card. We would get together to talk about the opponent's weakness and strengths. Then he would add 'If I was coaching....' He was always accurate on how he would attack an opponent. I've never known him to be wrong. Then I would schedule our practice time based on his information. Many times he would come by and watch practice and might offer suggestions. He had a photographic memory and always had a great feeling for the coming game."

Marv Hiebert, Mt. Hood C.C. Coach

- In 1979 –80, Kawasoe became an assistant coach to **George Rallis** at Grant. He took over the head coaching post in 1981after Rallis moved to David Douglas.

GRANT HIGH SCHOOL (19-11-0)

1981	5-5-0	
1982	7-3-0	
1983	7-3-0	

MAJOR SURGERIES:
- 1977- had 2/3rds of his stomach removed and double by-pass heart surgery
- 1978-brain neurosurgery
- 1985-another double by-pass heart surgery

Kawasoe is retired and resides in Portland.

Larry Lee Keck

- Born: Jan. 30,1931 in Levant, Kan.
- Parents: Bryon and Emma Keck
  Father was a farmer
- Married: Geraldine McBride Oct. 1, 1950.
- Children: Mike 1/29/53, Alexa Baltz
  8/20/54, Julie 9/22/62, Scott 4/1/66
- High School: Kanorado, Kan., 1944-1948
- Coach: Charles Curry, 1944-1945,
  Jim O'Toole, 1946-1947
- College:Trinidad State Junior College
  Trinidad, Colo. 1948-1949
  Coach: Jack Walton and Robert Riddell
  Football: Starting DB and backup QB
  League champions 1948-1949
  Played in "Salt Bowl"
- Colorado State College of Education,
  1950-1952
  Coach: Football- John Hancock
  Football: All-League DB in 1951
- Degrees: Associate of Arts: Trinidad Jr.
  College '50
  B. A.: U of Northern Colorado 1952
  Physical Education;
  M.A.: U of Northern Colorado 1959 in
  Educational Psychology
- Baseball Honors: Outfielder on two Rocky
  Mountain Conference champions, 1951-52
- Service: Drafted in to U.S. Army in 1952;
- First job: Elementary school in Lamar,Colo.

THE JOURNEY

Larry Keck grew up on a farm near the small border town of 300, Kanorado, Kansas. He attended a one-room school during his grade school years. Being the oldest, he learned early how to milk cows, drive the tractor and what it was to work until dark. So by the time he was to attend high school Keck knew he didn't want to be a farmer.

High school was a big thrill for Keck, an opportunity that he could be a three-sport athlete. However, it wasn't until his junior year that his journey to be a coach started to crystallize, when **Jim O'Toole** arrived to coach at the 45-student school. The new coach tutored all three sports besides the summer American Legion team. His influence motivated Keck to the point that "The coach" became a role model.

Larry Keck: The consummate high school football coach. He developed a football philosophy and enjoyed 37 years applying it.

Keck's senior year, O'Toole personally took him to Trinidad Junior College to recommend him for an athletic scholarship. The college opportunity became a reality, and Keck became determined to make the best of it. Besides his athletics, he worked part-time washing dishes and sweeping the library floors. He studied hard earning himself an academic scholarship later to Colorado State College of Education (University of Northern Colorado).

Keck had both scholastic and athletic success at Colorado State. His senior year, he made all-conference as a defensive back on a team that played in the 1950 "Bean Bowl." The baseball team played in the College World Series.

Immediately after graduation, Keck was inducted into Korean War Conflict with an appointment to Officer's Candidate School. He earned a "Distinguished Graduate" commendation that placed him at a leadership school at Fort Chaffey. Arkansas. It was there, that he had his first coaching experience. He coached the basketball team.

The commanding general wanted Keck to make the Army his career, but Keck remained determined to be a coach. He returned to Greeley, Colorado to do his student teaching.

THE OREGON CONNECTION

In 1953, Larry Keck did his student teaching at College High School in Greeley. At that time he became the JV basketball coach for **Cy Butterfield** and a varsity football assistant for

Jim Malone. The next school year, Keck was placed at Lamar High School as a PE teacher.

Keck's first coaching job at Fort Lupton was made by the one recommendation of **Martin Smith**. He was hired to coach football, wrestling and baseball .

FORT LUPTON H.S. COLORADO (31-11-0)

1955	5-4-0	
1956	5-3-0	
1957	6-2-0	
1958	8-1-0	**League Champions**
1959	7-1-0	

Larry Keck had a successful five winning seasons, before he became anxious in advancing his career to the next level. It was at that time he reconnected with **Cy Butterfield** who was in Colorado recruiting teachers for the Portland, Oregon high schools.

"Do you want to come to Oregon?" Butterfield asked Keck as he filled out an application for him.

Frustrated that the larger schools would not interview him for coaching openings, Keck responded to Butterfield's next invitation in February of 1960. He was offered an opening at Portland's Lincoln High School to coach wrestling and assist **Bob Signor** in football.

WASHINGTON HIGH SCHOOL. (4-12-1)

1962	3-5-0	
1963	1-7-1	

MADISON HIGH SCHOOL (16-15-4)

1964	4-4-0	
1965	1-7-1	
1966	4-3-2	
1967	7-1-1	**Division Champs**

REYNOLDS HIGH SCHOOL (53-27-1)

1968	8-1-0	2nd lost to State Champs Jesuit
1969	6-3-0	
1970	6-3-0	
1971	5-4-0	
1972	6-2-1	
1973	6-3-0	
1974	4-5-0	
1975	7-2-0	
1976	5-4-0	

COLUMBIA HIGH SCHOOL (3-15-0)

1977	0-9-0	* No senior class
1978	3-6-0	

MADISON HIGH SCHOOL (81-23-0)

1979	5-4-0	
1980	6-4-0	
1981	9-1-0	**PIL Champions**
1982	10-1-0	**PIL Champions**
1983	9-1-0	**PIL Champions**
1984	8-3-0	
1985	10-1-0	**PIL Champions**
1986	10-1-0	**PIL Champions** **Oregon Coach of the Year**
1987	9-2-0	
1988	5-5-0	

WILSON HIGH SCHOOL (39-13-0)

1989	5-4-0	
1990	9-2-0	**PIL Champions**
1991	8-2-0	**PIL Champions** **Nat HS Coach of Year Reg. 7**
1992	8-4-0	
1993	9-1-0	**PIL Champions** **PIL Coach of the Year**

COACHING RECORD (227-116-6) 37 yrs

PHILOSOPHY

"My coaching career was extremely gratifying. After a few immature years, I put things in the proper order of priority," remembers Keck. "I used football as the vehicle to teach proper values of life, teachings that actually came from the Bible."

"Our goal was for everyone to have a good experience in football and let the wins take care of themselves. The motto of 'For the Team' became the operating agenda for the players and the coaches. It served for the players attending classes, keeping training rules, and their conduct and leadership in school."

PACIFIC NORTHWEST FOOTBALL COACHES CLINIC

"**Ron Phiester, Bob Brown** and I, with the help of my wife **Geraldine**, ran the coaches clinic for 22 years. We brought the top college coaches to Portland each year as speakers for a 2-day clinic. We had John Robinson, Johnny McKay, Lou Holtz, Bobby Bowden, Bill Walsh, the Alabama staff, the Nebraska staff and the Notre Dame staff to name a few."

Larry Keck is retired and resides in Portland.

Roy Servais "Spec" Keene

- Born: July 1, 1894 in Hopewell, Ore.
- Died: August 24, 1977
- Parents: Granville and Sophie Keene
- Occupation: Father was a farmer who died when Spec was 8; mother worked at Fairview
- Family: Married Marie Mendenhall Daughters: Madeleine Swarbrick 10/30/29, Jerri Corbin 5/7/35
- High School: Salem, 1915
- Honors: earned 13 letters in four sports
- College: Oregon Agriculture College '21
- Degree: OAC Animal Husbandry
- Played baseball, student body president
- Service: Oregon National Guard, Sgt 3rd Inf., 1917-1919 WWI--trained recruits in France with gas mask techniques; WWII US Navy Lt. Commander–in charge of 12th Naval District physical fitness program

THE NICKNAME "SPEC"

Keene's nickname, "**Spec**," was given to him by **Leon (Doc) Barrick**, a baseball player from Salem. "It happened one day when I was playing shortstop and he was at first base. He told me my throws looked like 'specks' coming at him."

Spec Keene excelled as an athlete at **Salem High School** in the class of 1915. He earned 13 letters, four in football as an end, four in basketball as a center, four in baseball playing shortstop and one in track as a sprinter.

Spec enrolled at **Missouri Wesleyan College** in Cameron, Missouri, but returned to Oregon after a year and joined the **National Guard**. He entered active duty during World War I, serving 19 months with the "41st Infantry Division" in Contres, France.

At **Oregon Agriculture College**, Spec "lettered three years in baseball as a pitcher, but skipped basketball and football because he had his sights on a pro diamond career." Spec stated "It didn't take me long to learn that I would get no place in baseball… I hurt my arm when I fell from a troop train in France, and it never came back."

COACHING

"I guess I went into coaching because I liked athletics and working with growing kids," remembered Keene. His degree was in animal husbandry.

Spec Keene: "The Father of Willamette Athletics." He coached football, basketball, and baseball for 44 seasons during his 17-year tenure.

Keene's experience under **Paul Schissler** prepared him for his coaching career. He was also exposed to many of the **Knute Rockne** summer "coaching schools" that were held in Corvallis between 1924 –1928.

1921-1923	Corvallis H.S.	Coaching combination football, basketball, baseball and PE teacher
1924-1925	OAC	Freshman, then varsity assist. to **Paul Schissler**

"The Father of Willamette Athletics"

Beginning in 1926, the initial year of the Northwest Conference, Keene coached football 17 seasons, baseball 16 years and basketball 11 seasons. During one remarkable year, 1929-30, Keene's football, basketball, and baseball teams each won conference championships with undefeated records. In his 17 years and 44 coaching seasons at Willamette, Keene's squads won or shared 19 NWC titles. His Bearcat gridders won 27 straight conference games in the 1930s, his baseball team won 13 in a row and his final basketball squad (1936-37) won 22 games.

WILLAMETTE UNIVERSITY
17 Years (84-51-6)

1926	2-4-0	
1927	3-3-2	
1928	3-5-0	
1929	6-2-0	
1930	5-3-0	
1931	5-4-0	
1932	4-4-1	
1933	6-3-0	
1934	8-1-0	
1935	5-2-0	
1936	7-2-1	
1937	6-3-0	
1938	5-3-0	
1939	3-4-2	
1940	4-5-0	
1941	8-2-0	
1942	4-1-0	

Two men played a large supporting role for Spec Keene in his coaching journey at Willamette:

JOE KASBERGER

A major help to Keene developing the football program at Willamette was **Joe Kasberger**, a fraternity brother and close friend from OAC. Kasberger had been the coach at Mt. Angel College before it burned down in 1926 joined Keene's staff as his line coach in 1927. Since Spec didn't have the football experience as a college player or coach, Kasberger, an indirect "Rockne pedigree," became a very valuable addition. He provided him with an experienced perspective that he could trust in building the Willamette football program.

When Kasberger went to St. Benedicts in Newark, New Jersey, he took over a prep school that became a New Jersey power. The connection also became a "New Jersey pipe line" for some good players that Kasberger encouraged to come west to the Salem, Oregon school.

St. Benedicts' **John "Scooter" Oravec** was the first to enter Willamette. He was followed by **Dick Weisgerber** the next year. They became the "Touchdown Twins from New Jersey," both earning Little All-American honors.

HOWARD MAPLE

Howard Maple, a star football and baseball player at OAC in the late 20s, came to Willamette University to assist Keene in 1938. In 1937, he coached freshmen football, basketball and baseball at Oregon State.

Maple was a strong asset to Keene's football program through the 1942 season.

> Spec set high standards at Willamette. The 1932 year book reported " Keene won a place of respect for himself in the hearts of the Willamette students and alumni."
> "His teams were representative of our school and have stood for the best qualities of inter-collegiate sports."
> "Spec Keene Day" was celebrated Nov. 8, 1952 at Willamette University

> **The fur coat story**
> "Mom wanted a fur coat, so dad gave a pep talk before one of the games when he told the players, 'If they win the game, I'll buy a fur coat for Marie.' " The team won 70-0.
> **Daughter Jerri Corbin**

OREGON STATE COLLEGE
ATHLETIC DIRECTOR 1947-1964

When Keene returned from World War II, he found his Willamette coaching position wasn't saved for him. He joined Howard Maple in the sporting goods business in Salem until a unique opportunity arose.

When **Percy Locey** the Oregon State Athletic Director resigned, Spec Keene didn't apply for the job. He was "drafted."

The Spec Keene legacy was strong:

- His contacts and personal friendships enabled him to arrange one of the most **representative schedules** in the country.
- Keene started an expansion program unparalleled on the Pacific Coast. By 1950, **Gill Coliseum** with a seating capacity of 11,000 replaced the Men's Gym 2,500. In 1953, **Parker Stadium** with a seating capacity of 27,000 replaced Bell Field.
- Hiring of **Tommy Prothro** in 1955 to lead the football fortunes.

HONORS

1960	**NAIA Dist. Hall of Fame**
	Willamette U. Hall of Fame
1988	**Oregon State University Hall of Fame**
1982	**State of Oregon Sports Hall of Fame**

Spec Keene retired as A.D. in 1964. He died in Corvallis August 24, 1977 at the age of 83.

Jerome Cecil "Jerry" Lillie

- Born: Sept. 4, 1908 in Portland, Ore.
- Died: Oct 18, 1991
- Parents: Cecil and Nina Lillie
- Father's occupation: Owned Albina Fuel
- Married: Ida Mae Nickels 12/26/36
- Family: son Jay Lillie 10/12/40, daughters Nancy Danmann 6/15/42, Dina Chadwick 6/17/44, and Brenda Griffen 4/21/49
- High School: Grant, 1926, school's first graduating class
- Coach: Albert Runquist
  Played tackle on the "baby" of the Portland High School League championship team.
  All-city basketball team
- College: University of Oregon 1931
- Coach: Clarence "Doc" Spears
- Three year starting guard in football
- Degree: B.S. and M.S. in Education

COACHING CAREER

Jerry Lillie was one of the few coaches who got a job during the Great Depression years. Lillie's contribution was more than that of a coach. He was the community morale booster.

ST. HELENS HIGH SCHOOL (32-13-5)

1931	7-1-1	
1932	6-3-1	
1933	6-2-2	
1934	7-3-0	
1935	6-4-1	*George Pasero was a track athlete

A 1990 Jerry Lillie reunion offered testimonies when they saluted their former coach: "Genuine, heartfelt thanks for the spirit he imbued in them, the values and hope he gave them in those most difficult times."

"I tried to stimulate spirit in St. Helens," Lillie said.

BEND HIGH SCHOOL (8-0-1)

1936	8-0-1	

Lillie had graduated from Grant High School in 1926 and returned as a coach with a well-earned reputation when the coaching job opened in 1937. Principal **A.F. Bittner** told Lille he could have the position if he would teach chemistry in addition to biology. He received some help with chemistry class and began an eight-year career at Grant succeeding **Ted Rohwer.**

Jerry Lillie, a high school coaching legend of the 30s and 40s, led Willamette University to the 1947 NWC Championship.

GRANT HIGH SCHOOL (47-15-9)

1937	5-3-1	
1938	5-2-1	
1939	5-2-2	
1940	6-2-1	
1941	5-2-2	
1942	5-2-1	
1943	9-1-1	**PIL and State Champions**
1944	7-1-0	

Sheldon Jones recalls the 1943 season when the Portland high schools were first invited to participate in the state playoffs: "Jerry Lillie was a man who commanded tremendous respect from his players. He was an innovative coach. He was the first to introduce the T-formation while all others played either the single and double wing offenses. Grant used a lot of quick openers and **Dick McGregor's** passes to **Art Milne** and **Glen Kasch** to win the PIL and edge Klamath Falls 6-0 in the finals at Multnomah Stadium.

"The 1944 team didn't have a lot left over from the championship team of 1943, but Jerry Lillie's team played football to win. They played fair and they played hard. They were licked, but Jerry and his boys didn't offer any alibis. He accepted defeat and victory in the same gentlemanly fashion.

"One of the major reasons Lillie was so popular with fans and players was his concern for his athletes."

> "He was successful because of his main purpose was in developing the spirit of a champion in the teams he guided."
> **Marlowe Branagan , *The Oregon Journal 1945***

Central College of Education at Ellensburg, Washington pursued Lillie to start their football program at the end of WWII. But the men were late arriving at the college after being separated from the service, preventing Central College from establishing a team for the 1945 season.

Lillie taught at Central that year and coached the Ellensburg High School football and basketball teams. In the spring he coached the college track team.

ELLENSBURG, WA. H.S.

1945		* no record available

Lillie's father-in-law informed him that the elite Hawaiian high school, **Punahou,** was looking for an assistant to help new coach **Harry Fields**, the former Oregon State and Chicago Cardinal football player. The one year experience began the "Punahou connection," a flow of Hawaiian players, that would follow Lillie to his next coaching stop at Willamette University.

PUNAHOU H.S. Hawaii

1946	Assistant coach to Harry Fields

Ed Averill, a Board of Trustees member at Willamette University who was a fan of Lillie at Grant, encouraged the coach to apply for the Willamette coaching opening to replace **Walter Erickson.**

WILLAMETTE UNIVERSITY (13-7-0)

1947	7-2-0	Northwest Conf. Champions
1948	6-5-0	

> As Willamette's coach, **Al Stump** reported in a *Saturday Evening Post* piece: "Jerome (Jerry) Lillie, a bald, cheerful T-formation disciple who serves as combined varsity and jayvee head coach, athletic director, equipment manager, purchasing agent, trainer, rubber, ticket manager, promotion man and employment bureau."

Oregon's Cotton Bowl coach **Jim Aiken** recruited Lillie to assist him as his backfield coach in 1949. In 1950 when Johnny McKay was added to the staff, Lillie coached the ends. It marked a return to his alma mater after 17 years of coaching the game of football.

UNIVERSITY OF OREGON ASSISTANT

1949	For **Jim Aiken**	Backfield coach
1950		End coach

When Jim Aiken was fired at Oregon in 1951, Jerry Lillie found a home at Milwaukie High School where he would stay until he retired in 1974. He coached one year before he went into administration. The school's auditorium is named the ***Jerome Lillie Fine Arts Building***.

As the principal at Milwaukie, he had the foresight to hire a young aspiring coach to his first head coaching football job, **Darrel "Mouse" Davis.**

MILWAUKIE H. S.

1951	2-7-0	

> " Jerry Lillie combined toughness with imagination and understanding…qualities which undoubtedly have helped make him a most successful administrator."
> **George Pasero, *Oregon Journal 1968***

Vice principal at Milwaukie High School 1952
Principal at Milwaukie High School 1953-1974

Jerry Lillie died October 19, 1991 at the age of 83.

Gerald E. "Jerry" Lyons

- Born: Dec. 27, 1930 in Salt Lake City, Utah
- Parents: DeLloyd and Winnifred Lyons
  Father was a carpenter for *CE Stevens*
- Children: Mike, Vicki Sue, Karen
- Married: Julie
- School: Llewelyn grade school
- High School: Washington , 1945-49
- Coach: Gerald Exley in football and track
- Football: 6'1" 190 pound fullback   team tied for city title in 1947
- Track: High jump and hurdler
- Junior College: Grays Harbor JC 1950
  Coach: Dan Melincovich
- Service: Enlisted in the US Navy during the Korean War as a hospital corpsman
- College: U of Oregon 1955
  Coach: Len Casanova – as a tackle
- Degree: B.S. Health and PE 1957; M.S. Health and PE 1964

When Jerry Lyons was growing up in Portland, he was interested in sports. The grade school did not have organized team sports, so Lyons had to wait to play for the Washington High School teams.

Coach **Gerald Exley**, a 12 letter-winner at Washington State himself, had a big influence on Lyons. He instilled the belief that it was best to play as many sports as possible.

Lyons worked for a year after graduation, before he joined a group of friends to attend and play football at Grays Harbor JC in Aberdeen, Washington. He played fullback in 1950 for coach **Dan Melincovich**.

SERVICE FOOTBALL

- In 1951, Lyons played 7-man football at Oak Knoll Naval Hospital where they were 11th Naval District champions.
- In 1952, Lyons replaced **Joe "The Jet" Perry** as the fullback on the Alameda Naval Air Station team, where he had the opportunity to play and compete with many pro players.
- In 1954, Lyons was brought out of Korea to play for an all Marine Corps team in Kanahoe, Hawaii.

UNIVERSITY OF OREGON

Lyons returned to college at the University of Oregon in the fall of 1955. He had moved to

Jerry Lyons created an atmosphere that allowed the players to have fun, enjoy the game and win.

tackle by that time. "I learned more football at Oregon in two years than I had in my whole career."

"**Bill Hammer**, the line coach was a great influence as he was very tough and worked us double hard," remembers Lyons. He started the spring game, but chose to give up playing due to family responsibilities and hopes of graduating in three years.

PHILOSOPHY OF FOOTBALL

- "I always believed in having a good time with my team and that football was meant to be fun. In order to have fun, the more you won, the more fun it was. I liked having large numbers turn out for my teams, and I tried to keep everyone in the program.
- I felt my teams always played aggressive, but clean football. We hit hard and worked on fundamentals. I felt the game was for the players not the coaches.
- The coaching staff was given a lot of responsibility and I treated them as head coaches of their areas.
- I love football, but I always supported all sports and school events. I never encouraged my players to give up other sports to concentrate on football."

MADISON HIGH SCHOOL

Jerry Lyons was hired as the school's first wrestling coach in 1957. He served as the frosh football coach before he became the varsity coach in 1961.

MADISON HIGH SCHOOL (10-4-2)

1961	4-2-2	
1962	6-2-0	

PORTLAND STATE UNIVERSITY

When the Portland State football job came open following the resignation of **Tom DeSylvia** in 1963, Lyons convinced athletic director **Joe Holland's** selection committee that "he was a green coach that could grow with the PSU football program." He was hired.

"This was a hard job as I was teaching health and PE full time, but it was rewarding. We had the first championship and started the move to the Big Sky Conference and a better level of football," remarked Lyons.

PORTLAND STATE UNIVERSITY (20-25-1)

1963	6-2-0	**Oregon Collegiate Champs**
1964	4-4-1	**Oregon Collegiate Co-Champs with SOCE**
1965	3-6-0	*Independent
1966	4-6-0	
1967	3-7-0	

Lyons coached such players as **Billy White, Jim Hollingsworth, Andy Berkis, Tom Oberg** and **Jim Gorman.**

JACKSON HIGH SCHOOL

"Jackson was a great school to teach and coach. Although it was one of the smallest schools in the Portland Interscholastic League (800-950), it was one of the most successful in athletics.

From 1969-1973, Lyons was the athletic director and coached freshman football. In 1974, he became the head football coach.

JACKSON HIGH SCHOOL (47-29-0)

1974	2-7-0	
1975	5-4-0	
1976	7-2-0	**Division Champs**
1977	8-2-0	**PIL Champs tie Div. Champs**
1978	6-3-0	**Division Champs**
1979	6-4-0	**Division Champs**
1980	7-3-0	**Division Champs**
1981	6-4-0	**Division Champs**

In 1982, when Jackson closed, the faculty merged with Wilson and Lincoln. Lyons became the Wilson football coach.

WILSON HIGH SCHOOL (38-27-0)

1982	7-2-0	
1983	3-6-0	
1984	6-3-0	
1985	5-5-0	
1986	4-5-0	
1987	5-4-0	
1988	8-2-0	**PIL runner up to Benson**

In 1989, Lyons retired from teaching and coaching in the PIL at the age of 58. He decided to go to Germany to teach for the Department of Defense as "a fun thing to do."

PATCH HIGH SCHOOL

Patch High School was a small school in Stuttgart Germany, whose football teams had to play in leagues with bigger teams. "The program grew in size while the school got smaller," reflected Lyons. "At Patch, I only had my players two years and then they were gone."

PATCH AMERICAN HIGH SCHOOL (7-21)
STUTTGART, GERMANY

1990	2-5-0	
1991	1-6-0	
1992	2-5-0	
1993	2-5-0	

STUTTGART BATS

The Bats was a German American football team of 19-37 year old players. The Bats participated in a semi-pro league from April to July against other teams throughout Germany. There were four levels or divisions of competition.

Jerry Lyons comments: "We had great success, and this was one of the great experiences of my coaching career." His wife, **Julie,** served as a trainer and manager.

STUTTGART BATS (34-3-1)

1993	10-1-1	*Co Champs L-2
1994	13-2-0	*Co Champs L-1
1996	11-0-0	**League Champs L-4**

Jerry Lyons is retired and lives near Brightwood, Oregon

Don Frances Mabee

- Born: Sept. 5, 1917 in McMinnville, Ore.
- Died: Nov. 14, 1996
- Parents: Olivier and Eva "Darr" Mabee
- Father's occupation: Farmer and barber; Married: Suzanne Barendrick in 1941
- Children: Judy Endecott 4/1/46, Jeri Kost 8/23/49, Mike 4/24/57
- High School: McMinnville 1937
- Football Coach:
- Honors : 4 year letterman in football, basketball and track. All-state basketball in 1936-1938
- College: University of Oregon 1938-1941
- Football coach: Tex Oliver
- 3-year letterman in football ('38,39,40)
- Service: U.S. Army 1943-46 World War II – served at Ft. Ord as a POW guard.
- Degrees. BS in PE and Masters in Ed U of Oregon 1942

Don Mabee was unique in his brand of coaching an unorthodox mixture of discipline and fun.

THE ATHLETE

In 1936, the McMinnville paper noted that the high school was "led by the versatile **Don Mabee**, a natural halfback, was shifted to fullback at the beginning of the season to fill a hole at that position. He provided the scoring punch, making 84 points. His defensive work was excellent whether at safety or at the backing-up job, but it was on offense that the 170 pound back really shone."

Although Don Mabee played and coached football most of his career, he truly loved basketball. The three-time all-state basketball player from McMinnville High School made the traveling team for the 1939 "Tall Firs" NCAA championship team. He dropped from the team after the tournament due to grades and his commitment to football. Coach **Howard Hobson** wanted him back the following year so bad that he offered to make him the team captain.

But Mabee was also a very talented football player. In his four years at Oregon, he was a triple-threat player, a runner, a passer and a receiver for coach **Tex Oliver's** offense. As an end his sophomore season, Mabee had multiple games in which he gained over 100 yards on end around plays.

EARLY COACHING EXPERIENCE

- Assistant freshman football coach at University of Oregon in 1941 under **Tex Oliver**
- The Dalles High School – taught PE, coached baseball 1941-42 and basketball in 1942

LAGRANDE

Mabee was offered the football coaching and PE job at LaGrande for $3,100 per year by **Fred Patton**. He was assisted by **Ted Wilson** who later moved with him to McMinniville.

His best season in 1949, his team was led by **Wayne Berry** and **Charles Brackett**. He recognized La Grande's **Bill West** as the best athlete that he coached.

Mabee was offered jobs at both Whitman and Pacific, but he chose to remain a high school coach rather than test the college coaching waters.

LaGRANDE H.S. (31-16-0)

1946	3-6-0	
1947	4-5-0	
1948	8-2-0	**League Champs**
1949	10-1-0	**League Champs** **State Finals lost to Grant**
1950	6-2-0	**League Champs**

Mabee seemed isolated in La Grande. "Had it been in a better locale, I probably would have stayed." Mabee moved to McMinnville in 1951 and stayed 30 years as their high school football coach.

He captured nine league crowns. He also coached track and field for 20 years winning six league titles and was the basketball coach for a couple of years.

COACHING PHILOSOPHY

In explaining his success as a coach, Mabee remarked, "There's no secret. It's just a matter of doing what you can with what you've got," he explains. "You let them know what it's going to take to have a winning season. Then it's up to them."

"Football is mostly mental, no matter what people say. More teams have been beaten because of a mental frame than by some physical characteristic.

" You must keep the practices fun. Football is the only game that can be drudgery. You don't run two steps without getting hit by somebody. So if you don't have some fun in practices or else you lose the enthusiasm of the kids.

"If at all possible, we try to see that everyone plays and not just a token amount. We play 11 on offense and another 11 on defense. In the long run you're going to be better off because they can develop as players."

A master at strategy, Mabee figures his teams could use as many different offensive plays as any team in the state. " We change every week, so the kids have to be quick and sharp. If a kid concentrated on his studies as much as he does on our signal calling, he would be getting all As and Bs."

Then once on the field, Mabee strives for teamwork and tough play from his athletes, not for showiness to impress the fans.

Don Rutschman remembers Mabee as a coach who worked hard to make sports fun for his young players, but who also had a serious side: "Practices were always fun—we looked forward to them. But you could read him and you knew when it was time to get serious. He was unique. I never knew another coach like him. He even made our conditioning at the end of practice seem like fun."

"He was a very smart football coach, but his casual image didn't always convey that in public," Rutschman added

---

Coaching (1946-1980) 220-95-7 in 35 yrs

McMINNVILLE H.S. (189-79-7) 30 YRS

Year	Record	Notes
1951	3-5-0	
1952	5-4-0	
1953	5-2-1	
1954	5-3-0	
1955	7-2-0	**League Champs**
1956	8-1-0	**League Champs**
1957	9-1-0	**League Champs**
1958	7-1-1	**League Champs**
1959	4-4-1	
1960	5-3-1	
1961	7-2-0	
1962	7-2-0	
1963	6-2-1	
1964	9-1-1	**League Champs**
1965	8-2-0	**League Champs**
1966	8-2-0	**League Champs**
1967	9-1-0	**League Champs**
1968	5-4-0	
1969	6-3-0	
1970	6-3-0	
1971	8-3-0	**League Champs Semis**
1972	6-2-1	
1973	8-1-0	
1974	5-4-0	
1975	7-2-0	
1976	8-1-0	
1977	6-3-0	
1978	5-4-0	
1979	2-7-0	
1980	5-4-0	

Don Mabee wasn't as sophisticated as the modern day coach because he didn't have the written timed practice schedules, game plans, and play books. He was an "on the field coach."

His son Mike related a story during a 1972 Shrine game practice experience when assistants **John Allen** and **Dino Edwards** cornered him about their need for a written practice plan.

"Dad, at first, resisted. Then he pulled out a napkin and wrote out a plan with a timed table to satisfy them. He also asked both coaches for their input. Satisfied with his effort, Dad wiped his face with the napkin—practice schedule and all, tossed it in the garbage can and walked out to practice.

"His philosophy was to enjoy the game, teach in simplest terms how to win and to win."

Mike Cahill remembered Mabee as a coach and later as a co-worker, said Mabee's manner of always putting his players first has influenced his own coaching. "Don taught me it's definitely most important to be personable with your players and not take things too seriously."

"He showed me that how you work with young people is probably more important than all the X's and O's you diagram for them."

Every Friday night preceding home games, the football team has gathered at the Mabee household. "It's a way of getting closer to the kids," explained **Sue Mabee**, wife of the veteran coach.

When Don Mabee was being nominated for the **National High School Coach of the Year** in 1976, he was recognized for his unique brand of coaching, an unorthodox mixture of discipline and fun.

"I always wanted to be a coach," reflected **Don Mabee** in 1977 interview, " I always knew I wanted to be working with athletes and young people."

" There is nothing that I've ever been connected with that has given me such satisfaction as coaching has," commented Mabee.

Philosophically he commented: "There are three things necessary in anybody's life: One, something to do; two, something to look forward to and three, the brotherhood of man concept. With those three things, for the most part, you will be happy."

When former Hawaii football coach, **Fred vonAppen**, was doing graduate work at Linfield, he used to drop by McMinnville practice to watch Mabee in action. He once commented, "He's the only coach who can put in a new offense on Monday and have the kids run it on Friday like they've been running it for years."

Mabee always had a special place in his heart for the high school athlete. "It's an ideal age," Mabee said. "You see the things they accomplish, and you see improvement. You see these kids develop and grow....Every year's a new challenge."

It was his contention kids are no different today than they were when he first broke into coaching.

"I fondly recall his unique ability to make the game fun, " remembers an all-league lineman from the 50s, **Gary Bracelin**. "I don't even remember having a play-book to memorize. He taught on the field--feeding us plays three or four a day. After a couple of practice plays, it was full speed ahead."

"One of the joys of playing for Mabee was your knowledge that he never took himself too seriously. But what he really did was take a group of average athletes, mold them into a team and turn them into winners."

Perry Stubberfield played for Mabee in the 1950s and was a varsity assistant in the late 1960s through 1980.

"As a player I thought he was a great motivator," Stubberfield said. "Coaching under him, I realized the number one reason whey he was a success. He had the uncanny ability to look over a team (at the start of the season), put this player here and that player there and by the second morning, the squad was set."

"Despite what sociologists say, a young man needs discipline today just as he did way back when, and athletics are one of the few things in life that can offer it on a continual basis," stated Mabee in a newspaper interview.

Don Mabee at the age of 79, died November 14, 1996 in McMinneville.

Bill McArthur

- **William Dean McArthur**
- Born: July 28, 1918 in Keokuk, Iowa
- Died: April 24, 1997
- Married: Margaret "Maggie" Walker 1946
- Family: Mike, Steve, and Kelly
- High School: Wilson H.S., Long Beach, Calif. 1935
- College: UC-Santa Barbara 1937-40 Known as "Bullet Bill," he was an All-American halfback. Starred in swimming and track (eight events). Held school track records: 9.6 100 yd dash, and 21.9 220 yd dash. UC Santa Barbara Hall of Fame 1988
- Degrees: BS in PE UC Santa Barbara 1940; Masters in Ed U of Oregon 1941; Doctorate in Ed Oregon State 1955
- Service: Army Air Corps pilot in WWII Trained as a pilot, spent the war ferrying fighters and bombers to military theaters, and working as a flying instructor. Played military football

Bill McArthur: Retired in 1982 as the winningest active coach (180-116-6) in NAIA history.

COACHING

"I was a physical education major," McArthur said. "I'd known from the time I was 15 that I wanted to be a high school coach. It was the Great Depression. My ambition was just to get a high school coaching job where I could make $5,000 a year."

After graduation in 1940, he returned to Wilson High School a cadet teacher and got his first taste of professional football with the Hollywood Bears. The coaching job was elusive. So he headed off to the University of Oregon with a graduate stipend to be the UO's freshmen boxing and swimming coach and earn a Masters degree.

A SETBACK

McArthur, who had learned to fly as a collegian in 1938, joined the Air Force. He continued his football career in 1945 on a Nashville, Tenn., base team that was a member of the Air Force League. When the Nashville team scrimmaged the Chicago Bears, McArthur caught the eye of the pros. He opted for an offer as player-coach with the Chicago Rockets.

When he headed off to training camp, he was engaged to be married. His running mate at halfback was the legendary **Elroy "Crazy Legs" Hirsch**. The future looked good.

But in the last preseason game in 1946, in Santa Rosa, Calif., McArthur's left ankle was broken. He was sent to a hospital in San Francisco. "They set the leg, and the next day the toes were black," McArthur said. "Gangrene. They had to amputate the foot. Eight days later, they took most of my lower leg. And three or four days later they took the knee."

A few weeks later, he stood on crutches for his marriage to **Maggie Walker**. Fitted with an artificial leg, he accepted a teaching job at Gold Hill in Southern Oregon in January of 1947. He coached basketball, baseball and track

Later that year, the Grants Pass School Board turned McArthur down when he applied for their football job. "A man with one leg couldn't coach," they told him.

Before McArthur could plan a return to college for an advanced degree, he was contacted by **Henry Gunn**, the new president of Oregon College of Education. He needed a football coach.

McArthur was offered $3,000 a year. "I told Henry that I didn't think that was much to pay a college coach," McArthur said. "He told me: 'Bill, hiring a football coach is like buying a racehorse. First , you find out if he can run.'

"Gunn was interested in creating a more masculine imag for the school," McArthur said. "He thought a good football team would be a way to do it. He asked how long it would take. I told him three years."

McArthur got busy. He went after veterans getting out of the service and enticed a quarterback away from the University of Oregon, Abe Johnson, "with an opportunity to play."

McArthur had a 6-3-2 team his second season, and then went 9-0 in 1949. The three year promise to Gunn had been kept. President Gunn knew he had his "racehorse." And OCE had a football coach.

OREGON COLLEGE OF EDUCATION (WESTERN OREGON STATE COLLEGE)
36 Seasons (180-124-6)

1947	2-5-0	
1948	6-3-1	
1949	9-0-0	
1950	6-2-0	**OCC Champs**
1951	6-0-1	**OCC Champs**
1952	3-3-0	**OCC Champs**
1953	4-4-0	**OCC Champs**
1954	4-4-0	**OCC co-Champs**
1955		*Sabbatical leave
1956	3-4-0	
1957	5-3-0	
1958	5-4-0	**OCC Champs**
1959	1-7-0	
1960	3-5-0	
1961	4-3-1	
1962	4-4-0	
1963	3-6-0	
1964	1-6-0	
1965	5-3-1	
1966	6-2-0	**OCC Champs**
1967	4-4-0	**OCC Champs**
1968	7-2-0	**OCC Champs**
1969	6-3-0	**OCC Champs**
1970	5-5-0	
1971	8-2-0	
1972	6-4-0	
1973	6-3-0	
1974	3-4-1	
1975	9-1-0	**Evergreen Champs**, NAIA Texas A&I 37, OCE 0
1976	9-1-0	**Evergreen Champs**, Oregon Bowl I, OCE 43, Linfield 27
1977	7-2-0	
1978	8-2-0	**NAIA Playoffs** Angelo State TX 32, OCE 0
1979	8-1-1	**Evergreen Champs**, Oregon Bowl II, OCE 49, Linfield 28
1980	6-3-0	
1981	5-4-0	
1982	3-6-0	
1991	0-9-0	

McArthur pointed out the reason he stayed so long at one institution was that WOSC always kept in mind the original rationale for college athletics: that it have an educational value and that it be fun.

McArthur admitted that he had opportunities during his career to accept other positions. "Frankly the reason I stayed is that I felt the college and I fit each other. I was comfortable here and confident of our purpose."

LEGACY

Bill McArthur said he wanted to be remembered for his competency as a teacher and an imparter of knowledge, and the integrity of his football program. We didn't lie to the players, we weren't phony, and our coaches always tried to use positive reinforcement.

McArthur's most famous ex-player is **Darrel "Mouse" Davis**, the architect of the run-and-shoot. "He's been a strong influence for me and a lot of people," Davis said. "He's had an incredible influence on coaching all over Oregon. He is who he is. Mac doesn't pretend. He does what he wants to do.

"One of the things that helped me with my own philosophy as a coach was that I saw Bill was at his best when we lost. He was very positive and would not get down on his team. When we lost, he would say, 'That's history, let's get on with next week.' "

"He made sure a person didn't play just one position," said **Gale Davis**, who played or coached of almost all of McArthur's 36 seasons at Western Oregon.

"He'd move players around because he wanted them to learn football, not just the position. Most of them were here to become coaches and teachers, and that's the way Bill approached it. We weren't just teaching, we were giving the kids the opportunity to learn how to teach, and Bill's objective was to teach teaching."

LEGACY: HEAD FOOTBALL COACHES

Marv Hiebert	Douglas and Mt. Hood CC
Gale Davis	Redmond
Erv Garrison	Canby
Mouse Davis	Hillsboro and PSU
Gleason Eakin	Wilamina and Lebanon
Barry Adams	Lebanon, Nestucca
Jack Knudsen	Franklin
Wyman Gernhart	David Douglas

Steve Sears	Gladstone
Ron Simmons	
Kevin Moen	
Don Tomlin	Lebanon and Sprague
Tim Hundley	
Jack Flitcraft	Gresham
Craig Ruecker	Glencoe
John Olsen	West Albany
Mike Fagan	Crescent Valley
Craig Walker	Bend
Bill Griffith	Pacific and Grant
Randy Wegner	Reynolds
Mark Henderson	Junction City
Jay Minard	
Greg Lawrence	
Brad Bauer	
Kirk Miller	

"The secret to coaching, is to surround yourself with great people, and rise to victory on their shoulders."

Bill McArthur

"He was very, very intelligent and articulate, smarter than anyone in the room, always very eloquent in his speaking abilities." Said **Jon Carey, Athletic Director at Western Oregon**

"One of the things that I carried with me in my coaching, was remembering to keep your game goals in mind during practice. That was among the things I learned from Mac.

"Bill had another ingredient that made him a good coach. He was able to choose the right position for each player's ability."

Marv Hiebert

REGIS HIGH SCHOOL Head Coach

1986		Semis
1987		2A State Championship Beat Salem Acad. 14-13
1989		

CENTRAL HIGH

At 76, McArthur was a volunteer coach at Central High of Monmouth-Independence in 1994 and 1995. They were 21-2 in two seasons.

"He still had good rapport and good relations with the kids and he still had the fire and competitiveness that had been characteristic of his coaching over the years," remembers **Chuck Newkirk**, the athletic director at Central. Bill McArthur died at age 78 on April 24, 1997.

Back to WOSC

When **John Vogt** vacated the head coaching position at Western in 1990, **President Richard Meyers** invited McArthur at age 73, to return as the coach and re-establish credibility to the program. He coached in his sixth decade. He marveled at how things have changed. When he started coaching in 1947 he recalled that he was the only coach the first two years. "Now we have 11 coaches, four full time and seven part time."

It became an opportunity for McArthur to assess his philosophy:

- *Bring in freshmen*, the young talented players who have not been offered scholarships, and develop them as football players.

- He believed that for someone to be a better football player, they need to become *"physically educated"* or cross-trained.

- He believed the concept of a family philosophy and integrity in the program. *Give the kids a voice.* Captains for each unit act as sounding boards to solve problems. Discipline has to be imposed by the captains and seniors.

- *Teach the fundamentals of the game.* "Our success in the future, and the past, will be our ability to teach the young people the game."

Don Arthur McCarty

- Born: Dec. 20, 1940 in Albany, Calif.
- Parents: Mr and Mrs Arthur McCarty
  Father was a millwright while mother was a receptionist in a doctor's office
  Moved to Elmira, Ore. in 1946
- Married: Sue Grainger   June 2, 1962
- Family: Darren 6/16/66, Mike 2/20/64, Megan Peterson 2/7/72
- High School: Emira, Class of 1959
- Coach: Bob Leck
  All-league in football and basketball
  Running back and defensive back
  5'8" 150 pounds
- College: Lewis and Clark College '63
- Coach: Joe Huston
- Position: Defensive "monster back" or strong safety; started all four years
  Captain of the defense unit '61, '62
- Honors: First team All-NWC '61 and '62
  Selected outstanding Senior Athlete at Lewis and Clark in 1963
- Degree: B.S. Health and PE in 1963 L&C;
       Masters: Guidance and psychology in 1969 at OSU

Don McCarty rebuilt programs at Centennial, Oregon City and Sandy. *"If you work hard, you will be successful."*

ASPIRATIONS TO BE A COACH

Don McCarty knew in the 8th grade that he wanted to be coach. "I had a great basketball coach, **Richard McNulty**. He molded and guided me by telling me: ' *if you work hard, you'll be successful,* " McCarty recalled. "I became a better student because of athletics. Because if I didn't keep my grades up, I couldn't play."

Since his father died three weeks after he graduated from high school, McCarty credited his mother for providing the encouragement for him to get a college education. He was recruited to Lewis and Clark.

When McCarty arrived on campus, the 5'8" 150 pound running back found the competition, the likes of All-American **Mick Hergert,** too stiff to play offense. He settled for a defensive starting position. McCarty started four years as the strong safety, captained the defense and earned All- NWC honors his junior and senior years.

At age 23, Don McCarty was hired as the head football coach at Lebanon High School upon the recommendation of his coaches at Lewis and Clark.

"I learned the hard way and on the job," remembers McCarty. " I had to go out and get help from everybody. I went to a lot of clinics, and I read a lot of articles and books. Every coach I competed against helped me directly or indirectly. I also learned, I needed to outwork them."

LEBANON HIGH SCHOOL (3-13-1)

1964	1-8-0	
1965	2-5-1	

"Coach Wilson , I'm in trouble," remembered McCarty requesting professional advice. "I've got five ex-head coaches as assistants."

Within two years, Ex- L&C basketball player and Centennial athletic director, **Ken Servis**, hired McCarty .

CENTENNIAL HIGH SCHOOL (34-31-1)

1966	3-6-0	
1967	1-8-0	
1968	3-6-0	
1969	4-5-0	
1970	6-3-0	
1971	6-3-0	
1972	11-0-1	**Wilco League Champs** **AAA State Champions** Beat Wilson 25-21

ADMINISTRATION

After McCarty won the state championship in 1972 and coached the 1973 Shrine game, he stepped aside from football. He entered school administration at the encouragement of Principal **Ken Servis**. "I had set goals for myself and had met them. Now I needed to find out for myself about administration."

But, it didn't set that well for McCarty when the football seasons rolled around. He missed it. "I told Servis, I need to go back to what I really like," recalled McCarty. "And that's coaching." When the Oregon City coaching job opened, Oregon City athletic director **Frank Good** hired him.

OREGON CITY HIGH SCHOOL (43-34-0)

1976	2-7-0	
1977	2-7-0	
1978	0-9-0	
1979	8-2-0	**Timber Valley Champs**
1980	9-1-0	**Wilco Champs**
1981	9-2-0	
1982	6-3-0	
1983	7-3-0	

LEWIS AND CLARK

Don McCarty was anxious to be successful at Lewis and Clark, but it didn't work out. Besides having to take a cut in pay, there was a lack of talented football players on the campus. As **Fred Wilson** the retiring coach put it: "The cupboard was bare."

LEWIS AND CLARK COLLEGE (7-20-0)

1984	3-6-0	
1985	3-6-0	
1986	1-8-0	

The administration reneged on their promise of salary increases as the college moved into an endowment mode. The salary freeze caused McCarty to return to the high school scene, which he missed. "There was always a community that provided the excitement of the high school game."

BEAVERTON HIGH SCHOOL (20-20-0)

1987	5-5-0	
1988	5-5-0	
1989	4-5-0	
1990	6-5-0	

The McCarty's had bought property at the mountains and were considering the location for their retirement when they shared their idea with friend **Mike Kostraba**, who in turn mentioned it to **Randy Hutchins**, the Sandy athletic director.

"Why don't you come now?" asked Hutchins.

"The Sandy job is a diamond in the rough," thought McCarty. "I can rebuild it."

SANDY HIGH SCHOOL (42-37-0)

1991	4-5-0	
1992	1-8-0	
1993	6-4-0	
1994	5-5-0	
1995	7-3-0	
1996	5-5-0	
1997	5-5-0	
1998	9-2-0	
1999		
2000		

McCarty's *"I Believe"* card

I believe in myself
I believe in my teammates
I believe through hard work I will achieve success
I believe something good will happen.

For eight years Don McCarty has required his players to carry the card in their helmets. For 33 years, McCarty has required his players to carry the principal in their hearts.

At Sandy, McCarty has not only turned around an underdog program, he has proven that in fusing players with self-esteem in every bit as important as memorizing the playbooks.

Gene Morrow

- Name: Eugene Russell Morrow
- Born: June 27, 1929 in The Dalles,Ore.
- Parents: Frank and Lulu Russell Morrow
- Father was a pharmacist
- Married: Karleene Lee Kramer 2/14/53
- Daughter: Geni Lu Morrrow/Magee; Sons: Kory Dennis Morrow 6/6/57-4/92; Luke Russell Morrow 1982
- High School: The Dalles 1948
- Coach: Curtis French and Dick Sutherland
- QB and HB, called "Rifle-Arm Morrow" The MVP that led The Dalles to the state championship in 1947 with a 47-7 victory over Hillsboro
- College: Oregon State 1952
- Coach: Kip Taylor
- Starting QB in 1949,1950, 1951
- Degree: Human Biology and PE
- Drafted by Pittsburg Steelers, but played for the Calgary Stampeders

Gene Morrow: *"The Dean of Oregon's Coaches"* has an innate understanding of young people and a life long dedication to the game of football."

THE COACH ON THE FIELD

Gene Morrow's high school coach, **Dick Sutherland**, recognized the amazing savvy of his star quarterback early. Not only was Morrow utilized as a coach on the field, he was a coach during practice too. Since Sutherland lacked an assistant, he turned many coaching chores over to his football-minded senior.

Morrow's brilliant play calling and strategic mind also paid dividends as The Dalles won the State Championship in 1947. "Oh, I made suggestions now and then," noted Sutherland, "but Morrow called the plays."

COACHING

Morrow matriculated to Oregon State to play football and focused on a future in pharmacy. He prospered in football, yet he struggled in the classroom until his sophomore year when he met with Pharmacy Dean **George Crossen**: "Morrow, you may be first team on the football field, but you're sitting on the bench in pharmacy." At that time, Morrow began refocusing his college studies toward a career in education and coaching.

He worked well in the football scheme of new football coach, **Kip Taylor**. He became a starter his sophomore season and hence his football talents continued to thrive throughout his college career. Morrow credits assistant **Bump Elliott**, the former Michigan All-American, with his development as a college player.

NEWPORT HIGH SCHOOL

Morrow opted to play for the Calgary Stampeders of the Canadian Football League but he became disenchanted with professional football. He returned to The Dalles in 1955 until one day at his father's drug store, he got a phone call. He was offered the head football post at Newport High School upon the recommendation of Oregon State alum, **Marshall Simmons**.

Before Morrow accepted the position, he sought out the counsel of his former high school coach, **Dick Sutherland**, who was then coaching at Bandon. "If there is any chance you don't want the job," said Sutherland. "I will take it myself."

Reedsport coach **Rudy Ruppe**, a former teammate at OSC, told Morrow after his third season: "Gene, there are more good coaches in the smaller schools than in the bigger ones."

Morrow took the coaching post at Newport in 1955, and today has an unmatched tenure in the number of years teaching the game. He plans the 1999 season to be his 45th and final season.

What the win-loss table doesn't explain is the hard work, the dedication and utmost loyalty that Morrow has devoted to his players and his program throughout the years.

Newport High School, 44 years (275-145-3)

1955	7-3-1	Coast League Champs
1956	4-5-0	
1957	6-3-0	
1958	7-3-0	Coast League Champs
1959	2-7-0	
1960	8-2-0	Coast League Champs
1961	7-1-1	Co-Coast League Champs
1962	5-4-0	
1963	8-0-1	Co-Coast League Champs
1964	8-2-0	Coast League Champs
1965	8-1-0	Coast League Champs
1966	8-1-0	Coast League Champs
1967	7-2-0	Coast League Champs
1968	7-2-0	Coast League Champs
1969	10-2-0	Coast League Champs Lost in AA State Finals To St. Marys 28-12
1970	4-6-0	
1971	7-2-0	Coast League Champs
1972	3-6-0	
1973	8-2-0	Coast League Champs
1974	3-6-0	
1975	4-5-0	
1976	3-6-0	
1977	4-5-0	
1978	8-3-0	Valco Champs
1979	8-2-0	Co-Valco Champs
1980	9-2-0	Valco Champs
1981	6-3-0	
1982	9-1-0	Valco Champs
1983	5-5-0	
1984	8-1-0	Co-Valco Champs
1985	8-1-0	Valco Champs
1986	5-4-0	
1987	8-2-0	Valco Champs
1988	7-2-0	
1989	4-5-0	
1990	8-4-0	Valco Champs
1991	6-4-0	
1992	5-5-0	
1993	4-5-0	
1994	4-5-0	
1995	5-4-0	
1996	6-3-0	
1997	9-3-0	Valco Champs
1998	5-5-0	
1999		

Morrow has always enjoyed the challenge each year at Newport. *"I've always had good kids that were willing to work hard and give that extra effort,"* he states. *"They become winners in the long run, in later life. It's been confirmed over and over."*

Care often ranks with winning....

"One knows that he still loves the game and most importantly, his players. After a rousing applause at a football banquet (led by his players) after he was introduced, Morrow fought back the emotions in talking about his team.

" At that moment it didn't matter that the Cubs hadn't made the playoff. What mattered was that he cared."

Tim Sullivan, Sports Editor, *News Times*

Morrow has built a program which not only wins with skill, but with class. Cub opponents often praise Newport for their behavior displayed on and off the field.

"We really stress clean playing, dedication, how to win, how to lose, sacrifice, team spirit---things that will make the kid a better person," said Morrow.

The players take these messages to heart. **Mark Collson**, Mayor of Newport, played for NHS in 1963 during Morrow's only undefeated season where the Cubs went 8-0-1 and didn't go to the playoffs because of that tie.

"You live with those memories for the rest of your life," said Collson about the heartbreaking season. "He (Morrow) will explain to you that those are lessons in life. They make you look at life in a certain way. He's good about interpreting the lessons away from athletics," added Collson.

Tim Sullivan, Sports Editor, *News Times,***1988**

"I retired in 1994 after 38 years of teaching. I taught almost everything from physics to remedial math," related Morrow. "Since then, I've enjoyed coaching football more than ever. I should have retired from teaching earlier."

HONORS

1970 1990	Head Coach East-West Shrine Games
1993	Oregon Coach of the Year by the Oregon Coaches Association Western Region "Coach of the Year"
	League Coach of the Year numerous

James Edward "Jim" Nagel

- Born: Feb.9, 1946 in Lynnwood, Calif.
- Parents: Fremont and Verlin Nagel
- Father worked as a painter for City of LA
- Married: Alice Whitley June 17, 1972
- Family: Eric Nagel 9/25/79, Michelle Nagel 12/1/84
- High School: Pius X, Downey, Calif., 1963
- Coach: Farley Day
- Honors: All-Conf. Linebacker and Center Team captain
- Jr College: East Los Angeles C.C. '63-'64
- Coach: Ron Smith
- Honors: All-Metro
- College: Long Beach State College '66
- Coach: Don Reed
- Degrees: B.S. PE Long Beach State '68 Masters from San Jose State '74

COACHING

Jim Nagel's football playing days ended with a knee injury early his junior year at Long Beach State. It was at that time that he focused on a career as a football coach. He returned to his former high school Pius X as a football assistant during the three years he finished college.

It would be the start of a long coaching journey that would eventually lead to Ashland, Oregon.

VILLANOVA PREP, Ojai, CA (5-12-1)

1969	1-8-0	
1970	4-4-1	

ST. BONAVENTURE, Ventura, CA (11-7-0)

1971	5-4-0	
1972	6-3-0	

1973 1974	San Jose State	Grad assistant and receiver coach for **Darrell Rodgers**
1975	UC Riverside	Assist to **Bob Toledo** in spring before school dropped football
1975	San Francisco State College	Offensive coordinator for **Vic Rowen**
1976 1977	San Jose State	Passing coordinator for **Lynn Stiles** *won conf. and led nation in pass efficiency with QB **Steve DeBerg**
1978 1979	New Mexico State	Offensive coordinator for **Gil Kruger** *won Mission Valley Conf.

Jim Nagel understands his coaching role and relishes the yearly challenge to apply his football wisdom. His success speaks volumes.

1980	Sunnyside Jr Hi Tucson, AZ	Football Coach
1981	Canyondel Oro H.S., AZ	Assistant to **Bob Smith**
1982	Amphitheater H..S. Tucson, AZ	Assistant to **Vern Freidli**

ASHLAND, OREGON

In 1979, Jim Nagel visited Ashland, Oregon to interview for an opening at Southern Oregon College. He was impressed with the community. A few years later, a brother-in-law who had taken a BLM job in Medford, informed Nagel that Ashland High School football coach **Craig Hastin** had taken another post in Medford. Nagel seized the opportunity and became the Ashland High School football coach in 1983.

Ashland High School not only got a football coach, they got a very good football coach. They got a coach that understands his role and relishes the yearly challenge to apply his football wisdom.

Nagel's record at Ashland speaks volumes to the success of his coaching philosophy. After 16 seasons at one of Oregon's smallest 4A high schools, 62nd of 76, his football teams have won 79% of their games. The Grizzlies have been to the playoffs 14 straight seasons, been in five state championship games winning three.

They have won the strong Southern Oregon Conference Championship seven times. In a conference with the two Medford schools,

Roseburg and Grants Pass, that is almost unbelievable. But how does he do it?

Jim Nagel is a student of football and a student of coaching the game. Always has been.

- His high school coach **Farley Day** taught him the importance of discipline and respect, and the value of weight training.
- He took every opportunity to learn from other coaches. He read everything he could get his hands on about the game. He shared with other coaches and attended as many clinics as he could. "There were a ton of good coaches in California."
- He recalls **Sid Gilman**, "the Guru of the Passing Game" helping him with his thinking. "He used multiple sets while spreading the offense around."
- Nagel's successful experience as the passing coordinator at San Jose State when **Steve DeBerg** led the nation in passing efficiency established him as a top offensive football coach.
- Nagel enjoys the yearly challenge, particularly at the high school level. He compares it closely with the game of chess. The need to know the strengths and weaknesses of your players similar to understanding what each of the chess pieces are capable of doing. With the **proper placement of his players**, he can tailor his offensive, defensive and kicking game to **maximize their potential**.
- Nagel tries to provide an atmosphere of **positive expectancy** for the players by utilizing *visualization* and *positive affirmations.*
- He believes in **goal setting**. Concrete goals for each player both athletically and academically.
- Nagel also understands **team goal setting**. He turns the ownership of the team goals over to the seniors. He believes that despite how much the coach wants to win, it's really the players that must want to work hard enough to make it happen. "I can spark the motivational fire that burns within each player, but they must fuel the fire themselves," comments Nagel.

Philosophically, Nagel believes strongly that coaches have a unique opportunity to serve as mentors. "Football provides a classroom or learning lab in which coaches can get the student-athlete's attention and focus better than any other classroom on campus. I want to take advantage of that opportunity.

"The great thing that I have found is that the better I teach the life skills and the skills needed to build resiliency, the more football games we seem to win."

ASHLAND HIGH SCHOOL,16 yrs(150-38-0)

1983	4-5-0	
1984	1-8-0	
1985	7-3-0	
1986	7-3-0	
1987	12-1-0	**SOC Champs**
1988	10-2-0	
1989	14-0-0	**SOC Champs** **State 4A Champions** **Beat Roseburg 24-22**
1990	10-3-0	
1991	13-1-0	**SOC Champs** **State 4A Champions** **Beat South Salem 28-0**
1992	13-1-0	**SOC Champs** **State Finals** **Lost to Marshfield 36-21**
1993	13-1-0	**SOC Champs** **State Finals** **Lost to N. Medford 27-24**
1994	5-5-0	
1995	9-2-0	
1996	9-2-0	
1997	9-1-0	**SOC Champs**
1998	14-0-0	**SOC Champs** **State 4A Champions** **Beat Roseburg 29-23**
1999		
2000		
2001		
2002		
2003		

Some of Nagel's better players were:**Ean Lombard, Scott Mimnaugh, Lance Mimnaugh, Chad Cota, Bert Peterson, Damian Jackson, Kirk Strait, Kyle Strait, Matt Wells, Cy Aleman, and Eric Nagel.**

COACHING HONORS

	Southern Oregon Conference Coach of the Year

Tillman "Ted" Ogdahl

- Born: Oct.1, 1921 in Glenwood, Minn.
- Died: July 29, 1988
- Parents: Tillman and Irene Ogdahl
  Father was a farmer who moved from
  Minnesota to Montana to Portland
- Married: Jean Donaldson 8/21/43
- Children: Wally 2/3/45, Greg 7/27/46,
  Tracy Valley 2/4/54
- School: Franklin 1936-1940
  Coaches: Chappie King '36-'37, Roy
  Sandberg '38, Johnny Londahl '39
  Position: Guard first 3 years, All-City
  halfback
- College: Willamette University 1940-43
  Coach: Roy 'Spec' Keene
- Honors: 2nd team Little All-American 1942
  Track: NWC 100 yard champ
- Degree: W'45 B.S. Education, W'48
  Masters Education, OSU'72 Doctorate in
  Education
- College of Pacific- V-12 Program 1943
  Coach: Amos Alonzo Stagg
- Service: 1943-1945
  Capt. USMC in the Okinawa invasion
  Two Purple Hearts and a Silver Star
- Pro football: San Diego Bombers 1946
  Coach: Mike Percarovich

Ted Ogdahl was smart and competitive. He coached with the same passion he played the game.

FRANKLIN HIGH SCOOL

Ted Ogdahl loved the game of football, and he loved to compete. His first years in high school he played guard, but as he grew stronger and faster, he became a running back.

In 1939, the new Franklin coach **Johnny Londahl** installed the double wing formation with a lot of reverses and double reverses. It was a "razzle-dazzle" offense that was perfect for Ogdahl's speed and talents.

The Portland prep league took immediate notice as Ogdahl developed into one of its finest backs. He earned All-City honors and was chosen by his teammates as their most valuable player.

WILLAMETTE UNIVERSITY

After Ogdahl graduated from Franklin in 1940, he accepted an academic-football scholarship to Willamette University. He played for **Roy S.'Spec' Keene** who had coached the Bearcat fortunes since 1926.

Willamette played the intricate man in motion offense, with Ogdahl at the left halfback. He would start in motion before the ball was snapped to the fullback. Either running or faking, Ogdahl was the key to the team's success.

In 1941, Willamette became the second highest scoring team in the nation, winning the Northwest Conference championship. But world events would soon alter the lives of many.

Pearl Harbor Day, Dec. 7, 1941 and the World War II battle for Okinawa in 1944, became major events in his life.

PEARL HARBOR

After the successful 1941 season, Willamette had scheduled two season-ending games in Honolulu. It was to be a series of games called the Shrine Bowl with Hawaii and San Jose State.

Hawaiian hospitality greeted the Willamette group after the five-day voyage with the traditional hula dancing and leis. It began as a travel experience for fun and football for the team, but it became a major witnessing event as the Japanese air attack brought the United States into World War II the day after the first game. The second game was never played.

The University of Hawaii beat the Bearcats 20-6 on Saturday December 6th. One of the game's highlights, remembered **Marshall Barbour**, was the play of Ted Ogdahl.

"Ted made the defensive play of the game," said Barbour. "He caught from behind Hawaii's top runner, Nellie Smith, reputed to be the fastest man in the Islands."

While the team and boosters were waiting in the lobby of their hotel the next morning for a day-long tour of the island, the Japanese air force was attacking Pearl Harbor sinking many of our Fleet in its harbor. The Willamette football players were immediately dispersed to do guard duty at Punahou High School with 1916-era Springfield rifles for the next two weeks.

The island waited for an anticipated invasion. Ogdahl later told the *Statesman-Journal*, "There was no question in our minds that the Japanese were going to invade us. They didn't come. But we thought we could see them coming many times-with every wave that came onto the beaches."

The team left the islands on the *President Coolidge*, December 19th. The ocean liner had become a floating hospital as it transported 125 seriously wounded servicemen. As an extra precaution, they were escorted by a cruiser and a destroyer for the five-day voyage back to San Francisco through submarine- infested waters.

ALL-AMERICAN

In 1942, Ogdahl enrolled in Willamette's V-12 program for officer training for the Marine Corps for his junior year.

The football team played a shortened five game schedule that year. Ted Ogdahl earned **Little All-American** honors on what was to be coach Spec Keene's last team

In the fall of 1943, Ogdahl was sent to the College of Pacific in Stockton, California under the V-12 program. There, he was able to play a season of football for the legendary **Amos Alonzo Stagg.**

"Amos Alonzo Stagg had put together a ragtag squad of 4-Fs and Naval trainees and watched it pay off in 1943, when he used a flanker formation. That club whipped UCLA, 19-7. California, 12-6, and upset Del Monte Pre-Flight, 16-7. College of the Pacific finished in the nation's top ten, and Stagg was voted America's coach of the year at age 81.".

Edwin Pope *Football's Greatest Coaches*

OKINAWA

Ogdahl's training led him to Paris Island and Quantico , Virginia, for officers training . As a second lieutentant, he joined the 2nd Marine Division at Camp Pendleton in August of 1944. By November, the Division was sent to the South Pacific for the invasion of Okinawa.

Although the Division met little resistance during the landing, Ogdahl's platoon was over run by the Japanese troops when they made their counter attack in the darkness of night. Most of the Marines encamped in the large foxhole were slashed and killed by the Japanese sabers leaving only Ogdahl with arm and shoulder wounds.

During a later skirmish, Ogdahl took a bullet in his chest while trying to take out a Japanese machine gun emplacement.

The medics rescued him and returned him to the field hospital where he remained unconscious for several weeks.

Immediately after Ogdahl regained consciousness, he asked the doctor, "Will I be able to play football again?"

Ogdahl's burning desire for rehabilitation was to play football again, but for his war effort, he was awarded two Purple Hearts and the Silver Star for bravery.

From the Naval Hospital in Guam, Spec Keene, his college coach, now a ranking officer in the Navy, got Ogdahl moved to Mare Island for rehabilitation and again later to Camp Adair near Corvallis as an out patient.

"AUGIE OGDEN"

Ted Ogdahl did get his wish to play football again. Perhaps thinking he would have another year of college elgibility remaining, he played pro football for the San Diego Bombers using the alias, "Augie Ogden," in the fall of 1946.

Ogdahl returned to Willamette the next season, but it wasn't to play football, but to coach for **Jerry Lillie** while he worked on a Masters degree.

GRANT HIGH SCHOOL

With his playing days out of the way and his teaching certificate and Masters degree under his arm, Ogdahl took to the coaching with the same passion he had as a player.

He was recommended for the Grant coaching job by Willamette coach Jerry Lillie, who had also coached at the northeast Portland school.

And what an impact Ogdahl made. In four years his teams won three city championships and two state championships while a third state final game tie was decided by yardage.

He had talented players, the likes of **George Shaw, Ron Phiester, Al Hansen, Dale Duff, Johnny Keller and Jerry Exley**. His teams always had a fine mix of running and passing.

Ogdahl's best player was **George Shaw**. The multi-talented quarterback led the Generals to two undefeated seasons in 1949 and 1950. His high school, college and pro careers made him an Oregon legend.

GRANT HIGH SCHOOL (35-4-4)

1948	3-3-3	
1949	11-0-0	**State Champions** Beat LaGrande 24-0
1950	11-0-0	**State Champions** Beat Marshfield 12-7
1951	10-1-1	**State Finals** Tie Lost to Grants Pass on first downs

"Ted Ogdahl was an intense competitor and the most intelligent coach I knew. He tried to hide it and fool people."

Assistant coach , Jerry Frei

"Ted put together a lot of good athletes, and he made them believe that they could win without being arrogant about it. Each of us had an individual job. He was a low-key type of guy.

I can remember the Roosevelt-Grant game that was played at the stadium. We were told that the Roosevelt coach had his scouts watching our practices from the top of the Grant Bowl and supposedly knew everything we were going to do. Before the game he told us just to make sure, he had sent their coach a copy of all our plays. 'You guys are going to have to play just a little harder. I think you can do it.'"

George Shaw, Grant QB

WILLAMETTE UNIVERSITY

When Willamette looked for a football coach in 1952, they didn't have to look far. Ted Ogdahl's outstanding high school coaching record made him the leading candidate to replace **Chester Stackhouse** who had held the reins the previous three years.

It was now Ogdahl's opportunity to work his coaching magic at the college level. All of his teams in his coaching career reflected a certain spirit for the game. They were always well coached and reflected the enthusiasm and toughness of their coach.

Speed, deception, blocking, and an ever-constant aerial threat made the Willamette offense hard to contain. If an opponent stopped their end sweeps, they would move up the middle. Likewise, if an opponent would halt them on the ground, they would take to the pass. This is the way Ted Ogdahl coached.

His best players were: **Bill Long, Vic Backlund, Tommy Lee, Stu Hall, Stan Solomon, Walt Looney, Lee Weaver, Bob Bowman, Calvin Lee, and Gig Gilmore.**

"In 1958, our football team had a family atmosphere. We only had 26 people, so we never scrimmaged. We had kids from small towns as the program began to build. When we started to win, it was made possible by coaches, **Ted Ogdahl**, **John Lewis** and **Jerry Long**.

The biggest lesson I learned from Ogdahl was during the heat of an important game, he told us: *'Guys, remember this! The first time that you learn to quit will be your toughest. It will get easier each time after that'*

Stu Hall , NAIA All-American '61

WILLAMETTE U. 20 years (98-65-10) .570

1952	5-2-2	
1953	2-5-1	
1954	6-2-0	
1955	1-7-0	
1956	2-4-2	
1957	5-2-2	
1958	8-1-0	**NWC Champs**
1959	5-3-1	
1960	8-0-0	**NWC Champs**
1961	4-4-0	
1962	6-3-1	
1963	3-5-0	
1964	5-4-0	
1965	6-1-1	
1966	5-4-0	
1967	7-2-0	
1968	9-1-0	**NWC Champs NAIA Semis**
1969	2-7-0	
1970	4-4-0	
1971	5-4-0	

During his 20 seasons at Willamette, Ogdahl's coaching record is 98-65-10, winning or sharing seven Northwest Conference titles.

He was selected **Oregon's Man of the Year (Coach of the Year)** in 1960 by the Oregon Sports Writers and Broadcasters Association.

The football field at Willamette's McCulloch stadium is named after Ted Ogdahl in 1993. He was inducted into the **Willamette Hall of Fame** in 1991.

Ogdahl resigned in December of 1971 after 20 years as Willamette's head football coach and 13 years as the track coach

> " I joined Ted Ogdahl in the fall of 1955 at Willamette and coached with him through the 1960 season.
>
> . Ted was a quiet confident coach who taught in a firm manner. He never yelled at players on the field, which earned him their respect. He had an educated approach to the game. He was very good at putting his thoughts together and had the ability to put in an offense that would meet and compliment his player's talents. He was also very good at calling plays and attacking the weakness of the opponent.
>
> Ted was great to coach with. I learned a lot from him. He gave me a lot of freedom to coach and let me bump my nose. Then he would say 'Lets talk this over.'
>
> What an honor it was for me to coach with him. He was my idol since high school. He had such a sense of humor, it made coaching fun at Willamette. There were tears when I left Ted Ogdahl (to go to Oregon State). We had coached some great teams
>
> He never tooted his own horn, but I knew he was disappointed in not getting a job at the next level.
>
> Ted Ogdahl left his mark as one of the top coaches in the state of Oregon."
>
> **Jerry Long, assistant coach**

He had been working summers on a doctorate through Oregon State University. The doctorate allowed Ogdahl to join the faculty at Oregon Tech (OTI) to teach in the paramedical areas.

Ted Ogdahl did coach football again in 1977, but this time as an assistant for **Don Read** who took over the helm at Oregon Tech after being released at the University of Oregon.

> **Don Read** remembers Ogdahl as very popular with the players. "He would always have M&Ms in his pocket. If a player did well in one of his drills, he would hand them an M&M."

Ted Ogdahl died July 29, 1988 at the age of 66.

Jack Allen Patera

- Born: Aug.1, 1933 in Bismarrk, N.D.
- Parents: Frank and Dorothy Patera
- Father's occupation: baker
- Married to: Susan Bennett 6/17/53
- Family: Michael Patera, 11/26/55, Mary Patera 3/29/59, John Patera 10/5/61, Beth Patera 3/25/63
- High School: Washington H.S. 1951
- Coach: Gerald Exley
- Honors: Capt. and All-City Tackle, Shrine All-star
- College: University of Oregon 1955
- Coach: Len Casanova
- Honors: All-Coast, All-American mention, 4 yr letterman, East-West Game, Hula Bowl, College All-Star Game
- Degree: B.S. Education U of Oregon 1955
- Service: ROTC 6 mos active duty 1st Lt.
- Drafted: NFL Baltimore Colts (4th)
- Professional football: Baltimore Colts 1955-57 (Linebacker and guard.); Chicago Cardinals 1958-59 (Linebacker); Dallas Cowboys 1960-61 (Linebacker)

COACHING

Jack Patera did not set out to be a coach although he had graduated from Oregon with a degree in education. He remembered the Baltimore Colt GM **Don Kellet**, telling him that "coaching was the hardest way to make an easy living there is."

- **Len Casanova**

    "Cas probably influenced my life the most. His dedication to coaching, the U of O and life in general has certainly affected me for the better I hope." "I was asked to come back to the University of Oregon to coach in 1958," remembered Patera. "But I told him I planned to play football until I was 50."

- **Tom Landry**

    Patera was picked in the 1960 expansion draft by the Dallas Cowboys. "Being a middle linebacker in Landry's type of defense was a major cog, so I probably learned as much in that first year with Dallas than I'd learned during my previous six years," said Patera. "Landry was more like Cas than other coaches I was associated with and that was probably why we got along so well."

    When Patera's playing days were

Jack Patera: *"The best defensive line coach in the NFL,"* became the first Seattle Seahawk coach.

finished with Dallas, he parlayed that experience into his first coaching opportunity with the Rams in 1963.

- **Harland Svare**

    When Svare was named head coach of the Rams in 1963, he hired what was called *"Swede's Neophytes."* They were all young and would-be coaches. He hired Patera as the defensive line coach, who had no prior experience, on the recommendation of former Cowboy teammate **Don Heinrich**.

"The Fearsome Foursome"

The Ram front four were "a mountain range of menace and muscle." They were **Merlin Olsen, Lamar Lundy, Roosevelt Grier, Deacon Jones, and Roger Brown** (who replaced Grier when injury forced him to retire.)

"The Fearsome Foursome" made the pass rush famous, in fact they choreographed it. They perfected a series of maneuvers known as "twists" and "loops." They made a science out of rushing the passer.

It began Patera's legacy as *the best defensive line coach in the league.*

ASSISTANT COACH

1963 1964 1965	Los Angeles Rams For **Harland Svare** *"Fearsome Foursome"*	Defensive Line Coach
1966	Los Angeles Rams For **George Allen**	Defensive Line Coach
1967 1968	New York Giants For **Allie Sherman**	Defensive Line Coach
1969 1970 1971 1972 1973 1974 1975	Minnesota Vikings For **Bud Grant** *"Purple People Eaters"* (Four NFC champion- ship games and 3 Super Bowls)	Defensive Line Coach

- **Bud Grant**

   "Working for Bud Grant and being as successful as we were certainly formed the ways I handled my first head coaching job."

   At a 20 year reunion of the 1969 NFL championship team, Head Coach Bud Grant personally acknowledged Patera's coaching role with an overdue compliment: "Patera, you were really a key figure in our success."

"The Purple People Eaters"

When Jack Patera coached the Minnesota Viking's front four equivalent, they were called the "Purple People Eaters." They were **Carl Eller, Gary Larsen, Alan Page and Jim Marshall**. The Viking front four played a big part in leading the Vikings to four NFC championship games and three Super Bowls during Patera's seven years.

It was Patera's coaching for **Bud Grant's** Vikings that got him the recommendation for the expansion Seattle Seahawks.

Jack Patera at age 42, got his first taste of head coaching when he became the first head coach of the expansion Seattle franchise in 1976.

SEATTLE SEAHAWKS (35-57-0)

1976	2-10	
1977	5-9	
1978	9-7	**NFL Coach of Year**
1979	9-7	
1980	4-12	
1981	6-10	
1982	0-2	*Released during NFL strike

Patera never took the Seahawks to the playoffs, but he did lead them to a 5-9 mark in 1977, the *best second-year record for an expansion team in NFL history.*

The Seahawks won early under Patera, putting together back-to-back 9-7 records in 1978 and '79. Patera was named **NFL Coach of the Year in 1978.**

Unfortunately for Patera, Seahawk majority owner **Lloyd Nordstrom** died a month after he was hired. Brother **Elmer Nordstrom** took over. Elmer didn't want to be involved in football. It led to family arguments that eventually led to the unceremonious dismissal of both Patera and General Manager **John Thompson** during the strike-filled 1982 season.

When Patera left, **Chuck Knox** immediately took the Seahawks to the playoffs. It was no surprise to Patera.

"The things I started in 1982 were the way they continued the next two years," he remarked. "But I think we were certainly on the road to developing a football team that would be respectable." He felt disappointed that he didn't have a chance to finish what he set out to do.

Patera never returned to coaching football. He resides in Cle Elum Wash., retired to a life of hunting, fishing and golfing. His avocation is field-training German Shorthair Pointers.

HONORS

1978	**NFL Hall of Fame**
1982	**State of Oregon Sports Hall of Fame**
	PIL Hall of Fame

Tommy Prothro

- **James Thompson Prothro Jr.**
- Born: July 20, 1920 in Dyersburg, Tenn.
- Died: May 14, 1995 Memphis, Tenn
- Parents: James Thompson "Doc" and Catherine Cates Prothro
  Father was a major league baseball player and major league baseball manager with the Philadelphia Phillies (1939-1941)
  Doc Prothro played third base for the Portland Beavers in 1926 and 1927
- Married: Shirley Seagle
- Daughter: Ann (Mrs. Richard) Wilson
- High School: Central High in Memphis, Tenn 1934-36
- Competed in football, basketball, baseball and track
- Riverside Military Academy in Gainesville, Georgia , a prep school for college 1936-37
  Football coach: Henry "Red" Sanders
- College: Duke University
- Coach: Wallace Wade
- Position: Quarterback for Duke in the 1941 Rose Bowl against Oregon State
  Won the Jacobs Trophy in 1941 as the best blocker in the east
- Also competed in baseball and lacrosse
- Degree: Bachelors Degree Duke 1942
- Drafted in fifth round of 1942 NFL draft
- 1942: Line coach at Western Kentucky
- Service: WW II U.S. Navy- served as an officer in the Pacific theatre 1943-45

HENRY "RED" SANDERS

If the childless Sanders family ever "adopted" a son, he was Tommy Prothro. Sanders had first coached him as a boy at Riverside Military Academy in 1936 and kept in close contact with him during Prothro's college days at Duke University.

Sanders literally plucked Prothro from a semi-pro pitcher's mound in 1946 and sold him on abandoning a potential baseball career to coach for him at Vanderbilt. It launched a nine-year professional association that followed to UCLA in 1949 and lasted until Prothro was hired at Oregon State in January 1955.

Prothro learned to coach the game well under his mentor, Red Sanders.

As Prothro became more accomplished as a teacher, both in execution of the fundamentals and player development, Sander's teams prospered.

Tommy Prothro: "The Genius" brought winning football to Oregon State.

OREGON STATE COLLEGE

Spec Keene, Oregon State's athletic director, said upon Prothro's acceptance of the Oregon State appointment to replace **Kip Taylor**: " It is a great satisfaction to have a man who has such great qualities of leadership in charge of Oregon State's football program."

Prothro, having been turned down for other head coaching opportunities, was very focused when he was selected to lead the Beaver football fortunes.

In his deliberate Southern drawl, he informed his new team: "Gentlemen, this is going to be the toughest spring practice in the history of Oregon State football."

Of the more than 50 that turned out only 29 players survived and met the challenge for the opening game in 1955.

"We didn't kick anybody off the squad and we didn't mistreat anybody, Prothro recalled. "But boy, we worked hard, and they weren't used to working that hard."

In taking over at Oregon State, Prothro said, "The football situation at OSC was about as run down as it could have been...But due to the tremendous desire of our squad to come back, I believe we will be better than expected." He was right, but it wasn't easy.

OREGON STATE UNIVERSITY(63-37-2)

1955	6-3-0	PCC 2nd
1956	7-3-1	**PCC Champs Rose Bowl** Lost to Iowa 35-19
1957	8-2-0	**PCC Co Champs**
1958	6-4-0	
1959	3-7-0	
1960	6-3-1	
1961	5-5-0	
1962	9-2-0	**Liberty Bowl** Beat Villanova 6-0
1963	5-5-0	
1964	8-3-0	**AAWU Champs Rose Bowl** Lost to Michigan 34-7

In his first year, he used motivation, an emphasis on fundamentals and a single-wing offense to upright the program.

It was important that they won an early game, so the players could buy into his philosophy. That timely and strategic win was against a heavily favored Stanford team in a Portland evening game. The black-clad Beavers came away with a 10-0 upset. The victory unified the team and gave the young team the confidence it needed to compete.

Prothro recalled that very game when he assessed his career 33 years later, that **"the Stanford game was probably the most important game in my career at Oregon State.** We had worked the boys very hard, almost to a mutiny. I feel if we didn't win, my career at Oregon State might have lasted only a couple of years."

Prothro made the transition to head coach at Oregon State in 1955 and was an immediate success, coming in second to UCLA. He led them to the Rose Bowl the year afterward, and only the conference "no-repeat rule" kept their 1957 co-championship team from going to Pasadena again in 1958.

PROTHRO, THE MAN

The big genial coach with horned-rimmed glasses, a constant cigarette, and the ever-present briefcase, was tall and imposing. His deep resonant voice penetrated into his players demanding results. He appeared indifferent, yet he was confident, and consistent.

" Prothro was seen as aloof, and austere, but that was only on the surface," coach **Bob Zelinka** laughingly said. "It was because he had to look so close to recognize people because his glasses were so thick. To me, he was very warm, a wonderful friend, and as a coach he was a great competitor. He had the knack for exploiting the weakness of an opponent."

A former player once said Prothro used players like pawns. Prothro said in a 1972 interview: "That's right. Yet I don't think of players in that way- particularly off the field...I develop a real affection for football players that play for me. They put out a tremendous effort. But winning is the most important thing to most football players. To achieve that, a coach has to blot out any sentiment that would affect his judgment or his efforts toward helping the team win."

At a Seaside High School athletic banquet in 1957, Prothro in his slow Southern drawl, opened his talk by saying, "I am usually considered the oratorical equivalent of a blocked punt."

Prothro told of his college days under **Wallace Wade** at Duke. He said Wade never talked much to the freshmen players. He said Wade would come in and talking through his nose remarked, "You know there is not a man in this room whose friendship I want. I only want your respect." Prothro told that is what Wade got -- respect.

"My first year at Oregon State we didn't have an exceptionally strong team, but we tried our best not to beat ourselves. We were content to let our opponents beat themselves, and six out of nine found a way to do it," Prothro related.

"We won the championship in 1956 because we were willing to pay the price, in working harder and putting out a little more. Also, that year we had a goal, the Rose Bowl."

"This fall (1957) we became convinced that we're the best after the USC game. Then we got complacent, and got pretty beat up by UCLA. I am very proud of the team because of the way it came back, with personal pride being its only goal."

CHANGING TO THE T FORMATION

Prothro changed his offense from the single wing to the T formation when Oregon State, became an independent. There became major problems scheduling quality games. Most schools didn't want to play a single wing team.

To learn the T formation, Prothro spent two weeks with the Washington State coach, **Jim Sutherland**. He also hired former WSU QB **Bob Gambold** as a backfield coach.

Prothro took the best features from the single wing and blended them with the "T" to develop the **"Sprint-out-T,"** a winning system. It would be the offense that would produce two Heisman winners.

TERRY BAKER

Terry Baker, the most celebrated football player in Oregon State's history, came to Corvallis as an 18 year-old freshman in 1959 only to play basketball, until Prothro set the hook.

Always the psychologist, Prothro challenged Baker with the statement: "I don't know if you can be a very good football player." Baker gave it a try. The rest is Beaver lore.

By 1962, Baker became the first player west of the Rockies to win the Heisman Trophy. He won about every honor given his senior year.

> When Baker went on to play pro football, he recalled how well organized the program was during his three-year college career. "I saw first hand that we had been light years ahead in that way at Oregon State."

UCLA

Even though there was disappointment and resentment in Corvallis when Prothro departed for UCLA in 1966, assistant coach **Jerry Long** recalls Prothro debating that decision: "I think I've given OSU my best. I know I've given them 10 years of hard work and 10 years of good football." And that he had. He returned winning football to Oregon State

"I hated to do it, and Shirley really hated it, because those were some of the happiest times of our lives," Prothro recalled. "I think there are better places to coach, but it is a great place to live (Corvallis)."

Prothro had been offered the job at UCLA the previous year, turning it down because the school would have to fire the beleaguered **Billy**

PROTHRO PHILOSOPHY

On coaching from the press box –"When a play is successful, it is due to execution, not play calling."

On free substitution: "Leaving out the winning factor, I feel a boy should learn to play both sides of the ball. It's part of the game and part of paying the price."

On his winning methodology three parts: "One, mental and physical ability of the players. That is a result of recruiting. Two, the techniques taught. Not plays or formations but fundamentals of the hitting position. Three, morale. If you've got any two of those, you can win."

Barnes, his friend, to do it. In 1964, though, Barnes dismissal was inevitable.

UCLA (41-18-3) .686

1965	8-2-1	AAWU Champs Rose Bowl Beat Michigan State 14-12
1966	9-1-0	2nd
1967	7-2-1	2nd
1968	3-7-0	
1969	8-1-1	2nd
1970	6-5-0	2nd

In 1965 Prothro returned to UCLA, this time as its head coach. The team had a lot of talent, despite being picked for eighth by the "Skywriters." Prothro quickly restored the Bruins to football prominence. Not since 1961 had the Bruins had a winning team. But in Prothro's first year at the helm, UCLA went 8-2-1 and upset Michigan State, 14-12, in the Rose Bowl.

> "I anticipated a solid football program when I hired Tommy Prothro, but nothing like this," said UCLA athletic director **J.D.Morgan**. "He's three or four years ahead of schedule."

Prothro received the highest honor in his profession, the **National "Coach of the Year" Award** by the members of the **American Football Coaches Association.**

Prothro's career at UCLA was a memorable one. He returned UCLA football to the prominence once enjoyed in the fifties. He guided the varsity career of **Gary Beban**, earning him and the school its first Heisman Trophy.

His teams were predictably unpredictable. He would creatively punt on third down throughout this period, yet was just as capable of going for it on fourth down whether leading, tied or behind. His experiments were calculated. A failed play did not necessarily mean a mistake, as it might be just setting up the defense for a killer that looked just like its "failed" counterpart.

> " I had the unique fortune of playing for a coaching staff that got more talent out of the team than it really had. Tom Prothro got us thinking the same way. He treated young men as men. Football was important, but he made sure we exploited our college years to the fullest."
> **Gary Beban '66 UCLA Heisman winner**

COACHING HONORS

1965	**National Coach of the Year**
1989	**State of Oregon Sports Hall of Fame**
1991	**National Football Foundation College Hall of Fame**
1991	**Oregon State University Hall of Fame**
	Duke University Hall of Fame
	Tennessee Hall of Fame

> **John Ralston:** (on Tommy Prothro)
> " He might have been the most intelligent college coach of our time. By that I mean I.Q. I wouldn't be surprised if it was 160 or so. He puts a lot of us to shame.
> "He has always felt he teaches blocking techniques better than anyone. It's been his main forte. I'm not sure he isn't right."

PROTHRO'S LEGACY TO COACHING

Clay Stapleton	College coach
Bob Zelinka	College coach
Jerry Long	College coach
Bobb McKittrick	College and pro coach
Ernie Zwahlin	College and pro coach
John Cooper	College coach
Rich Brooks	College and pro coach
Earnel Durden	College and pro coach
Terry Donahue	College coach
Mike Dolby	College coach
Dick Vermeil	College and pro coach
Pepper Rodgers	College coach
Bill Walsh	College and pro coach

THE *CROWTHER* BLOCKING SLED

> Prothro, who was first exposed to the *Crowther* sled while playing for **Wallace Wade**, developed a progression and increased the use of the blocking sled. He believed there was no better drill on the football field to teach the fundamental uncoiling of the body that is desired in both blocking and tackling.
> The Prothro legacy is recounted by the many coaches and players that use the *Crowther* sled.
> **Bobb McKittrick, line coach, SF '49ers**

PROFESSIONAL FOOTBALL

In 1971, when Prothro left UCLA to accept the offer of **Dan Reeves** to step up to the pro ranks with the Los Angeles Rams, he violated three of his long standing rules about coaching.

- **College football is the ultimate in coaching.** Prothro credited "the media that convinced me pro football is bigger than college football."
- "I always felt that a coach, **if he's going to move, should do it where a team was losing, not winning.**" Former coach **George Allen** who had a winning, 49-17-4, record did not have his five-year contract extended. The Ram players resented the coaching change and always compared Prothro with Allen.
- **"Anyone who tries to be anyone but himself is going to get into trouble.** With the Rams I'm going to work my own way." Prothro's emphasis on fundamentals became a challenge. His college-experienced Ram staff met resistance from the seasoned pro players.

But be it, a bridge tournament, playing a touted team or whether a college coach can handle a pro job, Prothro enjoyed the challenges.

After the second season when **Carroll Rosenbloom** bought the team, he came out firing, and the first to go was Prothro despite the three years remaining on his five-year no-cut contract.

LOS ANGELES RAMS (14-12-2)

1971	8-5-1	
1972	6-7-1	

Prothro might have stayed out of football, except that **Gene Klein**, owner of the San Diego Chargers, saw the effects of Prothro's two seasons with the Rams manifest itself under the coaching of **Chuck Knox**.

While the former Ram coach was winning bridge tournaments around the world, his Ram draft selections were winning football games. The nucleus of the Ram defense, the front four, was a Prothro product. And what Klein needed more than anything else was a coach who knew how to pick players. Considering what was going on in San Diego, Klein not only needed a coach, he needed an entire new team.

From the outset, Prothro was the master of the draft process. Within three years, Klein was saying: "**Prothro is the best judge of talent I've ever seen.** There was nothing when he arrived in San Diego and now we have a team that's going to be strong for a good many years."

SAN DIEGO CHARGERS (21-39-0)

1974	5-9-0	
1975	2-12-0	
1976	6-8-0	
1977	7-7-0	
1978	1-3-0	* Resigned after 4 games

CLEVELAND BROWNS 1979-81

Rejecting Gene Klein's offer to work for the Chargers after his release as the head coach, Prothro chose to accept an offer from owner **Art Modell** to join the Cleveland Browns organization as their director of player personnel.

Modell said when Prothro was hired: "We wanted a little more stress in the personnel end, with a man to work closely with the coaching staff, and we found the one we wanted in Tommy."

"Oregon State gave me the opportunity to coach. I'll always be indebted to them."

To Oregon State, Prothro has given close to $2 million. The school has honored him by naming a practice field and locker room for him.

Tommy Prothro retired to Memphis, Tennessee in 1982. He died in May of 1995 from prostate cancer at the age of 74.

EULOGY

"True enough, he was a football coach. But he taught his boys enduring values as well as football fundamentals. His philosophy was just as sound for everything else as for football: Prepare, prepare, prepare. Be ready for good luck when it comes.

He was a 'gentleman for all seasons,' who could discuss plays of Broadway as well as plays on the goal line. He was a **teacher** who took **boys** and turned them into **men**. Prothro type men, of character and integrity."

Charlie Smith May 1995

Tommy Prothro's most satisfying victory, a bitterly contested 10-7 Civil War win over the 1957 Rose Bowl-bound Ducks, tieing for the PCC title. Bobb McKittrick, Ted Bates, Buzz Randall and Bob DeGrant carry their coach off the field.

George Harry Rallis

- Birth : April 23, 1940 in Ellensberg, Wash.
- Parents: Harry and Katina Rallis
- Father was a restaurant owner in Yakima
- Married Dana Vandeburg   April 11,1958
- Children: Ron Rallis 10/21/58, Ronda Rallis 1/24/60, Rena Gonzales 7/20/61
- High School: Lewiston, Idaho 1955-59
- Football coach: Bob Williams
- 6' 0" 205 pound tackle
- Honors: All-Conference and team co-captain
- College: Boise JC 1959-61
  Football coach: Lyle Smith
- College: Whitworth College 1961-63
  Football coach: Sam Adams
- Degrees: B.A. Whitworth 1963
  M.Ed. U.of Idaho 1966

FOOTBALL COACHING

George Rallis knew he wanted to be a football coach as early as the eighth grade. He had a special interest in boxing, but when he experienced tackle football, he said good bye to boxing. He liked football best and wanted to be a coach.

1963 1964	Sunnyside, Wash. H.S.	Line coach for **George Potter**
1965	U. of Idaho	Grad. Assistant

RICHLAND

Rallis' initial coaching choice Richland High School, but after three years, he moved to Portland. "I always wanted to coach in Portland, mainly because we didn't need to travel like we did in Eastern Washington."

RICHLAND HIGH SCHOOL (9-15-1)

1969	3-4-1	
1970	4-4-0	
1971	2-7-0	

GRANT

At Grant High School, George Rallis built one of the PIL's strongest football programs during his coaching era. He was directly responsible for the school's success. The Generals compiled a 53-23 record, complimented by many trips to the playoffs, in the eight years under his tutelage.

George Rallis: A dynamic coach who relished the challenge of rebuilding football programs.

GRANT HIGH SCHOOL (53-23-0)

1973	4-5-0	
1974	5-4-0	
1975	7-2-0	2nd PIL
1976	7-2-0	**1st tie**
1977	6-2-0	**1st tie**
1978	9-2-0	**1st**
1979	10-1-0	**1st**
1980	5-5-0	

Rallis relished the challenge of rebuilding programs by instilling a winning attitude and creating an enthusiasm for the game. He also believed in sound fundamentals.

He encouraged his players to participate in more than one sport. "Kids have to learn to compete, and the more they play, the more competitive they become."

Rallis' strong will to succeed was evident by his strong influence on the lives of the Grant athletes. He stressed strength and conditioning through a weight lifting program. His encouragement, always striving to compete at a higher level, was present the year round. "Get in better shape. Hit that weight room," was his message.

Once, the athletes tasted success, football became the vehicle to keep the kids on track at the urban Portland school. And it was Rallis' everyday presence that stabilized their lives.

Rallis enjoyed taking a group of players that hadn't experienced winning and molding them physically and mentally into winners. He installed the triple-option offense, and with the talent base at Grant he was successful.

His best players were **David Lewis, Kevin McMillin, Jay Kirschenman, Eric Bosworth, Pat Shaw and Darrell Motely.**

DAVID DOUGLAS

Although George Rallis was a finalist in 1972, his coaching success at Grant caught the Douglas administration's attention again when they sought a new coach in 1981. The Scots had just struggled through a 1-8 season and needed someone to upright their program and return it to the status it enjoyed in the 60s. This time, Rallis was hired.

When Rallis took the Douglas reins, he committed himself to rebuild the program within three years. It wasn't an easy task. It took three years.

DAVID DOUGLAS H.S. (42-48-0)

1981	0-9-0	
1982	1-8-0	
1983	7-3-0	**Mt. Hood Coach of Year**
1984	3-6-0	
1985	6-4-0	
1986	8-3-0	
1987	5-5-0	
1988	7-4-0	
1989	5-6-0	

But true to his word, after posting 0-9 and 1-8 records the first two seasons, the football fortunes of George Rallis and David Douglas prospered in the third year. They finished 7-3 in the 1983 season and became a playoff team for the first time since 1979. Rallis was selected the **Mt. Hood Conference Coach of the Year.**

"With Coach Rallis, even the practices were an adventure. He brought that level of energy and excitement every day. He's the most dynamic man I've ever been around."
Bill Volk, David Douglas, ' 88-89

Near his 50th birthday in 1989, Rallis felt that "it was time to do other things in life. Coaching football at the high school level today was all-consuming."

Donald "Don" Read

- Born: Dec.15, 1933 in Los Angeles, Calif.
- Parents: Charles and Emily Read
  Father was a pro baseball player in the PCL
- Married: Lois Tipton   August 21,1955
- Family: Beth 11/12/57, Bruce 1/21/62
- High School: Santa Rosa, Calif. 1953
  Coach: Jimmy Underhill
  Honors: Team captain, most inspirational
  player, North-South Shrine game, All-State-
  CIF as a 195-pound center
- College: Santa Rosa Junior College '53-54
  Coach: Bob Mastin
- University of Oregon 1955
  Coach: Len Casanova
- Sacramento State 1958
  Coach: Ray Schultz
- Degrees: Associate of Arts- Santa Rosa JC
  B. S. , M.S. Sacramento State 1961
- Service: Drafted into U.S.Army 1956-57;
  Ft. Lewis, Fort Ord, and Fort Irwin- Special
  Services – Football and baseball coach

DEVELOPMENT OF A COACH

Don Read remembers all of his playing experiences in high school, junior college, and at both Oregon and Sacramento State as learning experiences toward a career in coaching.

Jimmy Underhill, his Santa Rosa High School coach, influenced him in the area of discipline. "He was hard-nose and strong in preparation," recalled Read.

Although Read was undersized for major college football, he caught the attention of the University of Oregon when he was playing at Santa Rosa JC.

Read considered himself just an average player. "I recruited Don," needled Oregon assistant **Jack Roche**. "After we got him up here, I asked him for my dime back."

Following the two years in the army coaching football and baseball, Don entered Sacramento State as a non-scholarship player and as a student with the intention to get a teaching degree.

Don Read became a consummate teacher. He was highly organized and creative in his endeavor to coach the game of football.

Read saved some struggling and desperate situations at Portland State, Oregon Tech, and Montana. His record speaks volumes of his success, and the challenges he overcame in each program illustrate his coaching legacy.

Don Read was the consummate college football coach. He upgraded football programs at Portland State, Oregon, Oregon Tech and Montana.

In 1959, Don Read started a 37-year coaching career that culminated with the highest recognition given a coach, the **National Coach of the Year**. His team, the University of Montana Grizzlies, was the **1995 National Champion for Division I-AA** by defeating Marshall 22-20 in the finals.

COACHING START

1959	Placer High School	Assistant
1960	Petaluma H.S.	Assistant
1961	Petaluma H.S.	Assistant

PETALUMA HIGH SCHOOL (28-8-2)

1962	5-3-1	
1963	8-1-1	**League Champions**
1964	8-2-0	**League Champions**
1965	7-2-0	**League Champions**

Read took over a program at Petaluma High School that had never won a championship. In fact, the team did not win a single game the year before he became the head coach.

HUMBOLDT STATE

1966	Assistant to **Bud Van Duren**
1967	

Read worked as the offensive backfield and QB coach at Humboldt State. Within one year they were in the Camelia Bowl, and QB **Jim Costello** was selected to the All-American team.

PORTLAND STATE COLLEGE

Portland State Athletic Director **Skip Staley** was looking for a coach that could upgrade their football program. He chose Don Read.

Read looked at the move as an opportunity to be a head coach in a big city that had a good tradition for football.

Read recruited many junior college players to improve the talent and the team began playing their home games at Multnomah Stadium. He brought **George Dyer** a promising young assistant from Humboldt State with him, and with the arrival of quarterback **Tim Von Dolm**, the PSC grid fortunes improved. By 1969 they drew their largest turnout, 12,200, for a home game with Montana.

PORTLAND STATE COLLEGE (20-19-0)

1968	4-6-0	
1969	6-4-0	
1970	6-4-0	
1971	4-5-0	

UNIVERSITY OF OREGON

In 1972, Read moved to the University of Oregon to become the quarterback coach and offensive coordinator for **Dick Enright**. At the end of the 1973 season, Read was named the head coach after Enright was dismissed.

UNIVERSITY OF OREGON (9-24-0)

1974	2-9-0	
1975	3-8-0	
1976	4-7-0	

Although he inherited a losing program, Read's tenure at Oregon showed tremendous improvement with better play and recruiting. Six players went on to play in the NFL. But to his disappointment, Read wasn't retained long enough to get the Ducks turned around.

Read's initial charge "was to maintain a clean program." But despite satisfying that effort, he was released after three years.

OREGON TECH INSTITUTE (21-15-0)

1977	2-7-0	

1978	5-4-0	
1979	7-2-0	
1980	7-2-0	**Evergreen Conf Champs NAIA District III Coach of the Year**

Don Read opted immediately for another challenge, this time at Oregon Tech. When he took over their football program, the team was barely able to compete. Within two years, he had it turned around. The 1979 and 1980 teams established numerous team, conference, and national records. Oregon Tech became one of the small college powers in the United States.

PORTLAND STATE U. (19-33-1)

1981	2-9-0	
1982	2-9-0	
1983	3-7-0	
1984	8-3-0	**Western Conference Champs Division II Coach of the Year**
1985	4-5-1	

Read replaced **Mouse Davis** in 1981 when he returned to lead the PSU's football fortunes at another critical period in their history. With Portland State playing eight tough NCAA Division I teams, and operating with only 25 scholarships, Read was able to win the 1984 Western Conference Championship.

MONTANA

When Portland State went into Missoula, Montana in 1985 and walked away with a 21-13 victory over the Grizzlies, the Montana people took notice. They went after Don Read as their football coach.

Don Read took over a program that won only a total of five games in 1984 and 1985 under **Larry Donovan**. He immediately got the Grizzlies on the winning track with a 6-4 record. This made athletic director **Harley Lewis** happy because he strongly recommended Read's hiring to the selection committee. "He's got a great football mind, a great offensive philosophy and he's the kind of person Montana needs."

"AIR READ"

Don Read brought to Montana his knowledge of the passing attack.

Patterned after the successful program at BYU, **"Air Read"** is a controlled passing offense using multiple formations. It utilizes a single running back and four wide receivers.

Read prefers the passing offense for the same reason his practices are structured to insure his players' availability for games, the need to get an edge on the opponent.

"Today's rules encourage the passing game," Read said. "The blocking rules allow linemen to use their hands, the pass interference rules, and the playing surfaces are so fast now."

"I got to know him as a football coach at Portland State before he went to Oregon," said Lewis. "I had a chance to observe his coaching style and I always respected the way he handled young men. I liked his brand of football, it's always exciting, and also the way he dealt with people."

" He wasn't the type of coach to leave the hitting on the practice field, he didn't beat the kids up in practice, yet his teams always played hard and they played fair."

Montana A. D. , Harley Lewis

COLLEGE COACHING CAREER RECORD 26 YEARS (154-127-1)

At Montana, Read's teams won over 70 percent of their games, two Big Sky Conference Championships and a National Championship.

He retired from football in 1996 and resides in Castle Rock, Colorado.

Tribute to Don Read:
"One of the 'all-time nice people' that did well."

Anonymous

HALL OF FAMES

1998	University of Montana
1999	Portland State University

PUBLICATIONS

The Complete Passing Game
The Line of Scrimmage
The Making of a Quarterback

COACHED PROFESSIONAL PLAYERS

National Football League	39
Canadian Football League	19
United States Football League	9

UNIVERSITY OF MONTANA (85-36-0) .702

1986	6-4-0	
1987	6-5-0	
1988	8-4-0	Big Sky 2nd I-AA Playoffs
1989	11-3-0	Big Sky 2nd I-AA Playoffs **Big Sky Coach of the Year**
1990	7-4-0	
1991	7-4-0	Big Sky 2nd
1992	6-5-0	
1993	10-2-0	**Big Sky Champions** **Big Sky Coach of the Year** **Regional Coach of the Year**
1994	11-3-0	Big Sky 2nd
1995	13-2-0	**National I-AA Champions** **Big Sky Champions** **Big Sky Coach of the Year** **Nat Div I-AA Coach of Year**

DON READ'S COACHING LEGACY

John Becker	St. Louis Rams
George Dyer	Denver Broncos
John Marshall	SF 49ers
Bill Smith	Utah
Norv Turner	Washington Redskins
Dick Arbuckle	Arizona State
Vic Clark	Indiana State
Fred vonAppen	Hawaii
Tommy Lee	Utah
Joe Schaffeld	University of Oregon
Robin Pflugard	Arizona State
Jesse Branch	S.W. Missouri
Gene Dalquist	Texas
Jerome Souers	Northern Arizona
Brent Pease	Northern Arizona
Bruce Read	San Diego Chargers
Mick Dennehy	Montana

PLAYERS THAT READ HAS COACHED

Dan Fouts	San Diego Chargers-
Norv Turner	Washington Redskins
Fred Quillan	SF 49ers
Russ Francis	New England Pats
George Martin	NY Giants
Brent Pease	Houston Oilers
Mario Clark	Buffalo Bills
Tracey Eaton	Atlanta Falcons
Tim Hauck	Denver Broncos
Kirk Scrafford	SF 49ers
Larry Clarkson	BC Lions
Jay Fagan	Washington Redskins
Mike Trevathan	BC Lions
Matt Clark	BC Lions
Chuck Bradley	San Diego Chargers
Rick Olson	Detroit Lions
Hank Barton	New England Pats
June Jones	Atlanta Falcons
Scott Gragg	NY Giants
Tim Stokes	Washington Redskins
Shalon Baker	Hamilton
Dave Dickenson	Calgary
Mark Wilburn	Houston Oilers
Fred Osborn	NY Jets
Tim VonDulm	St. Louis Cards
Scott Camper	Philadelphia Eagles

Don Requa

- Birth: May 26, 1919 in Kimberley, Idaho
- Died: Aug. 14, 1987
- Parents: Elmer and Eva Requa
  Father was a farmer
- Married: Dorothy Finely , July 4, 1942
- Children: D. Scott Requa 9/45, David Requa 2/59
- High School: Wendell, Idaho '37
- College: Caldwell, Idaho –played football,
- College: Southern Idaho College of Education (Albion Normal) '46-'47-played football two years
- Degree: B. S. Education So Idaho '48, M.A from U. of Idaho '50.
- Service : WW II, Army Air Force Pilot Lt. Flew B-26s, A-20s and B-24s on New Guinea

Don Requa: "You wanted to play for him. He applied the lessons of football to the lessons of life."

BUHL, IDAHO H.S. (21-9-1)

1946	2-4-1	
1947	6-2-0	**League Champs**
1948	7-1-0	**League Co-Champs**
1949	6-2	**League Champs**

SOUTHERN IDAHO COLLEGE

1950	7-3-0	2nd place to Boise JC *College closed the next year

PENDLETON

Don Requa's success with generations of young people was remarkable. "You wanted to play for him," said **Dan Alderman** who played for Pendleton in the late 1970s. " A lot of people thought of Requa as a crusty old guy, but he wasn't. He was just very good with kids that age. He made you think you were more than you were."

"Requa was an educator and exactly what a high school coach should be. He was a winner, but more importantly, he applied the lessons of football to the lessons of life."
Don Peterson, OSAA Director

Requa continued coaching Pendleton football after he retired as a teacher and school administrator because he loved his lifetime's work. "That's why he stayed coaching those two extra years," said former Pendleton High School Principal **Joe Cole**.

Don Requa, the man who left a record that may never be matched in Oregon high school football, was a product of his time. There may be few people coming along with his self-discipline.

Gary Mires, former Baker player and coach, said this: "He was a great competitor. I think that's what made him. He was able to adjust to the times. He never got stuck with one thing like some coaches do. He always had a knack of staying ahead of you."

"I learned a lot from Requa, the value of being prepared…He out-coached most of us with his thoroughness. He appeared to have a simple approach to his offense, but it was more complicated than we realized because over the years it involved three or four options. His players were amazingly well drilled on how to run those options."
LaGrande coach, Doc Savage

"Requa believed in them as more than football players, but as people. It's quite evident that Requa made a huge impact on Pendleton as well as his players and not just because he won football games, but because he turned young teens into young man."
Asst. coach and AD Rollin Shimmel

PENDLETON HIGH SCHOOL (274-86-5)
36 years , 23 Intermountain Conference titles

1951	4-4-0	
1952	5-4-0	
1953	2-6-1	
1954	9-1-0	League Champs
1955	9-1-0	League Champs
1956	8-2-1	League Champs
1957	3-5-1	
1958	8-3-0	League Champs
1959	9-1-0	League Champs
1960	7-2-0	League Champs
1961	9-0-1	League Champs
1962	9-1-0	League Champs
1963	9-1-0	League Champs
1964	9-1-0	League Champs
1965	10-1-0	League Champs
1966	7-2-0	
1967	5-3-1	
1968	8-2-0	League Champs
1969	8-2-0	League Champs
1970	9-2-0	League Champ
1971	7-3-0	League Champ
1972	8-1-0	
1973	9-2-0	League Champ
1974	8-1-0	
1975	7-3-0	League Champ
1976	3-6-0	
1977	9-3-0	League Champ
1978	8-4-0	
1979	10-1-0	League Champ
1980	10-2-0	League Champ
1981	8-3-0	League Champ
1982	11-1-0	League Champ
1983	7-3-0	
1984	5-4-0	
1985	10-1-0	League Champ
1986	7-4-0	

BOB LILLEY

In the summer of 1956, a tall husky 17 year old kid from drought-suffering West Texas moved to Hermiston, Oregon to live with relatives. When his dad found a job in Pilot Rock, the family moved to Pendleton. Thus, Don Requa got his best and well-known football player in the person of **Bob Lilley.** Lilley became an All-American at TCU and an All-pro defensive tackle with the Dallas Cowboys. He has been inducted in the NFL Hall of Fame.

Since Bob Lilley wasn't recruited by either Oregon or Oregon State, Requa would always greet their recruiters with the same ridicule: "I don't know why you're interested in this boy, you weren't interested in Bob Lilley."

"Requa was a master of the game of football," said Pendleton graduate **Tim Temple**, who went on to a successful college career, then returned to Pendleton as an assistant.

"He was ahead of his time. He looked at his players and saw what was coming up, saw what the talent was, and changed the style to fit the material." Temple said.

Requa died the summer after he retired from coaching at age 68. He was eulogized by former Principal **Don Fossatti:** "Requa leaves behind a legacy many people believe will not be equaled. He truly was, and for all of us will remain, the winningest of them all."

HONORS

1992	State of Oregon Sports Hall of Fame
1997	National High School High School Coach's Hall of Fame (2nd class)

" Requa players often received applause that was misdirected. It should have been on Requa, the man who deserved it.

Req… the Buckeroo we will never forget!"
Former player, Don Whitney

Adolf "Ad" Rutschman

- Born: Oct. 11, 1931 in Hillsboro, Ore.
- Parents: Evelyn and Adolf Rutschman II
- Father's occupation: School maintenance
- Married: Joan Mason June 7, 1952
- Family: Donald 4/11/53, Cindy Bellville 7/16/55, Ross 12/23/56, Randall 5/12/59, Mary Jo Nichols 1/1/61.
- High School: Hillsboro
- Football coach: Jim Davis
- Honors: All-league, Shrine team
- College: Linfield '51-55
- Coach: Paul Durham
- Honors: Earned the nickname *"The Flying Dutchman"* Lettered four years in football, basketball and baseball. Three time All-NWC selection in football. **1st team All-American** selection his senior year. Set Linfield rushing record (3,761 yards) that still stands. Linfield retired his jersey, #32 NAIA Dist.2 Hall of Fame 1966.
- Degrees: B.A. in '54; Masters in PE and Math '58
- Full Professor in 1983

HILLSBORO HIGH SCHOOL

Despite being drafted by the Detroit Lions, Ad Rutschman took his first teaching and coaching job at Hillsboro High School in 1955. He started the first three years as their baseball coach before he was hired as the head football coach in 1958.

HILLSBORO H.S. (58-30-8) (64.6%)

1958	4-5-0	
1959	2-7-0	
1960	5-4-0	
1961	4-3-2	
1962	5-3-1	
1963	4-4-1	
1964	7-1-2	
1965	7-2-0	
1966	12-0-0	**AAA State Champions** Beat South Salem 17-2
1967	8-1-2	

Hillsboro H.S. Baseball Coaching Record

1955-1968	246-79-1 (75.6%)
1962,1966, 1968	**Oregon State baseball champions**
Five	Conference championships

Ad Rutschman: *"The Man,"* taught lessons about life in his laboratory, the football field.

LINFIELD COLLEGE

Ad Rutschman inherited a winning program when he succeeded his college coach **Paul Durham** in 1968. Not only did he continue the success, he made it even better.

> In 1998 when Ad Rutschman was inducted in the **College Hall of Fame** in South Bend, Indiana, he was honored for his coaching career at Linfield. It brought the highest honor of recognition to both him and the school.

THE RUTSCHMAN PHILOSOPHY

When Ad Rutschman retired from coaching at Linfield after 24 remarkable winning seasons of football, his legacy was huge and far-reaching.

He applied his philosophy, owned it, and lived it. He was respectively referred to as **"The Man."**

Rutschman believed football could be part of the college experience. That the gridiron was simply a big outdoor classroom on the Linfield campus. His former players are known to recall the countless *lessons about life* they learned as a student in "Rutschman's laboratory."

Rutschman would welcome the players each fall with everyone, sometimes 130 of them, down on one knee. "When I'm talking," he told them. "Look at me. I want you to pay attention, so keep your eyes on me. When you walk across the campus, look people straight in the eye.

When you are in the classroom, pay attention. Don't assume anything. Listen and learn."

> "He would tell a recruit: Don't ever forget that your number one priority is your schooling," **Ken Williams**, the school's registrar remembers. "And then he would say 'I hope your number two priority is football.' "
>
> "As a registrar, I saw him (Rutschman) as a teacher and a faculty member, and I saw his total dedication to the classroom, to his thoroughness, to how he ran his program and handled the responsibilities he believed were his."
>
> "He somehow managed to practice 130 kids, whether they had scholarship help or not, with no cuts. Rutschman felt that if a kid wanted to come to Linfield and be involved in athletics, then he should have that opportunity." Rutschman maintained such a large program because of the loyalty and respect of his paid assistants and the 15 or so volunteer assistant coaches.

• Teach values

"I've always felt the most important thing I could do as a coach was to have a player leave my program a better person than when he arrived," Rutschman said. "I had the best classroom going, which doesn't say athletics are more important than academics. But as coaches, we can teach integrity, trust, accountability, getting along with each other and living within a set of rules. Kids aren't being taught values anymore. They need to be."

• Teach preparation

"Tomorrow, you will face adversity on every single play," Rutschman would say during Friday night pep talks. "How you react to that adversity will determine who wins. It will be that way tomorrow, five years from now, every single day of your life."

"When you come back from being down, that's not just something that happens," Rutschman said. "You prepare for that situation the previous week in practice, and the previous month and the previous years so that when crisis hits, you're ready. You believe in yourself. It gets in your blood and stays there, even when your football days are over."

Linfield Baseball Coaching Record

1971-1983	244-198-2	**Nat. champs in 1971**
13 years	55.2 %	7 conference champs

*Only coach to win national championships in football and baseball.

With the unmistakable Linfield baseball hat on his head and a pencil protruding from the cap, he was always the teacher, the coach, the father figure and the motivator of the program.

LINFIELD COLLEGE 24 yrs (183-48-4) .780

Year	Record	Notes
1968	6-2-1	
1969	6-3-1	NWC Co-Champions
1970	8-1-0	NWC Co-Champions
1971	5-4-0	NWC Co-Champions
1972	6-3-0	NWC Co-Champions
1973	7-2-0	
1974	9-1-0	NWC Champs (9-0 reg. season)
1975	6-3-0	NWC Co-Champs
1976	7-3-0	NWC Champions
1977	8-1-0	NWC Champs (8-0 reg. season)
1978	9-1-0	NWC Champs (8-0 reg. season)
1979	6-3-1	
1980	9-1-0	NWC Champs (9-0 reg. season)
1981	8-2-0	
1982	12-0	NAIA Div II National Champs Beat William Jewell, Mo. 33-15
1983	6-2-1	
1984	12-0	NAIA Div II National Champs Beat Northwestern ,Iowa 33-22
1985	8-2-0	Columbia Southern Div champs
1986	12-0	NAIA Div II National Champs Beat Baker U. of Kansas 17-0
1987	5-4-0	
1988	7-2-0	
1989	6-3-0	
1990	7-2-0	
1991	8-3-0	Mt. Hood League Co-Champs

"I couldn't have had a better experience anywhere else. My experiences in football have mirrored my work experiences. We were taught values and how to be a team player. Like a lot of the corporate world, Levi-Strauss has decided to operate their company like a football team. They want diverse top management people to work together like a team to achieve a common goal. Because of my Linfield football experience, it was easy for me to make the adjustment."

Drake Conti '75

"He's the finest teacher of sports technique I've ever been around," said ex-**Oregon State** coach **Mike Riley** who coached for Rutschman for six years. "I can still see the veins popping out of his neck as he crouched to show the hitting position. He was intense."

In 1991, a car accident in Los Angeles left **Jim Winston**, a starting nose guard on Linfield's 1982 championship team, paralyzed from the waist down. Within days of the accident, Rutschman was on the phone, encouraging Winston not to give up.

"I've never forgotten how he would tell the team that self pity leads to self destruction," said Winston who owns a TV production company and recently got married. "Remembering his pep talks still gives me chills."

"Here I am paralyzed, and yet I feel like I did when I was strong and fast playing for Rutschman," Winston said. "I've been winning ever since that 12-0 season, all because of one man."

Damon Liles '86 remembers Rutschman as a dynamic motivator because of the manner in which he treated players. "He never did or said anything in a demeaning way. It was never personal. It always turned out to be positive for you," recalls Liles.

"He also has the utmost respect of anyone whoever played for him because of the values he taught. He just didn't teach us the game of football. Traits picked up from him will be used forever. They will help you work hard and be successful."

HAYWARD BANQUET OF CHAMPIONS

The Oregon Team of the Year
(George Pasero Award):
Linfield winner in 1982, 1984, and 1986

COACHING HONORS

- **National Football Foundation Hall of Fame (NAIA Coach) 1998**
- **Oregon's Coach of the Year, the "Slats Gill Man of the Year Award" in 1978, 1982, 1984, 1986, and 1991**
- **Northwest Football Coach of the Year, seven times**
- **Kodak District 8 Coach of the Year twice**
- **NAIA Baseball Hall of Fame**
- **State of Oregon Sports Hall of Fame 1993**
- **NAIA Div II Football Coach of the Year in 1982, 1984, and 1986**
- **Oregon High School Coach of the Year 1964**
- **Distinguished Service Award 1995 at the Banquet of Champions**
- **National Football Foundation's "Walk of Champions Award" (1966 Hillsboro H.S.)**

THE ATHLETIC DIRECTOR

When Rutschman arrived at Linfield as coach in 1968, he dreamed of the kind of facilities that would pull new students and coveted high school athletes to the school. At the same time, he didn't try to gloss over the poor playing areas.

Rather than being recognized as a convincing fund-raiser, Rutschman is acknowledged for the lessons about life and morals that he taught his players. Those former players are the ones who now financially support Linfield athletics.

BEHIND THE SCENES: Joan Rutschman

When her husband worked as head football coach, head baseball coach and athletic director, **Joan Rutschman** kept the athletic department organized in her job as secretary/receptionist. She gained the nick name **"Mama Cat."**

The $1.2 million field house on the Linfield campus was dedicated in the fall of 1995, and is unique among northwest small college facilities. It was built because of the respect and admiration for Ad and Joan Rutschman, and it bears their name.

COACHING LEGACY

"When you work with the kids for all those hours, every coach is going to have an impact," Rutschman said. "I hope that I've had a positive impact on people. In fact, the most satisfying thing is to see your kids have success after they graduate." Nothing illustrates this better than the way Rutschman's eyes light up when he talks about former players who have gone on to become coaches.

Head Coaches that have played or coached for Ad Rutschman at Hillsboro HS or Linfield

Shawn Aguano	Kapaa, Hawaii
Tim Arthur	Toledo
Jeff Basinski	Forest Grove
Larry Barnett	Yamhill-Carlton
Jay Beckman	Vale, Vancouver
Mark Bell	Oregon City
Larry Binkerd	Hillsboro
Jeff Bowman	Lake Oswego, Redmond
Tim Brown	Ashland
Mike Cahill	McMinnville
Larry Carlson	Yreka, CA
Scott Carnahan	Lower Col., Linfield
Rob Casteel	Aloha
Greg Cusick	Reynolds
Dennis Davidson	Perrydale
Pete Doumit	Moses Lake, WA
Jerry Dressel	Putnam, Tillamook
Sam Disch	Florida
Larry Doty	Linfield
Jon Eagle	Evergreen H.S., WA
Bob Edwards	Vale, Vancouver
Deno Edwards	Tigard, The Dalles
George Fairhart	Washington
Tim France	Powers
Leonard Gann	Carlsbad, CA
Wally Green	Reynolds
Jose Guevara	Monanalu, Hawaii
Bob Haack	Forest Grove
Steven Hall	Neah Kah Nie
Floyd Halvorsen	Sunset
Mark Hawley	Amity
Mark Henry	Canby
Randy Heath	Crater
Ted Henry	Linfield, Hillsboro
Terry Holmes	Toledo, WA
Craig Howard	Jesuit, OTI
John Howey	Maupin
Marty Hunter	Bend, Canby
Rod Ingram	St. Marys College. CA
Roger Ishizu	Maui, Hawaii
Steve Johnson	Tillamook Catholic

Dan Jones	Powers
John Knight	WOSC
Chris Knudsen	Centennial
Steve Kraus	LaSalle
Ed Langsdorf	Linfield
Rusty Law	Putnam
Jay Locey	Linfield
Tom Lopez	San Diego City Sch.
Greg Lord	Oregon City
Henry Mahi	Amity
Tony Mauze	Sprague
Byran Marmion	Texas Lutheran U.
Kelly Marval	Klamath Falls
Jim Massey	Yamhill-Carlton
Bob Mewhinney	Sunset, Stayton
Marco Min	Hawaii
Shawn Mosley	Dallas
Brian Mullan	McMinnville, Concordia
Norm Musser	Grants Pass, No. Medford
Tom Niebergall	St. Helens, Oregon City
Donald Ng	Hawaii
Rick Pass	Knappa
Kip Patterson	Lake Oswego
Dan Paulino	Amity
Bernie Peterson	Hawaii
Mike Procter	Page, AZ
Bill Parrish	Astoria, Hillsboro,
Mike Rex	Days Creek
Kent Rilatos	Toledo
Jim Reynold	Alaska
Mike Riley	OSU, SD Chargers
Dave Robertson	Taft J.C.
Brad Robins	Sheridan
John Rogers	Nestucca, Arlington
Rob Roesner	Centennial
Don Rutschman	McMinnville
John Sadowski	Leilehua, Hawaii
Doug Sawyer	Hood River
Wendell Say	Hawaii
Ralph Staley	Hillsboro
Todd Shirley	Riddle
Pat Silva	Hawaii
Mike Springer	Glencoe
Wes Suan	Linfield, Hawaii U.
Steve Sugg	The Dalles
Ed Trochim	Texas
John Voorhies	Newport
Ron Webb	Century , Glencoe
Bill Wallin	Hillsboro
Jeff Weins	Reynolds
Mark Whitehurst	Alaska
Bobby Williams	Alaska, California
John Woodward	Tillamook

Lorence "Doc" Savage

- Born: Feb. 8, 1933 in St. Francis, Kan.
- Parents: Robert Monroe and Blanche Savage
- Father was a farmer and a carpenter. The family moved to Fruitland, Idaho in 1937. "We were like the 'John Steinbeck's family' in the *Grapes of Wrath.* We crammed in a Model A and headed west."
- Married: Muriel Hilliker in 1989
- Sons: David 9/6/57, and Dan 12/10/59
- High School: Ontario H.S. 1951
- Coach: Jim Atterbury (Col. Of Idaho)
- Football: Tailback in a single wing
- College: Eastern Oregon College of Education 1955
- Coach: Roy Tatum (Missouri)
- Football: Running back in college
- 1965: NAIA Hall of Fame
- Degree: Masters in Education EOCE 1962

Doc Savage: An intelligent and dignified coach, who always got the optimum from his players.

> **"DOC SAVAGE"**
>
> Lorence Savage was tagged with the nickname, "Doc," at football practice by his college coach. It was a direct reference to the **"Doc Savage"** of *The Doc Savage Stories,* a pulp fiction character from the 40s who spoke many languages and was super human physically, "a man of bronze." The nickname stuck.

COACHING

Doc Savage always felt his career would lead to coaching when he matriculated to Eastern Oregon.

After a year as a graduate assistant, Savage was recommended for an opening at Elgin High School by EOCE president **Frank Bennett**. He became the head football and track coach for a school of 160 students.

ELGIN H.S.   Class B 11-man football

1956	2-6-0	

After one year of coaching, Savage realized he needed more coaching experience at a larger school when he took an assistant job at Redmond High School. His first tutor was **Joe Proulx**.

The next four years, Savage spent learning from **Gale Davis**, who became Redmond's coach in 1958. When Davis moved to OCE, Savage became Redmond's head football coach.

> **"Gale Davis** had the best football mind I've ever known," remembers Savage. "I spent many hours learning from him. What evolved for me was the importance of simplicity and thoroughness. My goal became not to run a play unless it was practiced 100 times."

REDMOND HIGH SCHOOL 16-20-0

1963	4-5-0	
1964	2-7-0	
1965	6-3-0	
1966	4-5-0	

Savage moved on to La Grande in 1967 feeling it was a greater opportunity, and he liked the idea of a college town.

THE STATE CHAMPIONSHIP 1974

1974 was a special year for Doc Savage and the La Grande Tigers football team. The only blemish on their record that season was an early loss to Burns.

Savage remembers the championship game against the **Chuck Solberg**-coached Corvallis team was a game when "everything went perfectly." Recovered fumbles and seized opportunities brought a 26-7 win. Quarterback **Loren Huntsman** and running back **Bob Kirk** were outstanding.

"Our offense featured a run oriented ball control attack with play action passes from the I-formation or split backs."

LA GRANDE HIGH SCHOOL (110-83-2)

1967	4-2-2	
1968	8-1-0	
1969	7-2-0	
1970	6-3-0	
1971	1-8-0	
1972	5-4-0	
1973	6-3-0	
1974	11-1-0	**AAA State Champions** Beat Corvallis 26-7
1975	7-2-0	
1976	7-4-0	**League Co-Champions**
1977	3-6-0	
1978	8-1-0	**League Champions**
1979	5-4-0	
1980	2-7-0	
1981	5-4-0	
1982	6-4-0	
1983	3-5-0	
1984	5-5-0	
1985	8-3-0	
1986	3-5-0	
1987	0-9-0	

COACHING HONORS

1974	*Oregon Journal's* **Coach of the year**
1975	**Oregon's Coach of the Year** **The Slats Gill Award**
1975	**Shrine Game head coach**

Doc Savage got involved in politics after he retired from coaching. He enjoyed two terms as a Union County Commissioner from 1989-1997. He resides in La Grande.

"Doc was a great man. He was quiet, not a showman. He very seldom got excited. He was to stay calm and maintained his dignity.

" He was very intelligent person in football. We practiced hard and always had a practice plan. His strength was getting the optimum out of the kids. He got his players to believe.

"He dealt with discipline in a gentleman way. He very seldom chewed a kid out.

"He was a great influence on me."
20 year defensive assistant, Roland Bevell

Tom Smythe

- Born: December 13, 1940 in Omaha, Neb.
- Parents: Dana and Hazel Smythe
  Father was a salesman
- Married : Nancy Sheperd May 1987
- High School: Lake Oswego H.S. 1959
- Coach: Cliff Giffen and Vince Dulich
  Football: 3 yr letterman as a quarterback
  Basketball 3yrs and Baseball 4 yrs
  Honors: All-League in three sports
- College: University of Oregon 1959
  Frosh football, basketball and baseball
  Coach: John Robinson
- College: College of San Mateo 1960
  Coach: Doug Skovil
- College: University of Oregon 1961
  Football manager
- College: Lewis and Clark
  Coach: Joe Huston
  Assistant coach in 1962
  QB and end in 1963-64

COACHING

"We moved to Oregon from Nebraska when I was two years old and lived in a house across from the Canby High School field,"recalls Tom Smythe. "My bother Jerry and I would spend hours watching football practice. I knew from that time on that I wanted to be a football coach."

COLLEGE

After Tom Smythe graduated from Lake Oswego High School, he went to the University of Oregon. He had what he called "an awful football experience." It bothered him. Although he admitted his own immaturity, "It was the football system that stripped me of my self confidence," he recalled. "I even questioned my value as a person."

The next fall, Smythe left for the College of San Mateo in California. There, former Lake Oswego Coach **Cliff Giffen** provided him with encouragement. Meanwhile, the junior college team also needed his playing services.

Smythe quarterbacked the College of San Mateo team to the league championship in 1960. He was chosen as his team's most valuable player.

The spring of 1961 found Smythe back on the University of Oregon campus. Assistant coach **Jerry Frei** wanted him as the football manager for spring practice, while **John Robinson** saw him as a backup quarterback. But the transfer credits didn't match up for Smythe to be eligible.

Tom Smythe: *"Good quarterbacks sort of follow me around,"* is a huge under-statement. He develops them.

Still feeling a desire to play football, Smythe transferred to Lewis and Clark where he credited coaches **Joe Huston** and **Fred Wilson** with getting his football act together. It would also start him on his life-long career.

Smythe gained his first coaching experience in 1962 helping Huston until he regained his eligibility. He played quarterback and end for the Pioneers in 1963 and 1964.

ASSISTANT COACHING

1965	Willamina H.S.	Asst football coach For **Gleason Eakin** and
1966		For **Chocktaw Smith**
1967	Tigard H.S.	Asst football coach
1968		For **Ron Parrish**
1969	Lake Oswego H.S.	Asst football coach For **Boyd Crawford**

LAKE OSWEGO H. S. (6-3-0)

| 1970 | 6-3-0 | |

In Smythe's many years of coaching high school football, he's never had a losing season.

"It's never been a goal to win a state championship, or 'X' number of them. Every time we get into the playoffs, then it becomes a goal, but that's not why I coach."

"What tells you if you're doing things right, is the consistency of a program. We've always been ranked high. But if you don't win the big one, does that mean you don't have a great program? No, you don't determine it on how many state championships you've won."

Smythe's life centers on football but doesn't end with it. He has authored two football textbooks and has completed a golf travel guide to Europe. He has taken golf vacations every summer since 1970 to Scotland, Great Britain and Ireland.

LAKERIDGE H. S. 16 yrs (151-30-1)

1971	7-2-0	
1972	6-3-0	
1973	9-1-0	**League Champs**
1974	6-3-0	
1975	6-3-0	
1976	7-2-0	
1977	8-1-1	**League Champs**
1979	10-2-0	**League Champs**
1980	12-2-0	**League Champs**
1981	9-2-0	**League Champs**
1982	11-1-0	**League Champs**
1983	13-1-0	**League Champs** **Finals lost to Corvallis 24-7**
1984	13-1-0	**League Champs** **Finals lost to Crook Co 28-6**
1985	9-4-0	
1986	11-2-0	
1987	14-0-0	**League Champs** **4A State Champions** **Beat Roseburg 24-7** **Oregon H.S. Coach of Year**

COACHING PHILOSOPHY

- " I have fun coaching and I want the kids to have fun playing,
- "I want my players to have a life outside of football. If they'll give me two hours a day of great concentration, I'll give them 22 hours to live their lives. Our players play football from September to December and we don't do anything in the off season to play football"

> "A business professor at Lewis and Clark taught me the best lesson of my life when he went over the law of diminishing returns," Smythe said. *There is a point in everything that you do, where if you spend too much time on it, it becomes counter productive.*

LEGACY

Smythe's legacy at Lakeridge won't focus so much on his ability to work the X's and O's as it will his remarkable gift for *communicating with young men.*

> "As far as being a tactician and knowing the game of football, there are very few people of Tom's caliber in the state," said Redmond coach **Jerry Hackenbruck**, who served nine years on Smythe's staff at Lakeridge. "As far as his ability to work with kids and being able to motivate, get the most out of them and provide a positive experience for them, he doesn't have an equal."

QUARTERBACKS

Quarterback development has been Smythe's strong suit. " Good quarterbacks sort of follow me around," he says. And he has coached many of the best that have played in Oregon. **Todd Beahm, John Pigott, Todd Anderson, Eric Wilhelm, Mike Miadich, Jason Palumbis, Doug Nussmeier,** and **Mike Fanger** at Lakeridge; while he has tutored **Luke Atwood, Shawn Kitner and Steve Copeland** at McNary.

COLLEGE

Tom Smythe has coached at all the levels of football. In 1978, he left Lakeridge to join **Craig Fertig's** staff at Oregon State in hopes of working with the quarterbacks and the offense. Instead he worked with the linebackers and strong safeties. That coupled with the problem of some staff disharmony led Smythe back to Lakeridge.

PORTLAND BREAKERS

In 1985, Smythe took a short sabbatical to coach with the Portland Breakers in the United States Football League. He enjoyed working with Coach **Dick Coury** while handling running backs, **Marques Dupree** and **Buford Jordan**. But the USFL folded at the end of the season, and Smythe returned to Lakeridge again.

LEWIS AND CLARK

After his Lakeridge team won the state championship in 1987, Smythe looked for the challenge of coaching at the small college level. Lewis and Clark appealed to him. "It would be the place that football could be kept in its proper perspective," he felt.

LEWIS AND CLARK COLLEGE (29-25-2)

1988	2-7-0	
1989	7-3-0	**CFA Champs** **Coach of the Year**
1990	5-3-1	
1991	7-2-1	**CFA tie 1st**
1992	4-5-0	
1993	4-5-0	

Even though Smythe had good teams in his six years at Lewis and Clark, his success on the football field did not translate into a professional respect with the college administration. He resigned at the start of the 1994 season.

VIENNA VIKING FOOTBALL CLUB

While coaching at Lewis and Clark, Smythe was hired by the Vienna Viking Football Club of Austria to coach football during the spring.

The Vienna Viking I team whose average age is 27-28 is part of an Austrian league that has three levels of play. Four Americans are allowed on each team. **Mike Fanger**, the former Lakeridge and L&C quarterback, led the 1994 team to the Austrian National Championship. The 1998 team also made the finals.

VIENNA (AUSTRIA) VIKING FOOTBALL CLUB

1994	10-1	**National Championship** **National Coach of the Year**
1995	11-2	Quarters finals of the European Championships
1998	9-4-0	Runner-up in Nationals
1999		
2000		
2001		

MCNARY HIGH SCHOOL

Smythe returned to high school football at McNary High School and continues to produce winning teams. "It's the level I enjoy the most," he reflected.

Smythe teaches half the year and returns to Austrian football in the spring. "To re-energize myself," he claims.

McNARY H.S., (42-7-0)

1995	8-3-0	
1996	11-2-0	
1997	14-0-0	**4A State Champions** **Beat Beaverton 51-48**
1998	9-2-0	
1999		
2000		
2001		
2002		
2003		

Prologue to a 1984 diary, Smythe chose to quote **Theodore Roosevelt** and **John Kennedy**, and by his selection, gave an insight into himself:

"The credit belongs to the man who is actually in the arena, who face is marred by dust and sweat and blood, who knows the great enthusiasms, the great devotions, and spends himself in a worthy cause: who at best, if he wins, knows the thrills of high achievement, and if he fails, at least daring greatly, so that his place shall never be with those cold and timid souls who know neither victory or defeat."

WHAT IS A COACH?

A COACH.....

Is a politician, a judge, a public speaker, a teacher, a trainer, financier, a laborer, a psychologist, a psychiatrist, and a chaplain. It also helps if he is an astrologer or at least understands numerology.

He must be an optimist and yet at times appear a pessimist, seem humble and yet be very proud, strong but at times weak, confident and yet not over confident, enthusiastic but not too enthusiastic.

He must have the hide of an elephant, the fierceness of a lion, the pep of a young pup, the guts of an ox, the stamina of an antelope, the wisdom of an owl, the cunning of a fox, and the heart of a kitten. It will also be to his benefit to develop the acting ability of a poker player with a pat hand.

He must be willing to give freely of his time, his money, his energy, his youth, his family life, his health and sometimes even life itself. In return he must expect little financial reward, little comfort on earth, little privacy, little praise but plenty of criticism.

However, a good coach is respected in his community, is a leader in his school, is loved by his team, and makes lasting friends wherever he goes.

He has the satisfaction of seeing boys develop and improve in ability. He learns the thrill of victory and how to accept defeat with grace. His association with athletes help keep him young in mind and spirit; and he, too, must grow and improve in ability with his team.

In his heart he knows that, in spite of the inconveniences, the criticisms, and the demands of his time, he loves his profession, for he is.....

A COACH!

by: Walter Gillett

Chuck Solberg

- Name: Charles Maynard Solberg
- Born: Dec. 27, 1935 in Hunter, N.D.
- Parents: Willard and Ruth Solberg
- Father's occupation: Father was a coach for 20 years and a school administrator for 28 years in North Dakota
- High School: Hettinger, H.S., N.D. 3 yrs
- Coach: Father Willard Solberg
- School's first four sport letterman
- High School: Bowman H.S., N.D. 1953
- Coach: Eric Strobel
- School's first four sport letterman
- College: Valley City State, 1953-54
- Coach: Bill Richter
- Service: US Army 1954-56 Fort Sill, OK as an artillery instructor during Korean conflict
- College: Valley City State, 1956-59
- Coach: Vern Gale
- Played TB and QB until an injury requiring lumbar disc surgery his sophomore year that ended playing career. Turned to track, setting conference 440 and 880 records.
- Degrees: B.S. in PE Valley City State and M.S. in P.E. Washington State 1966
- Family: Married Gloria Harrison 1958-84 Daughter Viki Stewart 5/16/59, son Jim Solberg 4/26/61

Chuck Solberg: A career football coach, whose legacy would be his Corvallis tenure; four state finals with two crowns in 10 winning years.

WILLARD SOLBERG

"My dad was my first coach and was definitely my inspiration. He coached me in all sports from grade 5 through 11. When he left coaching and went into school administration my senior year in high school, I played for my first coach other than Dad. He was both a supporter and critic until he passed away Oct. 13, 1998."

COACHING

"After deciding I wasn't going to be a fireman or a cowboy, I wanted to be a coach," recalled Solberg. "I was impacted throughout the years by the many former athletes that came by the house to see Dad. I realized how special it was to be a coach."

After college, Solberg's first coaching experience was a three year stint as an assistant football, wrestling and track coach at Moses Lake H.S., Washington from 1959-62.

TONASKET H.S.

1962	5-3-0	

After a year as head football coach at Tonasket High School, Solberg was encouraged by Moses Lake's **Roland "Red" Smith** to apply for an opening at Vancouver's Evergreen High School. In fact Smith drove him to the school after a football clinic in Portland. Athletic Director **Al Lemcke** called him a week later. "Are you going to apply for this job? You are my choice."

EVERGREEN HIGH SCHOOL (25-32-0)

1963	1-8-0	
1964	5-4-0	
1965	3-6-0	
1966	6-3-0	
1967	7-4-0	
1968	3-7-0	

The next coaching opportunity presented itself in a different way. Solberg a summer recreation director at Camp Colton, was looking forward to a first time golf outing with camp friend Corvallis pastor **Ivor Pihl**, **Jim Barrett** and **Dee Andros** to discuss a Beaver Club Boys Camp. At that time, he found out that Corvallis football coach **Paul Seal** had resigned.

Solberg applied for the job in which he called "The best place in all of football to coach."

CORVALLIS H.S. (83-21-1)

1969	8-4-0	**State Finals** Lost to Medford 27-0
1970	11-1-0	**Valley League Champs** **AAA State Champions** **Beat Medford 21-10**
1971	5-4-0	
1972	7-2-1	
1973	7-2-0	
1974	10-2-0	**Valley League Champs** **State Finals** Lost to LaGrande 26-7
1975	6-3-0	
1976	8-1-0	**Valley League Champs**
1977	8-2-0	
1978	13-0-0	**Valley League Champs** **AAA State Champions** **Beat Roseburg 21-14**

Chuck Solberg beams when he recalls the 1970 championship team. **"Gary Beck, Mike Riley, Jay Locey, Donny Reynolds and Jerry Hackenbruck** are all successful coaches. The 1977 champs were also special with **Dick Oldfield, Harold Reynolds, and** son **Jim Solberg."**

OREGON STATE ASSISTANT

After his second state championship, Solberg was hired by Oregon State's **Craig Fertig** to help his struggling team. After the 1979 season, Solberg was the only coach retained by **Joe Avezzano** when he took over the Beaver grid fortunes in 1980.

In 1982 Chuck Solberg went into a partnership with **Larry Hearing** when they took over The Gables Restaurant. It lasted a year before football coaching regained its appeal.

MARYSVILLE-PILCHUCK H.S., Wash.

Friend and Marysville Athletic Director **Ward Sayles** mentioned that he was looking for a football coach to upright his program. They had experienced seven losing seasons. It interested Solberg. He returned to high school coaching.

MARYSVILLE-PILCHUCK H.S., (24-21-0)

1983	5-4-0	
1984	5-4-0	
1985	5-4-0	
1986	5-4-0	
1987	4-5-0	

In 1988, Solberg got a call from **Tom Smythe.** The newly appointed Lewis and Clark football coach needed a defensive coordinator. "Chuck, here is a college coaching job where we could both enjoy coaching without the pressure of winning."

LEWIS AND CLARK COLLEGE

1988	Defensive Coordinator for Tom Symthe
1989	
1990	
1991	
1992	
1993	

When head coach Tom Smythe left the Lewis and Clark program abruptly before the season in 1994, Chuck Solberg became the interim coach. The next season he was named the head coach.

LEWIS AND CLARK COLLEGE (13-33-0)

1994	1-8-0	
1995	4-5-0	
1996	4-6-0	
1997	3-6-0	
1998	1-8-0	

Chuck Solberg, at age 63, retired after 39 years coaching football on January 27, 1999.

COACHING HONORS

1969	**Oregon AAA FB Coach of the Year**
1970	
1979	
1970	**Shrine Game Head Coach**
1986	**Washington East West Game Coach**

Fred Spiegelberg

- Born: Oct. 14, 1919 at Colville Indian Reservation near Okanogan, Wash.
- Died: March 22, 1996 in Medford, Ore.
- Parents: Ted and Katie Spiegelberg
- Married: Margaret "Mickey" Kelly 6/5/43
- Children: Mark 1/18/49 died at 6, Scott 7/1/53, Shawn Retzlaff 11/9/57, Barry 1/22/61
- High School: Omak, Wash., Played FB and basketball
- College: Washington State College '43 Football: End 1939-41
- Coach: Oren E. "Babe" Hollingbery
- Boxing: Pacific Coast Light Hwywt Champ in 1941-42; 2nd at '41 Nationals. Degree: B.S. in Ed in 1943
- Service: 1943-1946 U.S.Army WWII

Fred Spiegelberg: The Medford legend coached a high school football dynasty for 31 years.

THE SPIEGELBERG STORY

It was an amazing journey that Fred Spiegelberg took to coach football when his early interest was really boxing.

His father had immigrated to America on a tourist ship from Switzerland when he was 16. He met his wife-to-be in Seattle. They later homesteaded on a 160 acre ranch in the Okanogan in the state of Washington.

Fred was born in a log cabin on an Indian reservation. When he was school age, he rode on the back of his older sister's horse to a one-room school where he had many Indian friends.

As a youngster, young Fred was always busy working on the ranch, herding cattle and cutting wood (he cut off his right middle finger).

" I was a pretty tough kid when I was young," recalls Spiegelberg during a family video interview. "My aspirations were to be a cowboy or a boxer."

Although the first day at Omak High School was marred by a fight, he played other sports. Football and baseball were his best.

At age 14, Spiegelberg was fighting in "smokers" under the main tent when the carnivals would come to town. After a professional fighter from Seattle taught him to box, Spiegelberg began fighting the 19 and 20 year olds for $10 a bout.

Going off to college at Pullman was a big step for the shy country boy. He was the first family member who went to college.

At Washington State, Spiegelberg built a reputation as a boxer during an era that boxing was big. With aggressiveness as his strength, the redhead won the Pacific Coast Intercollegiate light heavyweight championship in both 1941 and 1942 with a national runner-up in 1941.

As a football player, Spiegelberg was a substitute end for Coach **Babe Hollingbery** playing behind two All-Coast ends. He remembers his coach as a "great motivator, who would raise the encouragement or pep-talks to a fighting pitch."

The advanced ROTC program at WSC allowed Spiegelberg to finish college in June of 1943 when he received his draft orders. Within a week, he married coed **Margaret Kelly** and reported to training.

His World War II tour took him to combat in France and Germany as a rifle company commander. He was awarded three medals (The Bronze Star, the Purple Heart, and the Oak Leaf Cluster).

At the war's end, Spiegelberg became the athletic director of the Berlin Command. He coached both the boxing and football teams. His Berlin Bears football team won the European Theatre Championship in 1946. It was an experience that propelled Spiegelberg into the coaching ranks.

After serving as a freshman coach at Washington State, Spiegelberg came to Medford in 1948 as an assistant to **Lee Ragsdale**. "No way," Spiegelberg once said. "I thought I would be in Medford for a few years and move on."

After four years as an assistant, he was promoted to head coach prior to the 1952 season when Ragsdale became the athletic director.

MEDFORD H.S. , 31 years (254-62-10) .780

Year	Record	Notes
1952	4-4-1	
1953	3-5-1	
1954	7-3-0	**SO Champs Quarters**
1955	6-2-2	**SO Champs Quarters**
1956	10-1-1	**SO Champs Finals** Lost to Marshfield 40-19
1957	5-3-1	**SO Champs Quarters**
1958	9-1-1	**SO Champs Finals** Lost to Jefferson 21-7
1959	12-0-0	**SO Champs State Champs** Beat Jefferson 7-6
1960	10-1-0	**SO Champs Semis**
1961	7-2-0	**SO Champs tie with KF,GP**
1962	11-0-0	**SO Champs State Champs** Beat North Salem 14-0
1963	7-2-0	**SO Champs Quarters**
1964	8-2-0	
1965	8-1-0	
1966	8-2-0	**SO Champs Semis**
1967	6-3-0	
1968	7-2-0	
1969	9-3-0	**SO Champs State Champs** Defeated Corvallis 27-0
1970	9-2-1	**SO Champs Finals** Lost to Corvallis 21-10
1971	8-0-1	
1972	7-2-0	**SO Champs GP forfeit**
1973	11-1-0	**SO Champs Finals** Lost to Hillsboro 35-21
1974	7-3-0	**SO Champs Quarters**
1975	5-4-0	
1976	6-3-0	
1977	11-1-1	**SO Champs State coChamps** Tied Churchill 7-7
1978	11-1-0	**SO Champs Semis**
1979	11-1-0	**SO Champs Semis**
1980	12-2-0	**SO Champs Finals** Lost to Beaverton 7-6
1981	7-4-0	
1982	12-1-0	**SO Champs Semis**

MEDFORD FOOTBALL

Friday night football was "king" at the Medford High School stadium where crowds were usually in the neighborhood of 8,000. Two radio stations would carry the play-by-play accounts of the games.

Medford drew from a large talent pool. It was normal to have up to 100 boys turn out for the team. Many times an underclassman not in the starting lineup in the opener would emerge as an all-conference or even an all-state player by the end of the season.

> "Spiegelberg produced the men of Medford," said former Black Tornado lineman **Fitz Brewer**. "He took a great tradition in football and made it better. He was a legend."

THE SPIEGELBERG LEGACY

During his 31 year coaching career at Medford, Spiegelberg left a legacy of winning football. With the reputation as an authoritarian mentor, he had strong organizational skills.

His program organization, which would extend into the grade and junior high schools, received national recognition.

Another mark of the Spiegelberg legacy was his wisdom to surround himself with good coaches. In his later years, the young coaches helped him stay relevant which extended his longevity.

"Fred had a presence, a way about him that made it easy to maintain discipline," former player **Dennis Hoffbuhr** remembers. "When he came around to where you were, you did your best to make a good impression."

Even though the man known as "Spieg" had great talent, and even though he wasn't known as an exceptional Xs and Os coach, he taught the players the fundamentals and motivated them to get the most out of their ability.

Opposing coaches often said they knew what was coming. But the Spiegelberg teams were so talented and well coached in fundamentals that they were difficult to stop.

Sizing up the rivals during his era, "The Grants Pass game was for the district championship," Spiegelberg remembered in a 1992 interview. "But it was Medford versus Marshfield and later Corvallis for the state championship. It was blood and thunder."

> " A lot of what I learned from him has shaped my life as a coach and a person. He touched so many people. He had a dedication and a love of the game," said **Bill Singler** a former star player and the present South Medford football coach. "But he also had plenty of time for those who weren't involved in football."

When **Fred Spiegelberg** retired as Medford's football coach in 1982, he had the most career wins of any coach in Oregon's football history. He had coached the Black Tornado for 31 seasons with a 254-62-10 winning record.

COACHING HONORS

1959	**Oregon's Coach of the Year** **Slats Gill Award**
1971	**National High School Coach of Year**
1980	**National High School Football** **Coach's Hall of Fame**
1983	**"Spiegelberg Stadium" named for him**
1983	**Washington State U. Hall of Fame**
1985	**Medford Hall of Fame**
1988	**State of Oregon Sports Hall of Fame**
	Head Shrine Coach 6 years

Fred Spiegelberg retired from coaching in 1982. He died at the age of 76, in Medford March 22, 1996.

Many top players for Spiegelberg were **Norm Chapman, Rocky Stone, Mike DeVore, Dick Copple, Dick McLaughlin, Neil Plumley, Jim Funston, Mike Murray, Gary Winetrout, John Frohnmayer, Al Funston, Skip Bennett, Phil Humphreys, Mike Hood, Dan Sieg, Ken Durkee, Jerry Anderson, Dick Ragsdale, Lowell Dean, Scott Eaton, Monte Jones, Lloyd Hammons, Gary Griffen, Danny Miles, Jeff Hadrath, Tim Murray, Brian Petersen, BobDames, George Dames, Dane Smith, Mike Cox, Bill Enyart, Doug Johannson, Mark Dippel, Larry Farris, Dan Pinkham, Lee Suksdorf, Charles Cobb, Scott Spiegelberg, Bill Singler, Jon Pappas, Ted Pappas, Mike Ritchie, Matt Reid, Eric Ronnander, Gary Orndoff, Matt Lawerence, Paul Chitwood, Lenny Griggs, Tom Critser, Don Casebier, Mark Mullaney, Steve Boyea,Mike Mangold, Eddie Singler, Eric Evensen, Mike Atwood, Andy Vobora, Rob Christian, Bobby Jones, Mike Barnes, Mike Chriss, Jeff Yarnell, and Tracey Eaton.**

Gary Lee Stautz

- Born: Jan. 1, 1953 in San Jose, Calif.
- Parents: Hazel and Oswald Stautz
- Father's occupation was a pipe fitter
- Married: Susan "Sunny" Hightower 6/7/75
- Family: Jeffery 7/28/81, Kristina 3/7/83
- High School: Grants Pass, 1971
- Coach: Gary Mires
- Offensive tackle for two co-champion teams
- College: Linfield 1975
- Coach: Ad Rutschman
- Did not letter in football at Linfield
- Degree: B.A. Linfield 1975; M.A. Lewis and Clark 1980
- Business teacher, PE/Health, and counselor

COACHING

Gary Stautz's preparation to be a football coach was unusual. A shoulder injury his sophomore year and a work related accident requiring 125 stitches to save a hand the following year ended his playing days.

An unexpected event before his senior year affected his career decision. Linfield football coach **Ad Rutschman** asked Stautz to consider coaching for him. He needed someone to handle the defensive ends.

Although, Gary Stautz didn't earn a football letter in college, his coaching opportunity with Rutschman propelled him into one of the state's finest high school football coaches.

1974-1975	Linfield	Graduate Assistant for **Ad Rutschman**
1976-1981	Gresham	Assistant Coach for **Dick Flood**

When Stautz arrived at Gresham High School in 1976, he found a strong cadre of coaches. Head coach **Dick Flood** already had **Larry Knudsen, Jack Flitcraft**, and **Sam Whitehead** on the staff. After two seasons as the freshman coach, Stautz became the line coach until Dick Flood resigned to become vice principal.

COACHING HIGHLIGHT

Gary Stautz said his best memory was a 10-7 state semifinal win over Medford in 1982 before his Gresham Gophers beat Lebanon 13-12 for the title.

"That was **Fred Spiegelberg's** final game as a coach, and they were rated No.1," Stautz said of the legendary Medford coach. "We held them to 6 yards in offense. That was a remarkable game by our players."

Gary Stautz had phenomenal coaching success in 11 seasons at Gresham.

GRESHAM H.S.,   11 yrs, (101-24-0)

1982	13-1-0	**Mt.Hood Conf. Champs** **Oregon 4A State Champs**
1983	10-2-0	MHC-2nd Quarterfinals
1984	8-2-0	**MHC- Co-Champs**
1985	11-1-0	**MHC Champs – Quarterfinals**
1986	7-3-0	MHC tie for 2nd
1987	5-5-0	
1988	12-1-0	**MHC Champs – Semifinals**
1989	11-2-0	**MHC Champs – Semifinals**
1990	10-1-0	**MHC Champs**
1991	8-2-0	**MHC Champs**
1992	6-4-0	

Gary Stautz's first season as head coach was magical. The Gresham Gophers won the **Mt. Hood League** and **Oregon State 4A Football Championships**. He was the **Coach of the Year.**

Stautz resigned after leading the Gophers for 11 years, winning seven championships while qualifying for the playoffs each year.

COACHING HONORS

1982	**Mt Hood Conf. Coach of the Year** **OHCSA Football Coach of the Year** **Shrine Game head coach**
1985	**MHC Coach of the Year**
1988	**MHC Coach of the Year**
1989	**MHC Coach of the Year** *Scholastic Coach Mag.* **Silver Award** **Shrine Game Head Coach**
1991	**MHC Coach of the Year**

Alonzo L. "Lon" Stiner

- Born: June 20, 1903
- Died: March 1985
- Parents: Alonzo Stiner
- Father's occupation: House mover
- High School: Hastings, Nebraska H.S.
- College: Lombard 1922-23
- Coach: Paul Schissler
- College: Nebraska 1925-26
- Coach: E. E. Bearg
- Honors: All-America tackle 1926
- Degrees: B.S. in Business
- Family: Married Caroline A. Parker 1/21/26
- Son: Alonzo Stiner 4/19/34 ;Daughters: Betty Jean Ingram 6/5/28 and Caroline Stiner 1930.

LOMBARD COLLEGE TO NEBRASKA

When Lombard College won their league championship in 1923, Oregon Agriculture College (OAC) hired their successful coach **Paul Schissler** to lead their football fortunes. The star young lineman on the Lombard team was Lon Stiner.

As a college player and student, Stiner transferred back to his home state and finished his career at the University of Nebraska. In 1925, the Nebraska team shocked **Knute Rockne's** Notre Dame team 17-0. Stiner's play in that game propelled him to All-America recognition his senior season when he captained the 1926 Cornhusker team.

COACHING

Lon Stiner's career interest was to be a football coach. His first job was at Colorado as a line coach. But it didn't take long before **Paul Schissler**, his former college coach at Lombard, invited him to join his staff at Oregon Agriculture College.

ASSISTANT COACHING

1927	Colorado	Line coach for **Myron Witham**
1928 1929 1930 1931 1932	Oregon State	Line coach for **Paul Schissler**

Stiner was an assistant for five years until Paul Schissler's resignation following the 1932 season.

Ln Stiner: His *"Iron Men"* and the 1942 Rose Bowl win put Oregon State on the football map.

While athletic director **Carl Lodell** went on a nation-wide search for a new coach, local support from the community and team members surfaced for the young assistant. "What about Lonnie as the coach?" they asked. Oregon State reconsidered and settled on Stiner for their choice.

The popular Lon Stiner would coach the Oregon State grid fortunes for 14 years with two years off for World War II.

OREGON STATE COLLEGE   (74-49-17)

1933	6-2-2	"The Iron Men"
1934	3-6-2	
1935	6-4-1	
1936	4-6-0	
1937	3-3-3	
1938	5-3-1	
1939	9-1-1	**Pineapple Bowl beat Hawaii 39-6**
1940	5-3-1	
1941	8-2-0	**Pacific Coast Conf. Champs Rose Bowl beat Duke 20-16**
1942	4-5-1	
1943 1944		**WWII No team**
1945	4-4-1	
1946	7-1-1	
1947	5-5-0	
1948	5-4-3	**Pineapple Bowl beat Hawaii 47-27**

"THE IRONMEN"

Stiners's first team, considered the weakest team in the conference at the outset of the season, grew into "the smartest, toughest and fightingest team seen on the coast for a long time." **Norm Franklin** and **Ade Schwammel** gained national recognition as All-Americans for their play.

Stiner spent a majority of his time that first season teaching the Oregon State football players his style of "the rock 'em and block 'em gridiron tactics."

The big impact on the college football scene in 1933 was a scoreless tie with **Howard Jones'** top-ranked Southern California team at Portland's Multnomah Field. It ended the Trojan's 25 game winning streak. Eleven OSC starters played the entire game without substitution, thus the nickname, *The Ironmen.* Today, it earmarks the 1933 team and is part of Beaver football lore.

> Christened the bunch **"The Iron Eleven"** and the name stuck. *"An astonishing feat of stamina, condition and courage, it was almost unprecedented in modern football."*
>
> *"Most vivid, unforgettable football dramas of Multnomah field's history."*
>
> **L.H. Gregory,** *The Oregonian*, **1933**

THE PYRAMID PLAY

The "pyramid play" was conceived when 6'6" **Clyde Devine**, Oregon State's tall center, was hoisted in the air to block field goals and extra points on the shoulders of **Harry Field** and **Ade Schwammell**. A rule was made the following year to rule out the step ladder-type play.

> "This team impacted the country, by holding the "Thundering Herd," beating Fordham and exploiting the 'pyramid play' during an era of time the northwest got very little recognition."
>
> **George Pasero,** *The Oregon Journal*

THE STINER SYSTEM

The Stiner system called for an unbalanced line with many of the plays starting from a short punt formation. The play developed depending on the situation. Variations from this conservative formation were gained through the uses of reverses, crossbucks, tricky laterals, and end arounds. To gain proper effectiveness in this system, the ball carrier had to be a triple-threat player with the ability to punt, pass and run the ball.

His Oregon State single wing teams used pass-run option plays with right-handed left halfbacks and left-handed right halfbacks.

"Every spring, I'd pick out a lad who could throw right-handed," remarked Stiner. "Then I'd scour the ranks for a boy who could throw left-handed. If he had any running ability, our offense jelled."

> Stiner's teams were noted for their exceptional spirit. He once pointed to a reason: "Our boys knew each other well," he said. "They went to classes together, turned out together and in general, shared the feeling of teamwork throughout the school year. The idea of team work and friendships, so necessary for success in football, cannot be obtained by a few workouts in the fall."

THE TRANSPLANTED ROSE BOWL

Stiner's most famous Beaver team, was the 1941 team that defeated Duke in the transplanted Rose Bowl game at Durham, North Carolina. It was moved to the East because of the WWII restriction of large crowds to assemble in West Coast cities.

. Oregon State Athletic Director **Percy Locey** coordinated and implemented a contingency plan. As host team, Oregon State had the choice of an opponent and desired to play the best team available. Although the top ranked team at the time was Minnesota, to play a game in Minneapolis was prohibitive due to the weather. Oregon State chose to play Duke.

The Duke players voted against playing the game because of the holidays. But **Wallace Wade** prevailed upon his players by allowing them to return home for Christmas, during which time the enthusiastic Beavers practiced hard.

It was the advantage that Stiner needed. They defeated Duke 20-16 on Jan 1, 1942. **Don Durdan**, the Oregon State halfback, was the MVP of that 1942 Rose Bowl. He was inducted into the Rose Bowl Hall of Fame in 1999.

Lon Stiner post-war teams were all strong and competitive. The 1946 OSC team was the best, losing only to the eventual conference champion UCLA in the season's opening game.

Following the Pineapple Bowl victory Jan.1, 1949, Stiner, at age 45, retired from football. He became the personnel director of the Hines Lumber Company in Westfir, Oregon.

He died in March 1985 at the age of 82.

Marion "Pete" Susick

- Born: June 27, 1920 in North Bend, Ore.
- Parents: Peter and Matilda Susick were Croation immigrants moving to North Bend in 1914 after a stop in Gallup, N.M.
- Father worked in the lumber mills
- High School: North Bend H.S. 1933-39
- Coach: Vic Adams
- Honors: All-league in football and basketball. All-state in basketball.
- College: University of Washington '43
- Coach: Ralph "Pest" Welch
- Degree: B.S. in Far Eastern History Education degree from U of Oregon
- Service: WWII U.S.M.C. (1st Lt.)
- Married: Marcella Nelson 12/29/41
- Sons: Kipp Susick 10/26/47, Rick Susick 10/17/49, Daughter: Nancy Girt 11/14/51

"PETE"

Marion Susick did not like his given name, so he adopted "Pete," a nickname that stuck. When he was young, he was called "Little Pete" after his dad.

FOOTBALL

At an early age, Susick was enamored with athletics, especially football. But it caused a bit of a rift between father and son. His father did not want him to play football in high school. He couldn't understand his son's competitive interest in sports. He felt it would interfere with his education.

Defiantly, young Pete told his father that he would not go on to high school unless he could play football. A compromise settled the issue. Susick went on to graduate from high school and had an outstanding athletic career in football, basketball and track. His parents only saw him play one football game, a college game.

Veteran sports writer, **Kenn Hess**, considers Susick one of the best athletes to come out of the Coos Bay area of Oregon. "Pete was a jack-of-all-trades player in football—a running back, blocking back, quarterback, passer, punter, receiver and defensive back in both high school and college. As captain of North Bend's undefeated team in 1938, he ran the ball for 1,880 yards in seven games, a per-game average of 270. The mark still stands as a school record.

As a basketball player, he led the only North Bend team to the state tournament finals.

Pete Susick: "It's a game of blocking and tackling." He never had a losing season in 33 years at Marshfield.

UNIVERSITY OF WASHINGTON

Art Derbyshire, a local booster from North Bend, wrote a letter to the University of Washington football coach, **James Phelan** extolling Susick's prowess as an athlete. It resulted in a scholarship.

Susick matriculated at Washington, where he played four seasons of varsity football in addition to his freshman season. Enlisting in the Marine Corps in 1942, he came under the Navy's V-12 program which made possible the fourth year of varsity football.

In 1942-43, Susick played for **Ralph "Pest" Welch**, the Purdue All-American halfback who followed Phelan to Washington as an assistant. Welch's six seasons were marked by the turmoil caused by World War II as the players came and left as their war duties allowed them to.

At 5' 9" and 179 pounds, Susick was named to the *Associated Press* All-Coast team in 1943 while leading the Huskies into the 1944 Rose Bowl game against Southern California. Susick scored eight touchdowns in winning four games against Whitman and three service teams. Due to the war, the Rose Bowl was to settle the winner of the conference.

But Pete Susick, the offensive leader of the team, did not play in the Rose Bowl game. He was ordered to active duty.

He received the **Guy Flaherty Medal** in 1943, symbolic of the Huskies' most inspirational player. It's considered even today the top award given annually to a football player.

THE MARINE CORPS

Instead of playing in the Rose Bowl of 1944, Susick was off to Quantico, Virginia where he was commissioned in the Marine Corps to serve with the 4th Marine Division.

Susick was severely wounded in his right arm on his 61st day on Okinawa. From the hospital ship, he was transported to the hospital in Guam, and ultimately to Oak Knoll for rehabilitation.

Susick was discharged due to his physical disability and returned to North Bend.

MARSHFIELD HIGH SCHOOL

Susick had not planned to teach, let alone coach. A history major at the University of Washington, he considered a career in foreign relations in the Far East.

But it was during the convalescent period with his wounded arm that his career took an unplanned direction. Susick was offered the football post at Marshfield High School.

But it required considerable persuasion by **Leonard Mayfield**, then Superintendent of the Coos Bay School District, to get Susick to enter the field of education. Another persuasive force was friend and former high school teammate, **Bill Borcher**. Borcher recently hired to coach Marshfield basketball.

There was nothing spectacular about Susick's first three seasons although the Marshfield Pirates earned a playoff berth for the first time in 1947.

> Marshfield football teams from 1954, through 1957 put together the longest string of consecutive games—40 without a defeat,   (37 wins and 3 ties), a state record.

As one of his coaching colleagues said emphatically: "Pete knew football. Sometimes I wondered if he needed any help (assistants) at all. He knew what he wanted from the players, the way he wanted it done, and he was determined to get it."

That was an overstatement because Susick readily gave his assistants credit. Often these men were a buffer between the head coach's demands and expectations of more sensitive players. At times in practice, the atmosphere had the air of a Marine Corps drill, which mellowed as the years rolled on. Few players ever dropped out after the first season or so.

However, a change in standards, lifestyles, values and attitude by teenagers in the late 1960s and the remainder of his coaching career resulted in an adjustment of Susick's techniques and psychology.

MARSHFIELD HIGH SCHOOL
33 years (231-65-17) .740, 13 District Titles

1946	4-4-1	
1947	5-3-1	
1948	5-4-1	
1949	8-1-2	
1950	11-2-0	**State Finals** Lost to Grant 12-7
1951	7-3-0	
1952	10-1-0	
1953	7-1-1	
1954	11-0-1	**State CoChamps** Tied South Salem 13-13
1955	11-0-0	**State Champs** **Beat Gresham 19-0**
1956	11-0-1	**State Champs** **Beat Medford 40-19**
1957	7-1-1	
1958	7-2-1	
1959	8-2-0	
1960	5-3-1	
1961	5-4-0	
1962	4-3-2	
1963	7-2-0	
1964	5-2-2	
1965	6-2-1	
1966	6-3-0	
1967	8-1-0	
1968	10-1-1	**State Finals** Lost to Jesuit 28-0
1969	8-1-0	
1970	8-2-0	
1971	6-3-0	
1972	6-3-0	
1974	7-2-0	
1975	7-2-0	
1976	6-3-0	
1977	7-2-0	
1978	8-2-0	

For the most part, Susick believed his teams could win every game. He was a motivator and the result was success three out of four times.

There was little doubt that his military experience forged strong leadership, discipline and values. He had respect for his players and they respected him.

Susick's philosophy for the game of football was simple: a game of blocking and tackling.

The team that blocked and tackled the best and effectively most often would win the game.

A meat and potato running attack, with, as the coach would say, "a few wrinkles here and there," was the Pirates' offensive forte during Susick's tenure. That, and stellar defense most years, proved to be a winning combination.

Susick in reviewing his coaching career believes he was in the right place at the right time during the first 15 years. "I had boys who wanted to play and I had great support from the parents and the community."

Susick never had a losing season as the Pirate coach. When he retired in 1978, the number of wins was a record for an Oregon high school coach.

1994	**State of Oregon Sports Hall of Fame**

The Marshfield stadium was named **Pete Susick Stadium** in 1980.

Susick resides in Coos Bay, Oregon.

Marshfield's Pete Susick carried off field after a state championship during the 50's

Kip Taylor

- **LeVerne HarrisonTaylor**
- Born: Nov. 25, 1907 in Jackson, Mich.
- Parents: William Arther Taylor and Mable Riemenschneider
- His father, at an early age, migrated to the United States from Canada. He was a linotype operator and a print mechanic
- High School: Ann Arbor , 1922-26
- Coach: Football Louis Hollway
- Honors: All-state in both football and basketball his senior year
- College: Michigan 1926-1931
- Coach: Ted Wieman
- Honors: Awarded the Michigan Alumni Trophy of Chicago (MVP in 1927 spring practice at Michigan)
- Degrees: B.S. Education Michigan 1931 Masters Columbia U. 1947
- Family: Married Josaphine Waidelich 1932-1962, and Amber Royce in 1965. Daughter: Sondra Lee Moore 8/8/37-1967

Kip Taylor's legacy at Oregon State will be the many players that became football coaches.

The Nickname "Kip"

Since Taylor grew up within a few blocks from the University of Michigan's Ferry Field, he and his buddies used to shag punts during the summers for **Harry Kipke**, a Michigan All-American football player.

"Harry Kipke was my idol during my high school years," shared Taylor. "I talked about him incessantly, much to the disgust of my friends. Eventually my friends started to call me Kipke to annoy me and as time went by, they shortened it to just 'Kip.' As a result, I have carried the nickname the rest of my life, and with pride I might add."

THE STADIUM'S FIRST TOUCHDOWN

Kip Taylor's claim to fame as a player, came in his sophomore season after he had gained the starting end position. He had made the switch from halfback to end while earning the MVP award during spring practice.

The first game in 1927 with Ohio Wesleyan was the opening of the new $1.2 million, 84,000-seat Michigan Stadium.

He remembered that day in detail. Beginning when teammate **Ray Baer**, an All-American tackle told him: "Taylor, when you pull that jersey on for today's game, always remember, you are Michigan and don't you forget it!"

Later teammate **Louis Gilbert** told him early in the game: "Listen sophomore, if I throw the damn ball to you, you better catch it!" Due to Michigan star end **Ben Oosterbaun** drawing most of the defensive coverage, Taylor found himself open and received a perfectly thrown pass from Gilbert. He stiffed-armed one defender and eluded another on the way to the end zone to score the *first touchdown in the new Michigan Stadium.*

But Taylor's playing days were numbered. Two weeks later, on October 15, 1927, while playing the University of Wisconsin, Taylor was injured. He broke his neck ending his playing career, calling the injury, "the biggest disappointment of my life." The resulting hospitalization and rehabilitation also delayed Taylor's education.

COACHING

In 1929, during the Great Depression, Taylor's high school coach, **Louis Hollway**, hired him to handle the grade school PE classes and to assist him coaching football, basketball and baseball at the high school. For his services, Taylor was paid $1,000, enabling him to complete his college education at Michigan.

Following graduation, the Ann Arbor School Board hired Taylor full time to teach and coach football and basketball at Ann Arbor High School with Hollway.

After five years as an assistant, Taylor moved on. He became the head football and basketball coach at Clark High School in Hammond, Indiana, an urban community near

Chicago. The school hadn't won a football game in four years.

CLARK H.S., Hammond, Indiana (29-20-0)

1934 -1939	Six years Head coach 29-20-0	*individual yr records unavailable

In 1939, **Louis Hollway** came up to Hammond to offer the Ann Arbor High School coaching job to Kip Taylor.

ANN ARBOR H.S., Michigan (37-4-5)

1940	7-0-1	**5A Champs**
1941	8-0-1	**5A Champs**
1942	5-1-2	
1943	8-0-0	**5A Champs** **Mythical State Champs**
1944	3-2-0	*Last 3 games canceled due to polio epidemic
1945	6-1-1	**5A Champs**

In 1943, Ann Arbor "Fighting Pioneers" claimed the Michigan mythical state championship. It was the first undefeated and untied Ann Arbor team since 1909.

It's become a tradition for the 1943 teammates to have a yearly reunion with their proud coach either in Ann Arbor or Lost Lake Woods in Northern Michigan. "This team is like a family," remarked Taylor. "To my knowledge, every member of the team turned out to be fine citizens." **Kip Taylor, 1998**

Taylor coached at Ann Arbor with a popular line coach, **Dobby Drake**, who was in the PE department.

"We worked good together," remembers Taylor. "If I would give a kid a chewing out, Dobby would give him a pat on the back. We were like the hatchet man and the healer."

COLLEGE COACHING

In 1946 Kip Taylor decided to try college coaching when **Clarence " Biggie" Munn** summoned him to his staff at Syracuse University as the end coach and in charge of scouting. He joined other assistants, future coaching legends **Forest Evashevski**, and **Duffy Daugherty**. The following two years they coached together at Michigan State.

1946	Syracuse University assistant coach to **Biggie Munn**
1947- 1948	Michigan State- assistant coach for **Biggie Munn**

"Munn was difficult to work with since he always used me as his whipping boy," remembers Taylor. Tiring of the abuse, Taylor jumped at the opportunity to coach the Oregon State grid fortunes when **Spec Keene** offered him the job in 1949. Keene had initially but unsuccessfully sought Forest Evashevski for that position.

Taylor also remembered, with some disappointment, a job offer he received a week later after accepting the Oregon State job. His former teammate, Michigan coach **Ben Oosterbaun**, had asked him to join his staff at the University of Michigan.

Kip Taylor's success at Oregon State didn't match his high school coaching successes, but he did leave his mark.

Beat the Ducks: "Upon my arrival in Corvallis in 1949, I asked Athletic Director **Spec Keene** what he would like to accomplish with the football program. His reply was most direct by stating that *they loved to beat Oregon,*" reflected Taylor. "During my six years at OSC, we defeated Oregon five straight years. However, the six and final year of my contract, we lost to Oregon and I resigned as the football coach."

OREGON STATE COLLEGE (20-36-0)

1949	7-3-0	
1950	3-6-0	
1951	4-6-0	
1952	2-7-0	
1953	3-6-0	
1954	1-8-0	

THE OREGON STATE LEGACY

- National recognition in 1949 with 25-20 upset of No.8-ranked Michigan State in Multnomah Stadium. The team finished with a 7-3 record.
- Taylor's dedication to fund raising for the new **Parker Stadium** which opened in 1953
- In 1994, Taylor returned to Corvallis when Oregon State University celebrated it's "*100 years of Football.*" He was warmly received by many of his former players. The testimonies of their own *career successes* enhanced his legacy:

COACHING LEGACY

Sam Baker	Pro football
Ken Carpenter	Coach and pro football
Herman Clark	Pro football
Jim Clark	Pro football
Tom DeSylvia	Coach
Wes Ediger	Coach
Bud Gibbs	Coach
Al Gray	Coach
Dick Gray	Coach
Jack Gotta	Coach and pro football
Wes Hogland	Coach
Doug Hogland	Coach and pro football

Andy Knudsen	Coach
Gene Morrow	Coach
Dave Mann	Pro football
"Duke" Moore	Coach
Arvid Niemi	Coach
Rudy Ruppe	Coach
Cliff Snider	Coach
John Thomas	Coach
Dick Twenge	Coach

1950 Oregon State Coaching Staff: Bump Elliott, Pete Elliott, Kip Taylor, Hal Moe, and Len Younce

After leaving coaching, Taylor ventured into the management field. From 1955-1963, he was the manager of the Columbia Edgewater Country Club in Portland. In 1964, Taylor returned to Ann Arbor to manage the University Golf Course and the Michigan Ice Rink.

Kip Taylor retired in 1972 and resides in Ann Arbor, Michigan.

Roy Malcom Thompson

- Nickname: "Bub" during his playing days
- Born: Jan. 22, 1927 Vancouver, Wash.
- Died: Feb. 20, 1993 Walla Walla, Wash.
- Parents: Basil and Bessie Thompson
- Dad worked for the Forest Service
- Family: Married Margaret Smith 6/12/48
- Son: Mark Thompson 3/1/52
- Daughter: Kristin Kirk 2/1/64
- High School: Vancouver , 1944
  Coach: Marshall "Dutch" Shields
  Captain and all-star center and linebacker
- College: U of Washington F'44
  Coach: Ralph "Pest" Welch
  Center and LB
- Service: Army Jan 1945
  FB in Tokyo, Pacific Champs '45 and '46
- College: Clark College F'47
  Junior College All American
- College: U. of Portland. F'48-'49
  Coach: Hal Moe '48, Harry Wright '49
- Degrees: BS History and PE Portland
  U.1951; MS Education U of O. 1966

COACHING LEGACY

At both Astoria and Roseburg high schools, Roy Thompson was credited with turning losing football programs into winning ones. "It would not be easy," said Thompson. "Because it takes hard work on both the part of the coaches and the others who believed in what we were trying to accomplish."

ASTORIA HIGH SCHOOL (25-27-0)

1952	2-6-0	
1953	2-7-0	
1954	2-6-0	
1955	6-3-0	
1956	8-1-0	**Metro League Champs**
1957	5-4-0	

THE LOCKER ROOM

During Thompson's first year, Astoria won two games and had but 19 kids turn out. The town's people, it seemed, were ready to ride the young coach out of town.

Thompson in the meantime had made friends with **Phil Weinstein**, a local clothing merchant. He had shared his dilemma with his new confidant who wasn't even a sports fan.

"Quit your whining and get something done," Weinstein said.

Thompson wanted a team locker room. "We need a fort that we can count our own."

Roy Thompson resurrected football programs at Astoria, Roseburg, Whitman and Sprague.

What transpired became a foundation of the turnaround effort that would earmark the Thompson legacy. Friend Weinstein had a load of lumber delivered to the football field. Thompson, with the help of two assistant coaches, built a new Astoria football locker room.

The kids turned out, and within two years, Astoria was beating perennial league favorites, Central Catholic and Gresham. **Larry Hill** and **Dave Urell** were his star players.

Thompson's creativity at building locker rooms to jump-start football programs followed him at both Roseburg and Whitman College.

LEADERSHIP

"One of the best lessons I learned in life, I learned while I was in the army," remembered Thompson. " It was based on leadership. *The only way I know that you can get people to follow you is to get out in front and lead them.* As an example, a platoon sergeant who grabbed a mop and showed the others what work was."

AN OFFENSE

In 1954, Thompson called University of Oklahoma coach **Bud Wilkinson** by telephone with a plea: " I need some help. I need an offense."

Wilkinson graciously responded by inviting the young coach to his summer football clinic in Wisconsin that featured his split-T offense. It helped him develop a winning offensive philosophy.

Later at Roseburg, Thompson spent countless hours with athletic director **Jim Aiken**, the ex-University of Oregon coach, adding a passing game.

At Roseburg, Thompson developed two good quarterbacks. They were both starters in the 1966 Civil War game; **Paul Brothers** for the Beavers and **Mike Brundage** for the Ducks.

> "Coach was a father, a friend, a counselor, a teacher, a psychologist, and a drill sergeant. When he came to Roseburg, he told us we had talent and potential, but no direction. He set goals and asked nothing less than our full potential—that was a state championship.
>
> "We got a chewing out, a hug or a pat on the back and learned that it took hard work with no short cuts."
>
> **Ray Palm, Roseburg '61**

ROSEBURG HIGH SCHOOL (44-15-1)

1958	6-2-1	
1959	2-7-0	
1960	7-2-0	
1961	12-0-0	**State Champions**
1962	8-2-0	
1963	9-2-0	

> "I played for the greatest high school coach there is, Roy Thompson. I just loved him to death. He took this country boy and showed him which way to go and taught him what to do." **Paul Brothers, Roseburg '62**
> **H.S. All-American QB**

The 1961 state championship season at Roseburg was one of those "magical years" that coaches dream about. After winning the Southern Oregon Conference, they blanked all the playoff opponents including Beaverton 25-0 in the finals.

> "Coach Thompson told me when I went to college at Willamette that I would have to really work hard, and maybe, by the time I was a junior I would be playing," recalls **Don Green**. " He set me up. I really worked hard and was playing my freshman year."

WHITMAN COLLEGE

Thompson earned his Masters in Education from the University of Oregon during the three years he spent as principal of Roseburg High School.

He also acknowledged to himself, he missed football. He would like to coach again, and would enjoy the challenge of a small college. When the Whitman College coaching job became available in 1967, Thompson applied for it.

Whitman College had decided to upgrade their football program in order to become competitive with other Northwest Conference schools. Wisely, they hired Roy Thompson to instill a new discipline and install a new style of football.

Taking a cut in salary, Thompson moved to the college town of Walla Walla, Washington. He taught PE classes, and coached football for eight seasons from 1967 to 1974.

When Thompson arrived, he was viewed as "a likeable person with an easy smile and a sharp sense of humor." He also left no doubt about his attitude toward football. " We're here to win football games," he said. "And that means we hit harder, execute better and want to win more than our opponent."

Thompson's tough conditioning program resulted in fewer injuries in early season games than in the past, and the Whitman team was in as good condition as anyone they met.

The offense with gold helmets, the defense with black helmets, and the "raiders" with red helmets, each had a role in the winning plan. Roy Thompson, the man with a goal, was behind that plan.

WHITMAN COLLEGE (26-42-2)

1967	2-6-0	
1968	4-4-1	
1969	6-3-0	**1st NWC** (4-way tie)
1970	4-5-0	
1971	4-5-0	
1972	0-8-0	
1973	3-5-1	
1974	3-6-0	

Within three years, he led Whitman to its first football title in 38 years. Thompson was named **District I NAIA Coach of the Year.**.

> After getting drubbed 60-7 by Whitman, Willamette coach **Ted Ogdahl** commented that, "Whitman not only has talent but they are well organized, well drilled and experienced."

> Coach Thompson taught us the principles of football and the lessons of life. "No one owes us anything," he would say. "Success is a product of hard work."
> **Eric Johnson, Whitman 1972**

"Basically, the reason for Roy Thompson leaving Whitman is his honesty and belief in perfectionism," wrote **Red Hurd** of the *Capitol Statesman Journal* following an interview in 1976.

Whitman held a high standard for its students staying at a 3.6 GPA level. For this Thompson answered: "The emphasis on grades is understandable, but there has to be more. There needs to be some encouragement from the faculty and there needs to be some fun too for a well-rounded program. There was neither. When it came to the point when I didn't want to sell Whitman (to prospective student-athletes on recruiting trips), it was a moment of truth for me."

He responded as everyone close to him knew he would. He resigned and accepted the Sprague job and returned to high school coaching.

SPRAGUE HIGH SCHOOL   (20-17-0)

1975	4-5-0
1976	9-1-0 **Valley Champs**
1977	3-6-0
1978	4-5-0

McKAY HIGH SCHOOL   (13-23-0)

1982	4-5-0
1983	4-5-0
1984	1-8-0
1985	4-5-0

Joe Schaffeld, the University of Oregon defensive coach for 20 years, remembered advice given to him by Roy Thompson when he first coached with him in 1959: *"If you think it can be done, and you can teach it, the kids can learn it."*

"I've used that philosophy for 37 years."

Roy Thompson retired from coaching at McKay High School in 1985. A few years later, he returned to Walla Walla to live.

Although he was suffering from prostate cancer, he managed to coach one more season to cap his career. In 1992 he coached with his son **Mark**, the Walla Walla High School freshman team to an undefeated season. Grandson, **Matt Thompson,** was the star running back. Roy Thompson called it, "the most enjoyable year of coaching I've ever had."

"Working with kids and trying to do the right thing is the most important thing, no matter what the level," remarked Roy Thompson.

> "What my dad was all about, was through the vehicle of football, he was about helping kids. He was the champion of the underdog.
>
> It was his philosophy as a coach that he treated every player on the team as if he were his own son."
> **Mark Thompson, Whitman '62**

Sizing up his coaching record (128-123-4) after 28 years, Thompson reflected: "Football is a lot like life, it's about 50-50. You win a few, and you lose a few."

Roy Thompson died February 22, 1993 at the age of 66.

Dallas Ward

- Born: Aug. 11, 1906 in Lexington,Oreg.
- Died: Feb. 14, 1983
- He was raised on one of the largest wheat ranches in the area
- Married: Jane
- Children: 3 girls, 2 boys
- College: Oregon Agriculture College (OAC)
- Coach: Football Paul Schissler '24-26 Played basketball and baseball also.
- Honors: Though one of the smallest football ends on the Coast, he started all 25 games as a receiver. 2nd team All-Coast as a senior. Team captain on all three sport's teams. Named to five honorary organizations for his academic achievements.
- Service: WWII- US Navy in 1944-45, Lt. Cmdr. Ward served as officer- in- charge of physical and military training at the U.S. Naval Air Station in Dallas, Texas.

Dallas Ward: The Oregon Stater who took Colorado football from relative obscurity into national prominence.

STUDENT ATHLETE AT OREGON STATE

In Oregon State University history, Dallas Ward holds a special distinction. He ranks as *one of the top scholar athletes of his time.*

As an OAC (Oregon Agriculture College) athlete, Ward is remembered as one of the senior stars of Coach **Paul Schissler's** 1926 football team, one of the best in Beaver history. The team posted a 7-1 record, losing only to Southern California, 17-7. The season closed with a 29-0 Thanksgiving Day victory over favored Marquette at Milwaukee, Wisconsin. Reports of the game praised Ward for sensational runs after receptions. Ward's teammates included the great tackle **Jim Dixon**, and backs, **Webly Edwards**, **Howard Maple** and **Wes Schulmerich**.

COACHING

Ward's first coaching job was a major high school in Minneapolis, Marshall High School, thanks in part to a recommendation letter from **Knute Rockne** (Rockne had annual summer coaching clinics at Oregon State 1924-28.)

MARSHALL H.S. Minneapolis,MN

1928-35	Won four City Championships

1936-1942	University of Minnesota freshmen coach under **Bernie Bierman**

1946 1947	University of Minnesota backfield coach for **Bernie Bierman**

> **Bernie Bierman** was cold, cryptic, confident—and very, very successful. It was he who brought Tulane's Green Wave into national prominence, leading them to the Rose Bowl, where the Greenies were defeated by one of the greatest Southern California teams. And it was he who made the Golden Gophers of Minnesota national champions for three straight years— 1934, 1935, 1936. All-American **Bud Wilkinson** played guard and quarterback.
>
> *The Story of Football by Robert Leckie*

On February 3, 1948, Dallas Ward accepted the job to become the 14th head coach at the University of Colorado succeeding **Jim Yeager**.

UNIVERSITY OF COLORADO (68-46-6)

1948	3-6-0	
1949	3-7-0	
1950	5-4-1	
1951	7-3-0	
1952	6-2-2	
1953	6-4-0	
1954	7-2-1	
1955	6-4-0	
1956	8-2-1	**Beat Clemson in Orange Bowl 27-21**
1957	6-3-1	
1958	6-4-0	
1959	5-5-0	

> "In Ward's first two years, which were also the University's first football seasons in the Big Seven, his teams finished 3-6 and 3-7. These were the only losing seasons in his tenure of 11 years at Colorado.
>
> "Beginning with the 1950 season, the Buffs were on their way. In 1951, they posted a 7-3 record, losing only to Oklahoma, the national champion, in conference play. In 1952, he was named **'Coach of the Week'** by UPI after Colorado played Oklahoma to a 21-21 tie, the only blemish on the Oklahoma record by any school in the league when Dal Ward was coach.
>
> " Dal Ward, more than any one man, took the Buffs from relative obscurity into national prominence with a bone-crunching brand of single-wing football that earned him as one of the top football coaches in the nation."
>
> **Bud Davis CU Alumni Director**

Steeped in the great single-wing tradition of **Bernie Bierman** , his Colorado teams used that offense until 1956 when he mixed in a T and Winged-T series for a devastating multiple offense. In 1957 his team led the nation in rushing offense and was second in total offense.

> "Dal Ward was an outstanding leader in Colorado athletics, " athletic director **Eddie Crowder** said. "He was one of the outstanding coaches of modern times, and also a great friend to all of us that worked with him."

Ward stepped down from coaching in the spring of 1959, but remained active in the athletic department as an assistant director.

Ward retired as Professor of Physical Education in 1975.

HONORS

1975	**State of Colorado Sports Hall of Fame**
1997	**Oregon State University Sports Hall of Fame**

Ward died of cancer in Boulder in February of 1983 at age 76.

Eric Leo Waldorf

- Born: Oct. 20, 1901 in Tyringe, Sweden and taken to the Yakima Valley when he was two. Grew up on a ranch seven miles from Kennewick, Wash.
- Died: Oct. 4, 1977
- Parents: Sven Peter Gudmundson Waldorf and Lilly Fredrika Svensson
- Father was a dairyman; mother was a beekeeper
- Marriages: Erma Schumacher 1926, Gladys Conner 1948
- Children: Jon 1930, Phyllis Kindt 1928
- High School: Kennewick, 1922
- Coach: George Kralowek
- Played football and basketball
- College: Washington State 1922-26
- Coach: A.A. Exendine (Carlisle)
  Played fullback in 1923,-24,-25
  Wrestling
- Degree: BA in Education WSC '26; Masters in Science Pacific U. 1963
- First job teaching and coaching at Dayton, Wash. in 1926-27
- WWII: Served with the Red Cross in Calcutta, India in 1945

THE SILVER FOX

Because his hair turned gray in his 30s Eric Waldorf was tagged by the media as "The "Silver Fox." But the students and his players called him "Mr. Waldorf," a type of respect that goes with a stern disciplinarian.

Waldorf: The Dean of the Democrats

"The maker of Jefferson champions has a tremendous desire to win, and has repeatedly transferred this desire to his players. Waldorf works his teams harder than most coaches and drills them hour upon end on fundamentals."

Pat Frizzell, *The Oregonian*

When Eric Waldorf was inducted into the **State of Oregon Sports Hall of Fame** in 1992 as a prep coach, he was honored for his coaching record at Portland's Jefferson High School. In 23 seasons, he won or shared 10 city championships.

Eric Waldorf was widely considered one of Oregon's best football coaches in the 30s and 40s.

JEFFFERSON HIGH (144-51-15) 23 years

1928	1-5-1	
1929	4-3-0	
1930	5-2-0	
1931	10-0-0	PIL 1st *unscored upon
1932	10-0-1	PIL 1st
1933	7-1-1	
1934	4-3-2	* forfeiture of three games
1935	6-2-0	
1936	9-0-2	PIL 1st
1937	9-2-0	PIL 1st
1938	9-1-0	PIL 1st
1940	6-2-0	PIL tie 1st
1941	8-0-2	PIL 1st
1942	5-1-2	
1943	5-3-1	
1944	4-4-0	
1946	7-2-0	
1947	7-2-1	PIL tie for 1st
1948	10-1-1	PIL 1st State finals Lost to Grants Pass 6-0
1949	3-6-0	
1950	3-6-0	
1951	4-4-0	
1952	8-1-1	PIL 1st Semis

JEFFERSON HIGH SCHOOL

Jefferson High School Principal **Hopkin Jenkins** went searching for a football coach in 1928. He finished an interview with Eric Waldorf at Dayton, Wash. by letting him know that he might not be capable to fill his coaching need.

Waldorf beat Hopkin Jenkins back to Portland and convinced him that he certainly was up to the task of leading the Jefferson gridiron fortunes.

Despite not being a first-year success with a 1-5-1 record, the young coach was called into Jenkin's office. "I didn't expect you to do much with those prima donnas," said Jenkins. "We will have new uniforms next year and I want you to have a championship within three years. Is that fair?"

The Kenton Bank went broke that year with all the school's funds, so Jenkins paid for the uniforms out of his own pocket. The 1929 team dominated with sophomores and juniors was 4-3. The 1930 season they were 5-2, and the 1931 team was *undefeated, untied, and unscored upon.*

In 1931, Waldorf's finest team was led by the incomparable **Bobby Grayson**. The team was awesome with Grayson scoring a league record of 117 points which stood until 1958.

> "**Bobby Grayson** brought 'em to their feet in 1931, when the curly-haired Jefferson lad was so brilliant that 26,000 people turned out for his last high school football game at Multnomah Field.
>
> Grayson didn't disappoint them. He scored four touchdowns, dropped a 57-yard punt onto the Marshfield one-yard line and completed an undefeated and unscored on season for the Democrats."
>
> **Dean Smith**, *Journal staff writer*

The 1932 football season was a repeat of the undefeated success of the preceding year. Never had two teams so dominated the competition allowing only one touchdown to cross their goal in the two years. Credit Waldorf with the success when the teams were more like college football machines than their rivals.

At one time, three Jeff alums were starting quarterbacks for the Pacific Coast Conference teams; **Bobby Grayson** at Stanford, **Ray Woodman** at Oregon State and **Roger Dougherty** at Washington State.

> "Eric Waldorf is the greatest high school coach in the United States."
>
> **Stanford's Bobby Grayson**
> **Three time All-American**

COLLEGE ASPIRATIONS

Waldorf's college coaching aspirations were dashed in 1938 when the University of Oregon hired **Tex Oliver** after the Portland press had made Waldorf the front-runner in the head coaching search.

> After **Prink Callison** quit the University of Oregon football coaching job after the 1937 season, Eric Waldorf was promoted by the media as his replacement:
>
> "Ninety out of 100 football fans in Portland put the O.K. on Eric Waldorf, Jefferson coach, to get the job at Oregon … folks that place their shoulders to the wheel in making Portland football-inded are hook, line and sinker for the brilliant Democrat mentor.
>
> "Waldorf wants the job and lays his past on the table for consideration. He has forgotten more football than all the present Duck coaching staff ever knew."
>
> **Billy Stepp**, *The News-Telegram*

In 1939, at the age of 37, the successful prep coach was granted a sabbatical leave to work on his Master's degree at the University of Oregon. It allowed Waldorf to taste the college level when he coached the freshmen football and wrestling teams in 1939-40. He returned to Jefferson for the 1940 football season.

> **Professional Football—WWII Style**
>
> In 1942, Waldorf added another coaching duty to his resume by leading the **Vancouver Warcos** of the War Industries League (Portland, Spokane and Seattle). The four teams were composed of former players of the many high schools and colleges of the Northwest.

Waldorf remained the respected football coach at Jefferson turning out well-coached players and winning many more than his share of city championships. The 1948 team lost to Grants Pass in the state finals 6-0.

After winning or sharing 10 football titles, Waldorf resigned in 1953 for a private business opportunity.

FOREST GROVE

In 1957, Waldorf returned to coaching after he had operated Pacific Cleaners in Forest Grove for four years. He replaced **Marvin Mellbye** at Forest Grove High School. "I've missed coaching and now that I have my business organized, I felt I would like to return to coaching," he said.

Waldorf coached football another four seasons and taught at Forest Grove until his retirement in 1967.

FOREST GROVE H.S. (17-17-2) 4 years

1957	3-6-0	
1958	6-2-1	
1959	4-5-0	
1960	4-4-1	

COACHING RECORD (161-68-17) 27 years

"An admiration for what can be accomplished by hard work probably has a great deal to do with the success of Eric Waldorf as a high school football coach.

Waldorf, a usually taciturn man of trim, athletic appearance, is known far and wide among college football coaches, who are eager to get Waldorf-trained men on their squads."

Paul Hauser , *The Oregonian*

" He was liked and well respected. You didn't argue with him, but he would listen. He was as important to the school as **Hopkin Jenkins**. I never went to Jenkins for help. I always went to Mr. Waldorf."

1933 All-Star player, Ben Ell

LEGACY OF PLAYERS

Bobby Grayson	Stanford All-American College Hall of Fame
Arnie Weinmeister	NFL Hall of Fame
Dave Patterson	Stanford Captain
Joe Wendlick	OSC , Pittsburg Steelers
Alan Bartholemy	Yale captain
Ray Woodman	Oregon State
Roger Dougherty	Washington State
Lief and Earling Jacobson	Oregon
Bunny Bennett	Willamette
Floyd Simmons	Notre Dame
Ben and Roy Ell	OSC and Oregon
Bobby Reynolds	Oregon
Jake Hergert	Portland U.
Bill Wetzler	Santa Clara
Ralph Davis	Oregon State
Hal Elmers	Lewis and Clark
Don Stanton	University of Oregon
Jim Inglesby	Oregon State
Larry Wisbaum	Portland U.
Walt Kelly	Oregon State
Norm Dversdal	Linfield
Monte Brethauer	Oregon and NFL Colts
Emery Barnes	Oregon and B.C. Lions
Caley Cook	Lewis and Clark
Tom Keele	University of Oregon
Roger Williams	Lewis and Clark

Eric Waldorf, died October 4, 1977, at age 76, in Forest Grove, Oregon.

In 1952, Eric Waldorf capped off his last season at Jeff with his 10th PIL title when his Demos beat Grant 6-0 in the mud.

Kenton James "Kent" Wigle

- Born: April 1, 1947 in Salem Ore.
- Parents: Cloid and Rita Kent
- Father was a heavy equipment operator while mother was a teacher
- Married: Susan Robert 12/20/75
- High School: Riddle H.S. 1965
- Coach: Dave Campbell
- Honors: As a running back, football all-league, baseball All-State
- College: Southern Oregon 1966-1970
- Coach: Al Akins Football, Ted Schopf Baseball All-League in baseball
- Degrees: B.S.in PE Southern Oregon, M.S. Uof Oregon

COACHING

Kent Wigle had early aspirations to be a big league baseball player. But his high school and college accomplishments weren't enough to make the grade.

After playing football his first three years at Southern Oregon for **Al Akins**, Wigle opted for an opportunity to coach the junior varsity football team his senior year. It helped him decide to be a coach.

SOUTH UMPQUA

Kent Wigle's first student teaching experience (one week) at South Umpqua was enough for Superintendent **Dea Cox** to offer him a teaching contract.

In the fall of 1970, he coached the South Umpqua frosh team to a perfect 8-0 season. It propelled him to the varsity post when **Dick Peterson** resigned.

Wigle built the football program when he increased the turnouts to 100, coordinated the junior and senior high teams, and solicited extra volunteer coaches.

Wigle attended many football clinics and worked in football camps during the summer. He loved sharing the game's intricacies with legends **Fred Spiegelberg** and **Chuck Solberg**.

South Umpqua's football fortunes prospered. Their teams won 7 league championships and 3 state championships in Wigle's tenure as head coach. His organization and team discipline were always the key to his success. After 17 years, Wigle felt "it was time to make a move."

Kent Wigle may establish an all-time winning record before his career ends. His Marshfield teams have not lost a league game in five years.

SOUTH UMPQUA (133-40-2) 17 years

Year	Record	Notes
1971	5-4-0	
1972	8-3-0	**Skyline League Champs**
1973	9-1-0	**Skyline League Champs**
1974	8-1-0	**Skyline League Champs**
1975	11-1-0	**Skyline League Champs** **State 2A Finals** Lost to Vale 24-20
1976	11-0-1	**Skyline League Champs** **State 2A Co-Champions** **Tied Gold Beach 8-8**
1977	12-0-0	**Sky-Em League Champs** **State 2A Champions** **Beat Tillamook 35-7**
1978	10-2-0	**Sky-Em League Champs**
1979	7-3-0	
1980	4-5-0	
1981	10-2-1	**Sky-Em League Champs** **State 2A Co- Champions** **Tied Siuslaw 0-0**
1982	6-3-0	
1983	7-3-0	
1984	7-2-0	
1985	5-4-0	
1986	5-4-0	
1987	8-2-0	

MARSHFIELD

Wigle had considered the Marshfield post earlier when **Pete Susick** retired in 1978, but "the situation wasn't right." Ten years later, the situation was right, and the town of Coos Bay and Marshfield High School got quite a football coach.

Wigle's winning formula is simple. It begins with numbers, gains momentum in the weight room and is anchored in fundamentals.

MARSHFIELD (104-24-0), 11 years

1988	8-2-0	**Midwest League Co-Champs**
1989	4-5-0	
1990	7-3-0	**Midwestern League Champs**
1991	8-4-0	
1992	13-1-0	**Midwestern League Champs** **State 4A Champions** **Beat Ashland 36-21**
1993	6-4-0	
1994	13-1-0	**Midwestern League Champs** **State 4A Finals** Lost to Glencoe 28-17
1995	12-1-0	**MW League Champs Semis**
1996	11-1-0	**MW League Champs** **Quarters**
1997	12-1-0	**MW League Champs Semis**
1998	10-1-0	**MW League Champs**
1999		
2000		
2001		
2002		
2003		
2004		
2005		

"There has always been tradition at Marshfield," commented Wigle. "They draw crowds well and it's an excellent town. We are now in the process of building a new grandstand on the visitors side of Pete Susick Stadium."

The football program averages 120 athletes. The kids know that they will have an opportunity to play. Wigle runs four teams—freshmen, sophomore, junior varsity and varsity, and the 12 coaches make every effort to start 22 players at each level.

"I believe that football is as valuable an education experience as any other activity. I believe in getting numbers involved and creating a positive atmosphere, " Wigle said. "We push pretty hard. But the kids respond because they know we sincerely care about them."

At 52, Wigle has built a dynasty at Marshfield. In 11 seasons, he has won 82 percent of the games, including 8 league championships and a state championship. Marshfield is undefeated in the Midwestern League play the past 5 seasons.

Kent Wigle looks forward to a minimum of 7 more years of coaching. He may become the winningest coach in the history of Oregon football.

HONORS

1971 1976	**Skyline League Coach of the Year**
1977 1978 1981 1987	**Sky-Em League Coach of the Year**
1977 1982	**Oregon AA Coach of the Year**
1976	**Head Coach West Shrine Game**
1977 1978 1982	**Head Coach East Shrine Game**
1990 1994 1995 1996 1997 1998	**Midwestern League Coach of the Year**
1992	**State 4A Coach of the Year**
1996	**Western Region nomination for National Coach of the Year**
1993 1995	**Head Coach of the Shrine Bowl**
1998	**Head Coach of the Oregon Bowl**

Fred Wilson

- **Fredrick Oswald Wilson**
- Born: Nov. 10, 1925 in Seaside, Ore.
- Parents: Francis M. "Doc" and Runa Wilson Father was a pharmacist and the Mayor of Warrenton
- Married: Virgina Taylor 6/15/63
- Sons: Terry 2/11/65, Daniel 5/14/66
- High School: Warrenton 1940-1944
- Coach: Romey Adams
- Quarterback on three state championship 6 man football teams. All-State Class B basketball player. Shortstop in baseball.
- Service: Tech Sgt. In U.S. Army Air Force 1944 for two years as a turret gunner on a B-17. Flew 3 missions over Europe.
- College: University of Oregon Fall of 1946 Lewis and Clark College 1948-1951 Football coach: Joe Huston 1950- All-NWC Safety , NAIA Dist II Hall of Fame as a player
- Degrees: B.S. Lewis and Clark 1951; Masters in Education U of Oregon 1957

After a strong coaching start at Lewis and Clark, **Fred Wilson** adjusted his philosophy to accommodate the changing attitude of the small college football player.

SPORTS

Fred Wilson became interested in sports at an early age. He remembers his father ordering a football out of the *Wilson Sporting Goods* catalog when he was in the third grade. He continued giving his son a new ball each year until he was out of high school.

Every free hour was spent playing football, basketball and baseball. As a seventh grader, Wilson boldly asked the football coach to give him football pads so he could work out with the high school team. He realized then, he wanted to be a good player.

Coaching was furthermost from his mind when he graduated from high school. "Boy, how I would hate to be a teacher," Wilson remembers saying.

OREGON

Wilson faced a career dilemma when he returned from the service. "Do I go to the Oregon State Pharmacy School to follow in my Dad's footsteps or should it be to the University of Oregon to major in PE?"

His father, Fred's avid supporter during high school, sensed his son's true interest and encouraged him to go to Oregon.

At Oregon, Wilson started well. He played ball on the three major junior varsity teams, but at 5'7" and 165 pounds, he "felt like a little fish in a big pond."

Wilson's anxiety about his athletic future at the big school was resolved when he met with basketball coach **John Warren** concerning playing time. When the coach became evasive, Wilson received the message he needed. He packed up his car and drove to the Junction City "Y" in the road, to contemplate a college change. "Should I transfer Linfield or Willamette?" Unable to decide, Wilson drove to Portland to look over Lewis and Clark.

LEWIS AND CLARK

Wilson was welcomed by the Lewis and Clark basketball coach **Eldon Fix**. Comfortable by his choice, Wilson practiced with the varsity and quickly earned the starting guard position by the opening game.

It was a good fit. Fred Wilson would start on every team in football, basketball and baseball in his three years on the Palatine Hill campus.

At Lewis and Clark, Wilson claims he "found himself" and started to enjoy college. Along with the athletic success, his grades and attitude improved. And according to him, "for the first time, the teaching profession began to make sense, and I started to work toward that goal."

ASSISTANT COACHING CAREER

1951	Assistant to **Bob Signor** at Rainier H.S.
1952	Assistant to **Jerry Long** at Rainier H.S.
1953	

RAINIER HIGH SCHOOL (10-8-0)

1954	7-2-0	
1955	3-6-0	

1956	Albany H.S. Asst football coach Head baseball coach

LEWIS AND CLARK

In the Fall of 1957, Fred Wilson was hired as the football assistant to his former college coach, **Joe Huston.** Wilson also became the head baseball and wrestling coach for the Pioneers.
He served as the top aide for eight years until he became the head coach in 1965 when Joe Huston retired to become the athletic director.

Fred Wilson got an initiation his first year as the head coach. Although The Pioneers had 20 returning letterman, Wilson found how tough it was to compete with the likes of Northwest Conference coaches, **Frank Buckiewicz, Ted Ogdahl, and Paul Durham.** His first season, he was 3-5 before a winning 5 year run.

LEWIS AND CLARK (79-98-2)

1965	3-5-0	
1966	8-1-0	NWC 1st Coach of the Year
1967	7-2-0	NWC 1st tie with Willamette
1968	6-3-0	
1969	5-4-0	NWC 1st tie Linf.,PLU, Whit.
1970	5-4-0	
1971	4-5-0	
1972	3-6-0	
1973	3-7-0	
1974	2-6-1	
1975	1-8-0	
1976	7-2-0	
1977	4-4-0	
1978	2-7-0	
1979	5-4-0	
1980	4-4-1	
1981	4-5-0	
1982	2-7-0	
1983	4-5-0	Retired
1987	0-9-0	Interim coaching year

APATHY AND ATTITUDE CHANGES

In 1971, Fred Wilson made a speech at the weekly meeting of the *Oregon Sports Writers and Broadcasters*, on his concern about the growing exodus of young men away from the game. He cited the missing 33 that didn't return that year for various reasons at his college. He exhorted the values of the game in a masterful fashion. The speech was printed in the *Oregonian* that week. The public reaction was broad and strong, but his biggest test as a coach would follow.

COACHING PHILOSOPHY

In the late 60s and the early 70s, Wilson recognized a dramatic change in the attitude of the football player. The authority and demands of the traditional coaching procedures were now being "questioned and doubted." No longer could an authoritative coach prosper. Respect for coaches, teachers and even their parents dropped to an all time low by the college student.

The coaching tactics needed to change. The old school of coaching, utilizing blind loyalty and fear tactics for motivation and demeaning players for non-performance wasn't working.

The players reacted negatively. Only at the higher level where scholarships and professional enticements became the motivator, would the college student athlete decide to turn out, let alone finish out the season.

Wilson recognized the relationship with his players needed to change. It was important that the athlete at Lewis and Clark have a more meaningful football experience. Wilson's philosophy:

- The coach/player relationship needed to improve. It needed more trust. It needed to be sincere.
- The program needed to be promoted and respected by students, faculty, the alumni and community.
- The program must attract an adequate number of good athletes from the community.
- The program needed to be a good product.
- The attitude of the players will be a direct reflection of the attitude of the coach.
- If the coaches work hard, the players will work hard. If the players are treated like "human beings," as having an interest in the individual on and off the field, the coach will earn the respect necessary to achieve their mutual goals.

"If a coach can achieve these aforementioned goals, they should win their share of games, remembering of course that a program is usually judged by the games it wins."

In 1974, Wilson experienced another player shortage. A team rule violation had decimated the team when L&C played Linfield. They suited only 18 players against the Wildcats, 60.

Chuck Charnquist, the L&C publicist honored the "Valiant Eighteen" with a poem called *"Charge of the Pioneer Brigade,"* ended his tribute with the question: "When can their glory fade?"

> "I played five positions that game; quarterback, wide receiver, corner, safety and tackle on the punt team," remembers **Rick Hennessy**.

"We had plenty of adversity, and that certainly was the lowest point of my coaching career," remembers Wilson. "People were on both sides of the fence," he said. "Loyalty was split among the players, student body and the faculty. But out of this adversity came unity."

L&C finished the 1974 season with only 18 players and a 2-6-1 record.

"The players who survived the 1974 season united the team toward a common goal," Wilson said. " I could see it coming a little bit last year, but something was still lacking. They put it all together this year (1976). Not only are we winning with our run-and-shoot offense, we attracted the student body, fans and faculty like never before. This is my most rewarding season ever."

Wilson had done a lot of soul searching. His self-diagnosis was that he had, as coach, become too involved in "individual differences." It took two years to restore the program. "Our team now believes in one another and what we are doing."

"We did a long analysis of our team last winter," says Wilson. "I felt last season our offensive line was the best I've had at L&C, but we won but two games. We felt we were the weak 'Oregon State' of the Northwest Conference. We were out muscled by four teams in our conference last year."

"After a time, we realized we were the 'Oregon State' of our conference, and for us to compete we had to go with the run-and-shoot offense."

Fred Wilson's gamble on a new offense paid off with seven wins in 1976 to earn him the Northwest small college **"Coach of the Year."**

Lewis and Clark posted a 7-2 record after being 1-8 in 1975, with a run-and-shoot offense that enabled quarterback **Scott McCord** to set national passing yardage records for the season. (6 national records in four categories and broke 10 conference records). Scott McCord was named NAIA Div II Co-player of the Year.

Wilson resigned his football post in 1983, but returned for an interim season in 1987 until **Tom Smythe** could take over the program. He recruited his competitive colleague friend ex-Pacific coach **Frank Buckiewicz** to help him.

Wilson retired from Lewis and Clark in 1989, but found his way back to the football field from 1994 to 1997 helping LaSalle High School's **Ray Baker** coach his team.

Wilson resides in Portland.

Bibliography

Beres, George, *Year of the 1995 Duck,*
Eugene:Northwest Sportscene 1995.
Brown, Jody, *Crosstown Crossfire,*Atlanta:
Gridiron Publishers 1994.
Evancho, Bob, *Pokey The Good Fight.* Boise:
Bootleg Books 1997.
Greenburg, John, *A Rose Bowl Story.* Chicago:
Greenburg 1993.
Joyce, Dennis, *Joe K.* Texas: Mondell Publishing
1998.
McCann, Michael, and others, *Oregon Ducks
Football.* Eugene: McCann Communications
Corp 1995.
McKay, John, *McKay: A Coach's Story.*New
York: Atheneum 1974.
Medford Linebackers, *75 Years of Medford
Football.* Medford: Gandee Printing Center
1987.
O'Brien, Michael, *Vince.* New York: Morrow
1987.
Oregon Daily Emerald Staff, *History of Oregon
Athletics.* Eugene: Oregon Emerald 1973.
Pope, Edwin, *Football's Greatest Coaches.*
Atlanta: Tupper and Love 1955.
Van Leuven, Hendrick, *Touchdown UCLA.*
Texas: Strode Publishing 1988.

Lewis and Clark College Football Media Guide.
Linfield College Football Media Guide 1998.
Oregon State University Football Media Guide.
*Oregon State High School Football Playoff
Records, OSAA.1998.*
Portland State University Football Media Guide.
UCLA Football Media Guide.
University of Colorado Football Media Guide.
University of Montana Football Media Guide.
University of Oregon Football Media Guide.
University of Washington Football Media Guide.
Western Oregon Football Media Guide 1998.
Willamette University Football Media Guide .

Photo Credits

Jim Aiken	University of Oregon
John Allen	Allan deLay Allen
Pokey Allen	Portland State
Dee Andros	Oregon State
Bill Austin	Oregon Sports Hall of Fame
Thurman Bell	Allan deLay, Bell
Hugo Bezdek	University of Oregon
Rich Brooks	University of Oregon, Falcons
Frank Buckiewicz	Lewis and Clark
Ed Burton	*Clackamas Review*
Prink Callison	University of Oregon
Len Casanova	University of Oregon
Mouse Davis	Portland State, Steve Brenner
Tom DeSylvia	Allan deLay
Bill Dressel	Bill Dressel
Paul Durham	Linfield College
Darrell Everett	Marshall High School
Jerry Frei	University of Oregon
Floyd Halvorsen	Allan deLay
Marv Heater	Allan deLay
Marv Hiebert	Allan deLay, Hiebert
Joe Huston	Huston, Allan deLay
Mel Ingram	Allan deLay
Dutch Kawasoe	Allan deLay
Larry Keck	Larry Keck
Spec Keene	Willamette University
Jerry Lillie	Willamette University
Jerry Lyons	Allan deLay
Don Mabee	Allan deLay
Don McCarty	Robert Gill
Bill McArthur	Western Oregon
Gene Morrow	Robert Gill
Jim Nagel	Robert Gill
Ted Ogdahl	Allan deLay
Jack Patera	Seattle Seahawks
Tommy Prothro	Oregon State
George Rallis	Allan deLay
Don Read	Don Read
Don Requa	Allan deLay, *East Oregonian*
Ad Rutschman	Allan deLay, Linfield College
Doc Savage	Doc Savage
Tom Smythe	Allan deLay
Chuck Solberg	Allan deLay
Fred Spiegelberg	Allan deLay, family
Gary Stautz	Gary Stautz
Lon Stiner	Oregon State
Pete Susick	Allan deLay,Susick
Kip Taylor	Oregon State
Roy Thompson	Allan deLay, Thompson
Dallas Ward	OSU Archives
Eric Waldorf	Jon Waldorf
Kent Wigle	Kent Wigle, Robert Gill
Fred Wilson	Lewis and Clark